The Iroquois Ceremonial
of Midwinter

A NEW YORK STATE STUDY

The Iroquois Ceremonial
of Midwinter

ELISABETH TOOKER

Syracuse University Press

ELISABETH TOOKER, received the B.A. from Radcliffe
College, the M.A. from the University of Arizona, and
the Ph.D. from Radcliffe College. She is a fellow of the
American Anthropological Association and the American Association for the Advancement of Science, a
member of the American Ethnological Society, American Folklore Society, American Society for Ethnohistory, and other professional groups.

Her articles have appeared in various anthropological
journals, and she is the author of *An Ethnography of
the Huron Indians, 1615–1649* (1964) and editor of
Iroqouis Culture, History and Prehistory (1967). She
is associate professor of anthropology at Temple University, Philadelphia.

Manufactured in the United States of America

Contents

Preface

The Iroquois have long fascinated white Americans. The image of the descendants of a once powerful "hunter state" reduced to living on a few impoverished reservations has proved to have an almost irresistible attraction. And as one result, probably more has been written about the Iroquois than any other American Indian group with the possible exception of the Navaho. Although in a sense Iroquois history has something for everyone, each student has his own reasons for his particular interest in the subject.

Of all the various aspects of Iroquois life that might be of interest, that which interested me most was religion. In dress, housing, employment, and the other externals of life, the Iroquois now resemble other Americans. What remains of older Iroquois culture is most apparent in religious practice, and those most knowledgeable about the old ways are often participants in its ritual. If we accept the seemingly paradoxical idea that the essential humanity of man is to be better understood through a consideration of cultural differences than through a consideration of cultural similarities, the religion of the Iroquois attracts attention—for it is in the religion of the Iroquois that these differences are most apparent.

As the Midwinter ceremonial is the longest and most complex of Iroquois rituals—the ceremonial reviews the year past and anticipates the year to come—it provides a most appropriate place to begin such an inquiry into Iroquois religion. This was in my mind when in January of 1958 I went to the Tonawanda Reservation outside of Buffalo to see the ceremonial. There I had the good fortune to be asked to stay at a house on the reservation for the week.

The complexity of the ceremonial turned out to be greater than I had anticipated. At Tonawanda, the Midwinter ceremonial proper lasts an entire week, and the activities of each of the seven days are different. It was quite apparent that the Indians knew what was going to happen next, and it was equally and painfully apparent to me that I did not. In consequence, my week's stay on the reservation produced only some rather disconnected notes. It seemed to me that there ought to be patterns underneath the ritual that governed its performance. The Indians, of course, do not have a printed program to aid them in following and remembering the order of events; nor do they have a printed liturgy comparable to The Book of Common Prayer or the Catholic missal. Although, in general, those peoples who do not use writing as a tool tend to be better at memorization than those who do, still, I thought, provision must have been made for those Indians who had not memorized the ceremonial. This problem was particularly evident to me as I had disregarded proper anthropological field procedure and had not written up my field notes until after I had returned to Buffalo. Proper procedure is to write up such notes each night before retiring, and some feel that an anthropologist in the field should always carry a notebook and jot in it anything of interest as it happens. Such good field practice seemed inappropriate among the Iroquois. After all, I was a guest in the house of a woman I had not met before, and to take notes on what happened would have made the occasion some sort of stage show. Further, no one—Indian or white—is permitted to take notes, sketch, tape record, or photograph in the longhouse, except on very few and unusual occasions. The objection is not to people—Indians or whites —coming to the longhouse to learn about the religion, but to the lack of respect that such behavior often implies.

Having seen the Midwinter ceremonial, the nature of the task before me was clear: to figure out how Iroquois ritual worked. The units out of which Iroquois ritual is built were readily ascertained. They are the limited number of songs, dances, games, and speeches which are used over and over again in various ceremonial contexts. Even the most naive observer is immediately aware that these are the ritual elements. It is, for example, quite immediately evident to one knowing neither the language nor the ritual when one dance ends and the next begins: the musicians and dancers leave the center of the longhouse and sit down, the speaker talks briefly, and a new group of musicians take their places, begin singing, and the dancers begin to dance. Each dance, as might be expected, has a name, and this name is easily obtained by asking for it. The task was to figure out how these units or rites combine into ceremonies. This apparently very simple task proved to be a long and frustrating one. It was quite evident, for example, that some of the rites in the first half of the Tonawanda Midwinter ceremonial are repeated in the second half, but—try as I might—I could not write the rules for the entire ceremonial. Despite all my efforts, I could not find—in the felicitous phrase of the mathematicians—the simple and elegant solution.

As it turned out, the solution to the problem was not to be found in the study of the Midwinter ceremonial alone, but in the entire ritual system of the Iroquois. Ritual, in a sense, is a language, and as a spoken language must be studied as a whole in order to see the general workings of the system.

Knowledge of the ritual system not only aids in understanding how the ritual is put together, but also how it changes. Given a particular structure, certain changes are simply easier to make than others. But not only do these ritual patterns shape the changes that do occur, they also influence where in the ritual such changes are likely to occur. Thus, knowledge of ritual structure is as useful in the study of ritual change as knowledge of the structure of language is useful in the study of linguistic change.

Some documentation of this change is provided by the earlier descriptions of ceremonial practice. By comparing earlier practice with present practice some idea is gained of the nature and kind of change. But even in this type of comparison some knowledge of ritual structure is mandatory: some differences in the accounts are not evidence of change or errors in reporting, but merely evidence of the kind and range of permissible variation.

Other documentation of this ritual change is provided by the present variation in practice in the various longhouses. The ceremonials of these longhouses did not arise quite independently of each other. Thus, differences in present practice may be evidence of changes that have occurred since the introduction of the original ritual or even that of change that occurred in the process of being introduced.

The Iroquois evidence indicates that changes are less likely to occur in the more fundamental ritual patterns than in the less basic ones and that these fundamental patterns are remarkably stable over time. Thus, for example, the New York Onondaga Midwinter ceremonial as now performed is virtually identical to that described in the 1880's by W. M. Beauchamp (1885, 1888, and 1895), Erminne Smith (1883), and De Cost Smith (1888); Frank G. Speck's (1949) account of the Sour Springs Midwinter ceremonial in the 1930's is virtually identical to that of Annemarie Shimony's (1961) for the 1950's; and William N. Fenton's (1941) data on performance at the Tonawanda Longhouse in 1936 agrees with that I obtained in 1958 and later years. Changes that do occur are likely to take place in the less significant parts of ritual practice, and, as Fenton (1936:20–22) has noted, it is these minor changes that result in local variations that the Iroquois feel strongly about. Although they are of little importance to the stranger, they are "the bones of contention which the old men chew."

While it cannot be assumed that knowledge of ritual patterns is also knowledge of what actually goes on in the participants' minds, any more than knowledge of the structure of language is also knowledge of what goes on in the speakers' minds, the two are probably not unrelated. Thus, for example, a classification of Iroquois ceremonials based on similarities and differences of the rites is probably closer to the classification the Indians themselves employ than one that seems most obvious to us. Here it should be recalled that the Indian faces some of the same problems as does the anthropological observer. He too, for example, must remember the order of events and the amount of variation allowable in each segment in order to act properly; he too is in need of some knowledge of the ritual structure—although such knowledge may be quite out of awareness—to take some of the complexity out of his religion.

Consequently, the reader should not suppose that the outline of Iroquois ritual structure presented here will allow him to "think Indian" or even act in accordance with the standards of Iroquois culture any more than he would suppose that merely reading a grammar of a language would allow him to speak a language fluently or think in it. Such outlines merely serve as a kind of guide, a kind of map for those who would travel in these realms. In the present instance, I would hope what follows will serve as such a map for those who wish to travel in the realm of Iroquois ritualism.

Acknowledgments

The field work that forms the basis of this study was done principally on the Tonawanda Reservation. This work, which began in 1958, consisted of brief periodic visits to the reservation over the last decade, and includes observation of virtually the entire Tonawanda Midwinter ceremonial in 1958 and 1964 and parts of the ceremonial in 1959, 1960, 1961, and 1966. I am indebted to William N. Fenton for first introducing me to several people on the Tonawanda Reservation and for his continuing interest in this study, to the late Elsina Cornplanter (widow of Jesse Cornplanter) for her hospitality over these many years, to Clarence and Dorothy Blueye for providing bed, board, and pleasant company on my recent visits to the reservation, to Chief Corbett Sundown for patiently trying to explain to me the ceremonial and for checking an earlier draft of the description of the Tonawanda Midwinter ceremonial, and to all the "Longhouse gang" for making the days I spent on the reservation many of the happiest of those years.

I am also indebted to the late Chief George Thomas of the New York Onondaga Longhouse for describing to me Onondaga practice. J. Joseph Pia kindly introduced me to Chief Thomas and made available to me a tape recording he had made of an interview with Chief Thomas on the Midwinter Ceremonial.

The libraries of the American Philosophical Society, Hamilton College, and the University of Rochester have been most generous in permitting me to use their manuscript collections. I also wish to thank Muriel Kirkpatrick for her work on the map.

M. H. Deardorff, William N. Fenton, Jacob W. Gruber, and Bruce G. Trigger read an earlier draft of this study. The present version has benefited much from their careful criticisms.

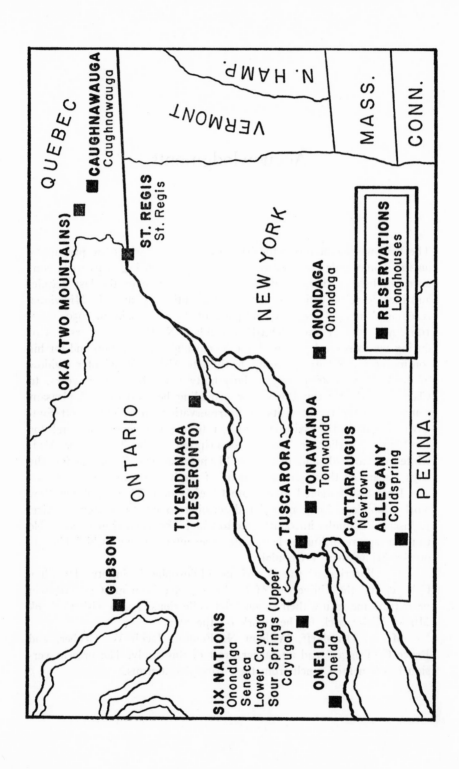

Introduction

The Midwinter ceremonial is still performed and other religious traditions upheld on a number of Iroquois reservations in the United States and Canada. The ceremonial itself is given in what is called a longhouse, also sometimes called a council house since political as well as religious councils may be held there. The religion takes one of its names from the name of this building; it is often called the Longhouse religion, and its believers are colloquially known as the "Longhouse gang."

The longhouses of the Iroquois religion are still to be found on the Allegany, Cattaraugus, and Tonawanda Reservations in western New York, on the Onondaga Reservation in central New York, and on the Six Nations and Oneida Reserves in Ontario. Although over the last century the number of longhouses on some of these reservations has declined, three new ones have been established in this century: one at the Oneida Reserve in Ontario, one at the Caughnawauga Reserve near Montreal, and a third at the St. Regis reservations on either side of the Canadian–United States border.

Followers of the Longhouse religion now constitute a conservative minority of the Indian population. So also some Iroquois reservations do not have longhouses; there are no longhouses on the Oka, Gibson, and Tiyendinaga Reserves in Canada, and none remain on the Tuscarora Reservation near Niagara Falls in New York. The few Oneidas who still live in New York State and the larger number who moved to Wisconsin in the last century also lack longhouses, although the Seneca-Cayuga in Oklahoma still hold some of the old ceremonies.

The religion practiced by Longhouse believers was reformed

in the early years of the nineteenth century by the Seneca prophet, Handsome Lake. These were years of great stress and change for the Iroquois. Earlier, during the seventeenth and eighteenth centuries, the Iroquois had risen to a position of power in the Northeast, controlling a significant part of the fur trade and striking terror in the hearts of a number of Indians and whites through their raids and wars. This Iroquois domination of affairs in the Northeast frequently has been attributed to their "political genius." Yet, it was a peculiarly favorable geographic location that allowed this political genius to flower. Iroquoia, the homeland of the Iroquois, was relatively close to the trading centers of the Dutch, English, and French, and consequently the Iroquois could play one off against another for more favorable market positions. Also, their geographic position was such that they could easily harass other Indians who, living further west, had to pass near Iroquoia on their way to the European trading centers, and they could by war establish and maintain their influence in the area (Tooker 1963). The League of the Iroquois—the confederation of the Mohawk, Oneida, Onondaga, Cayuga, and Seneca tribes—became a political force that could not be ignored.

The power the Iroquois had built and maintained in the seventeenth and eighteenth centuries was shattered during the American Revolution. Faced with the choice of siding with the revolutionary Americans or with the British, many Iroquois chose their old allies, the British, though some joined the American side and others remained neutral. General Washington's response to this threatening British-Iroquois alliance was to send a force under the leadership of Generals Sullivan and Clinton into Iroquoia. In the face of this army, the Iroquois abandoned their villages and crops which then were destroyed. After this defeat in their own homeland, many of the Iroquois fled to Canada and to the more westerly sections of what was to become New York State.

After the Revolution, the increase of white colonization of Iroquois land drastically reduced the Indian land base. Some members of the Sullivan-Clinton Expedition, having seen the fertility of Iroquoia, returned to settle there after the war—a movement that was merely a part of the general westward movement of the time. This trend was further accelerated by the completion of the Erie Canal. As the white population increased so also did the pressure on the Indians to give up what land had been set aside for them after the Revolution which, of course, reduced their reservation land.

The New Religion of Handsome Lake attempted to deal with the changes being forced on the Iroquois at the end of the eighteenth and beginning of the nineteenth century. The defeat of the Iroquois during the American Revolution had effectively curtailed not only their land base and political activities, but also their important trading activities. This meant that they had to adopt a new economy; the old one based on the digging-stick agriculture of the women and the hunting and trading activities of the men was no longer adequate. They were forced to accept the kind of economy practiced by the whites—one based on plow agriculture—in order to exist on their restricted land base. Among other things, the religion of Handsome Lake provided the moral code and the ritual underpinnings necessary to make this economy work. It seems probable that it was the Iroquois's recognition of this fact that led to the general acceptance of the New Religion by those Iroquois who were not Christians (Tooker 1968).

But the reforms introduced by Handsome Lake merely adapted Iroquois religion to changed conditions. They did not change the basic structure of the Iroquois ritual and belief systems. As will be seen, the basic principles on which Iroquois religion rests are quite different from those of the Judeo-Christian tradition. The reforms of Handsome Lake did make Iroquois religion more like Christianity in certain relatively superficial ways, and so in a sense permitted the old Iroquois view of the world to persist beneath the guise of a religion apparently much influenced by Christianity. Handsome Lake had preached a moral code that to a degree resembled that of the Christians, most obviously in its emphasis on drinking as immoral behavior, its vivid description of the punishments for wrong-doing in the afterworld, and its emphasis on a Creator and a Devil which gave the Creator God more importance than He had had previously in Iroquois religion. But Iroquois religion retained its old concern with maintaining harmony between mankind and the other creatures of the world. One important expression of this concern is the obligation felt by believers periodically to return thanks publicly to various beings —including the Our Life Supporters (corn, beans, and squash—the three important cultivated foods of the Iroquois), the Maple, the

Strawberry, the Sun, the Moon, and the Thunderers—in what are often but inaccurately termed the agricultural ceremonies. (Not all these ceremonies are in honor of cultivated plants.) Another expression of this concern is the "Feast of the Dead" in which the dead return to dance with the living. Still another are the ceremonies held to cure a sick individual, including those requiring performance of a song, dance, or game from the Iroquois ritual repertoire, a tobacco invocation to the dead requesting that the dead cease bothering the living, or a medicine society ritual.

Although the increasing acceptance of Christianity during the last century and a half has led to a decrease in the proportion of Iroquois who believe solely in the old Iroquois religion, the religion of the Longhouse holds a special place in Iroquois life for it is an outward symbol that the Iroquois are not merely slightly darker skinned whites either by history or culture. Indians of various Christian persuasions occasionally attend the Longhouse ceremonials to reaffirm this fact.

The religion of the Iroquois too holds a special place in white American life. The United States after the American Revolution was, of course, an independent nation, but it was also a nation without a history and a cultural identity independent from that of England. What the new Americans needed and wanted was a distinct heritage, and they turned to what they had that England did not— the Indians. But they could not ignore their own cultural roots in Europe. The result was, and is: white Americans both glorify the Indian as the "Noble Red Man" and despise him as an "ignorant savage" fit only for extermination. This ambivalent attitude is reciprocated by the Indians themselves: the Indians despise the injustices done them at the hands of the whites yet wish to partake of the benefits of Western civilization. White interest in things Indian was aided by the increased contact between the new and old Americans after the Revolution as more whites settled on lands in Iroquoia. One result was that the tide of books and articles on Iroquois life, customs, and history began to reach flood proportions.

For the whites, the Iroquois Midwinter ceremonial held particular fascination. This fascination was in large measure a result of their interest in the ritual sacrifice of a white dog, a rite that was part of the ceremonial in the nineteenth century. Some who saw the ceremonial wrote descriptions of it, and though these writers often erred in thinking that what they had seen was identical to that to be seen on other Iroquois reservations—they assumed no change had occurred in the ceremonial over the years—paradoxically their descriptions can now be used to document the ritual change they ignored.

With increased knowledge of Iroquois ceremonialism came increased recognition that ritual practice in the various longhouses differed. This led twentieth-century anthropologists—notably William N. Fenton and Frank G. Speck—to suggest that the variation in the ceremonials ought to be more fully documented, and they began this documentation themselves. As a result, ceremonial practice is now relatively well documented for five longhouses: the Coldspring Longhouse on the Allegany Reservation, the Newtown Longhouse on the Cattaraugus Reservation, the Tonawanda Longhouse on the Tonawanda Reservation, the Onondaga Longhouse on the Onondaga Reservation, and the Sour Springs Longhouse, one of the four longhouses on the large Six Nations Reserve. The kind of comparison envisioned by Fenton (1936:5; 1941:144) and Speck (1949:4) over a quarter of a century ago is now possible. I follow here, as Speck phrased it, Fenton's "marching orders"—the injunction that a comparison of ceremonial variations is necessary to understanding the history of the ritual.

Increased knowledge of Iroquois ceremonialism in particular and American Indian ceremonialism in general led not only to the recognition that ritual variation ought to be more fully documented in order to make more accurate historical inferences, but also to the recognition that ritual was patterned. Consequently, some anthropologists turned to the study of the structure of ritual, to the study of ritual patterns as well as cultural patterns as a whole. As Edward Sapir (in Mandelbaum 1949:546–47) observed some forty years ago:

All cultural behavior is patterned. . . . Let anyone who doubts this try the experiment of making a painstaking report of the actions of a group of natives engaged in some form of activity, say religious, to which he has not the cultural key. If he is a skillful writer, he may succeed in giving a picturesque account of what he sees and hears, or thinks he sees and hears, but the chances of his being able to give a relation of what happens in terms that would be intelligible and acceptable to the natives themselves are practically nil. He will be guilty of all manner of distortion. His emphasis will be constantly askew. He will find interesting what the natives take for granted as a casual kind of behavior worthy of no particular comment, and he will utterly fail to observe the crucial turning points in the course of action that give formal significance to the whole in the minds of those who do possess the key to its understanding. . . . It is the failure to understand the necessity of grasping the native patterning which is responsible for so much unimaginative and misconceiving description of procedures that we have not been brought up with. It becomes actually possible to interpret as base what is inspired by the noblest and even holiest of motives, and to see altruism or beauty where nothing of the kind is either felt or intended.

These anthropologists further recognized that knowledge of ritual patterns was important not only in understanding ceremonials actually witnessed, but also in understanding published descriptions of such ceremonials. As Kluckhohn and Wyman (1940:13) noted: "Many have been puzzled by the seeming conflict between various accounts of Navaho chants and by the apparent stupendous complexity of the whole system. . . . [But it is] evident that the intricacy of Navaho ceremonialism is not quite so overpowering once one has a clear view of the general workings of the system." Their observation applies equally well to the Iroquois instance.

However, although it is the intent of what follows to describe the "general workings" of Iroquois ritual in time and space, it should not be imagined that this is all there is to Iroquois ceremonialism, that this account is complete in those details it purports to describe, or even that it holds the key to understanding the ritual. I can only conclude, as does the Iroquois ritualist at the end of a ceremony:

And that is all that I myself am able to do; that is all that I learned of the ritual. That is it.

PART I

Principles of Iroquois Ritualism

The central intent of Iroquois ceremonialism is to return thanks to the beings of this world, both natural and supernatural. As one Iroquois ritualist told me, "We do not ask as you whites do; we give thanks." But, as Chafe (1961:1) has noted, the Iroquois "concept is broader than that expressed by any simple English term, and covers not only the conventionalized amenities of both thanking and greeting, but also a more general feeling of happiness over the existence of something or someone."

An important expression of this concern is the so-called Thanksgiving Speech or Address which systematically returns thanks to the beings on earth and those above. Most ceremonies begin with this speech, and it is repeated in an abbreviated form after the major rites of the ceremony have been performed. After the final recitation of the Thanksgiving Speech, the feast is distributed. The basic framework of an Iroquois ceremony, then, is: Thanksgiving Speech, performance of the rites appropriate to the occasion, Thanksgiving Speech, and distribution of the feast. If the ceremonial lasts more than one day, this pattern is repeated at each ceremonial gathering.

The Thanksgiving Speech, like all speeches delivered in the long-house and almost all announcements, is delivered in whatever Iroquois language the speaker knows. The songs are also in "Indian." As a rough rule, "Indian" is the first language of many older Iroquois; middle-age adults are often bilingual, speaking both "Indian" and English; children often know only English.[1] Change in language use reflects economic changes on the reservations: parents now teach their children English because a knowledge of English is essential to them. Most residents on reservations such as the Tonawanda Reservation find it necessary to find work off the reservation. Some commute to their jobs off the reservation and some live permanently in such nearby cities as Buffalo or more distant ones as Los Angeles. Formerly, work on the reservation itself provided a greater portion of its residents' livelihood, and much more reservation land was under cultivation than at present. Now what land is under cultivation on some reservations such as Tonawanda is rented out to white farmers. Small farms are no longer as profitable as they once were, and Indians usually lack both sufficient land and sufficient capital to engage in modern farming. As a result, they rely more on wage work than in the past and also on such benefits of white industrial society as unemployment insurance and welfare. Or, as one Seneca man put it to me, the gardens, chickens, and pigs once raised on the reservation were the unemployment checks of the time.[2]

The Thanksgiving Speech as well as other parts of the ceremonies are learned informally. There is little attempt made formally to instruct those who would learn the speeches and other rituals that make up the ceremonies. A would-be speaker knows the outline of the rituals from having attended the ceremonies since childhood, and probably if he suspects that he may become a speaker, he pays closer attention than he would otherwise. This lack of formal instruction may mean that the successor to the position is not obvious to the outsider until he is actually chosen (see, for example, Shimony 1961:128–29).

The Thanksgiving Speech, like other speeches and almost all announcements, is given by men. If a woman wishes to have an announcement made, she asks a man to make it for her.

Although not all those who deliver the Thanksgiving Speech follow exactly the same order, all begin with those beings on the ground and conclude with those above. The present principal speaker at the Tonawanda Longhouse uses the following order (Chafe 1961:6): (1) the people, (2) the earth, (3) the plants, including particular mention of the strawberries, (4) the water, (5) the trees, including particular mention of the maple, (6) the animals, (7) the birds, (8) the Three Sisters: corn, beans, and squash, (9) the wind, (10) the Thunderers, (11) the sun, (12) the moon, (13) the stars, (14) the Four Beings (the messengers from the Creator who appeared to the prophet Handsome Lake), (15) Handsome Lake, and (16) the Creator.

Chafe (1961:17–45) has translated a text of this speech by Corbett Sundown as follows:

And now, we are gathered in a group. And this is what the Four Beings did: they told us that we should always have love, we who move about on the earth. And this will always be first when people come to gather, the people who move about on the earth. It is the way it begins when two people meet: they first have the obligation to be grateful that they are happy. They greet each other, and after that they take up the matter with which just they two are concerned. And this is what Our Creator did: he decided, "The people moving about on this earth will simply come to express their gratitude." And that is the obligation of those of us who are gathered: that we continue to be grateful. This, too, is the way things are: we have not heard of any unfortunate occurrence that there might be in the community. And the way things are, there are people lying here and there, held down by illness; and even that, certainly is the responsibility of the Creator. And therefore let there be gratitude; we are always going to be grateful, we who remain, we who can claim to be happy. And give it your thought: the first thing for us to do is to be thankful for each other. And our minds will continue to be so.

And now this is what the Creator did. He decided, "There will be plants growing on the earth. Indeed, all of them will have names, as many plants as will be growing on the earth. At a certain time they will emerge from the earth and mature of their own accord. They will be available in abundance as medicines to the people moving about on the earth." That is what he intended. And it is true: we have been using them up to the present time, the medicines which the Creator made. He decided that it would be thus: that people would be obtaining them from the earth, where the medicines would be distributed. And this is what the Creator did: he decided, "Illness will overtake the people moving about on the earth, and these will always be there for their assistance." And he left on the earth all the different medicines to assist us in the future. And this, too, the Creator did. With regard to the plants growing on the earth he decided, "There will be a certain plant on which berries will always hang at a certain time. I shall then cause them to remember me, the people moving about on the earth. They will always express their gratitude when they see the berries hanging above the earth." And it is true: we see them when the wind becomes warm again on the earth; the strawberries are indeed hanging there. And it is also true that we use them, that we drink the berry water. For this is what he did: he decided, "They will always bring them to their meeting place and give thanks, all the people, as many as remain. They will be thankful when they see the berries hanging." That is what he did. And it is true: it comes to pass. When in the course of things it becomes warm again on the earth, we are thankful for everything. And give it your thought, that with one mind we may give thanks for all the plants, our medicines. And our minds will continue to be so.

And this is what the Creator did: he decided, "There will be springs on the earth. And there will be brooks on the earth as well; rivers will flow, and will pass by under the earth. And there will also be ponds and lakes. They will work hand in hand, the way I fashion them on the earth. And moisture will continue to fall." And it is true: fresh water is available in abundance to us who move about on the earth. And, in fact, to all those things which he provided for our contentment, fresh water is abundantly available too. And it is true: we have been using it up to the present time. It is the first thing we use when we arise each new time. And let there indeed be gratitude. It is coming to pass as Our Creator intended. And give it your thought, that we may do it properly: we now give thanks for the springs, the brooks, the flowing rivers, and the ponds and lakes. And our minds will continue to be so.

And now this is what the Creator did. He decided, "There will be forests growing on the earth. Indeed, the growing forests will be of assistance to the people moving about on the earth." He decided, "There will always be a certain period when the wind will become warm, and a certain length of time, also, when it will become cold. And the forests growing on the earth will provide heat for them." That is what the Creator intended. And it is true: it continues unchanged up to the present time. We are using them for heat, the forests growing on the earth. And this also he did: he made them medicines as well, the trees growing on the earth. He decided, "They can also be available as medicines to the people moving about on the earth." And he even did this as well: he decided, "Again, there will be a certain tree which I shall cause to remind the people moving about to think of me. The maples will stand on the earth, and the sweet liquid will drip from them. Each time when the earth becomes warm, then the sap will flow and they will be grateful for their happiness. When the time arrives again, they will attend to the maples standing there." And for those people who take notice of it, it continues unchanged: they do indeed tap them and store the sugar. For he decided that it would be available in abundance to the people moving about on the earth. And it is true: it continues unchanged up to the present time; we are still using it. And therefore again let there be gratitude that it all still continues as the Creator planned it. And give it your thought, that we may do it properly: we now give thanks for the forests growing on the earth. And our minds will continue to be so.

And now this is what Our Creator did: he decided, "I shall now establish various animals to run about on the earth. Indeed, they will always be a source of amusement for those who are called warriors, whose bodies are strong." He decided to provide the warriors, whose bodies are strong, with the animals running about, to be a source of amusement for them. "And they will be available as food to the people moving about on the earth." And up to the present time we have indeed seen the small animals running about along the edges of the forests, and within the forests as well. And at the present time we even catch glimpses of the large animals again. There were in fact a number of years during which we no longer saw the large animals. But now at the present time we again see the large animals running about, and at the present time they are actually available to us again as food. And we are using them as Our Creator intended. And therefore let there be gratitude that it all does still continue as he intended. And give it your thought, that we may do it properly: we now give thanks for the animals running about. And our minds will continue to be so.

And this is what Our Creator did. He decided, "I shall establish various creatures that will spread their wings from just above the earth to as far upward as they can go. And they too will be called animals. They will begin just above the earth, and will go all the way into the clouds. And they too all have names, the birds with outspread wings." And with respect to the small birds he decided, "There will be a certain period when they will stir, and they will turn back, going back to where it is warm. And it will become warm again on the earth, and they will return. With all their voices they will sing once more their beautiful songs. And it will lift the minds of all who remain when the small birds return." And he arranged as well that they are available to us as food, the birds with outspread wings. It is true: we are using them too, the birds with outspread wings. They are available to us as food. And we believe that they too are all carrying out their responsibility. They all, as I said, have names, according to their type. And give it your thought, that we may do it properly: we now give thanks

for the birds with outspread wings. And our minds will continue to be
so.

And now this is what Our Creator did. It was indeed at this time
that he thought, "I shall leave them on the earth, and the people moving
about will then take care of themselves. People will put them in the
earth, they will mature of their own accord, people will harvest them
and be happy." And up to the present time we have indeed seen them.
When they emerge from the earth we see them. They bring us contentment. They come again with the change of the wind. And they
strengthen our breath. And when the Good Message came we were
advised that they too should always be included in the ceremonies, in
the Four Rituals. Those who take care of them every day asked, too,
that they be sisters. And at that time there arose a relationship between them: we shall say "the Sisters, our sustenance" when we want
to refer to them. And it is true: we are content up to the present time,
for we see them growing. And give it your thought, that we may do
it properly: we now give thanks for the Sisters, our sustenance. And
our minds will continue to be so.

And now this is what Our Creator did: he decided, "Now it can't
always be just this way." And this, in fact, is what he decided. "There
must be wind, and it will strengthen the people moving about whom I
left on the earth. And in the west he made the thing that is covered
by a veil; slowly it moves and revolves. There the wind is formed, and
we are happy. It indeed strengthens our breath, for us who move about
on the earth. And the wind is just the strength for us to be content
with it and be happy. But the Four Beings told us: they said, "We
believe that your kinsmen will see that in future days it may happen
that it will be beyond our control. It is the most important thing for
us to watch. It may become strong in its revolving, and we believe
that it will scrape off everything on the earth. The wind may become
strong, we believe, and bring harm to the people moving about." That
is what they said. And indeed up to the present time we can attest to
it: the way it occurs, it destroys their homes. From time to time it is
destructive, for the wind can become strong. But as for us, we are
content, for no matter how strong the wind has been we have been
happy. And give it your thought, that we may do it properly: we give
thanks for the thing that is covered by a veil, where the wind is formed.
And our minds will continue to be so.

And now this is what Our Creator did: he decided, "I shall have
helpers who will live in the west. They will come from that direction
and will move about among the clouds, carrying fresh water." They will

sprinkle all the gardens which he provided, which grow of their own accord on the earth. And he decided, "There will be a relationship when people want to refer to them: they will say 'our grandparents, the Thunderers.' That is what they will do." And he left them in the west; they will always come from that direction. And truly they will always be of such a strength that the people, their grandchildren, who move about will be content with them. And they are performing their obligation, moving about all through the summer among the clouds, making fresh water, rivers, ponds, and lakes. And give it your thought, that we may do it properly: we now give thanks for them, our grandparents, the Thunderers. And our minds will continue to be so.

And now this is what Our Creator did: he decided, "There will be a sky above the heads of the people moving about. I must have a helper in the sky as well." And indeed he assigned him to be attached to the sky. There he will move about, and will cross the earth. He will always come from a certain direction, and will always go in a certain direction. And he also prescribed a relationship when we want to refer to it: we shall say "our elder brother, the sun." And it is true: he is carrying out his responsibility, attached there to the sky; there is beautiful daylight, and we are happy. And we believe that he too has done all that he was obligated to do; everything that he left to grow of its own accord is flourishing. He gave him the added responsibility of making it warm on the earth, so that everything he left to grow of its own accord would flourish. And we believe that he is performing his obligation up to the present time, the assignment he was given. And give it your thought, that we may do it properly: we give thanks for him, our elder brother, the sun. And our minds will continue to be so.

And now this is what Our Creator did: he decided, "There will be a certain period when it will be day." And indeed he saw well that the people moving about were taking care of themselves. And he decided, "They will rest. They will lay down their bodies and rest while it is in shadow." That is what he intended. "And perhaps it will happen that somewhere at a distance they will run into darkness. And I shall have another helper, another orb in the sky. People will say 'our grandmother, the moon.' That is how they will do it. It can be a sort of guide for their steps, providing them with light." And indeed it is a measure for us as we go along, we who move about on the earth. He decided, "The moon will change its form as it goes." They have called it "phases." And it is true: it is still a measure for us up to the present time, the way it is as we go along, we who move about on the earth. And we believe that they come from there too, that it continues unchanged: the little ones taking their places on the earth. They are here and they come from our mothers. And therefore we believe that she has done all that she was obligated to do, the assignment she was given. And now give it your thought, that we may do it properly: we now give thanks for her, our grandmother, the moon. And our minds will continue to be so.

And now this is what Our Creator did. He decided, "There will also be stars arrayed in the sky while it is dark." And he assigned to them certain things as well, the way it would continue to be. He decided, "They too will all have names, all the stars in the sky. And they too, in fact, will be indicators, to be used for measuring by the people moving about. If it happens that they run into darkness on their journey, they will use them, the people moving about. And indeed they will lift their faces to the stars and will be set straight. They will head back directly toward their home." And up to the present time they have had an added responsibility. While it is dark they will cause moisture to fall on everything that he left to grow of its own accord on the earth. And truly they enjoy water throughout the night, everything that he left to grow of its own accord. It comes from the stars arrayed in the sky. And we believe that they are performing their obligation, the responsibility that they too have. And give it your thought, that we may do it properly: we now give thanks for them, the stars arrayed in the sky. And our minds will continue to be so.

And now Our Creator decided, "I shall have the Four Beings as helpers to protect the people moving about on the earth." Indeed, he saw well that it was not possible for them alone, that they could not continue to move about alone. It was true: all sorts of things were going on on the earth where they would move about. It was inevitable that the people moving about on the earth would have accidents. The people moving about on the earth would have accidental things happen to them that would be beyond their control. And indeed we too can attest to it, we who move about on the earth: it will happen that people are involved in accidents that are beyond their control. It is the way with us who move about on the earth. And indeed they also have the added responsibility of keeping watch over those of his helpers called the Four Groups (the wind, the Thunderers, the sun, and the moon). They will continue to look after us whom he left on the earth, and will bring us contentment. And we believe that they too are performing their obligation, the assignment they were given, those who are called the Four Beings, our protectors. And therefore let there be gratitude, for we believe that we are happy. Give it your thought, that with one mind we may now give thanks for his helpers, the Four Beings, our protectors. And our minds will continue to be so.

And now this is what Our Creator did. He did indeed decide it, and it must happen according to his will. Indeed he was among us who moved about on the earth. Illness took hold of him, and he was confined to bed. For a number of years he lay helpless. And the way things were, he had to be thankful during the nights and days, and he thought that there must be someone there who made all the things that he was seeing. And thereupon he repented everything, all the things he thought he had done wrong when he moved about on the earth. And indeed he was thankful each day for each new thing that he saw. And now it happened that the Creator saw well how the people on the earth were acting. It seemed that nowhere was there any longer any guidance for the minds of those who moved about. And now it happened that he sent his helpers to speak to our great one, whom we used to call Handsome Lake, when he moved about. They gave him the responsibility to tell us what we should do in the future. And for a number of years he told about the words of the Creator. And the way things went, he labored until he collapsed. And let there indeed be gratitude that from time to time now we again hear the words of the Creator. And therefore let there be gratitude that it is still continuing as he planned it. And give it your thought, that we may do it properly: we give thanks for him, whom we called Handsome Lake. And our minds will continue to be so.

And now this is what Our Creator did. He decided, "I myself shall continue to dwell above the sky, and that is where those on the earth will end their thanksgiving. They will simply continue to have gratitude for everything they see that I created on the earth, and for everything they see that is growing." That is what he intended. "The people moving about on the earth will have love; they will simply be thankful. They will begin on the earth, giving thanks for all they see. They will carry it upward, ending where I dwell. I shall always be listening carefully to what they are saying, the people who move about. And indeed I shall always be watching carefully what they do, the people on the earth." And up to the present time, indeed, we people believe that we are happy. And therefore let there also be gratitude that we can claim to be happy. And give it your thought, that with one mind we may now give thanks for him, Our Creator. And our minds will continue to be so.

And that is all that I myself am able to do. What they did was to decide that a ritual of gratitude, as they called it, would always be observed in the future, when in the future people would gather. And that is all that I myself am able to do; that is all that I learned of the ritual which begins the ceremony. That is it.

Various of the spirits mentioned in this speech are addressed in particular Iroquois ceremonials. Important among these are: the Strawberry ceremony held when the strawberries ripen, the Maple ceremony held when the maple sap begins to rise in the spring, and the Planting, Green Bean, Green Corn, and Harvest ceremonies held in honor of Our Life Supporters, the Three Sisters—corn, beans, and squash. The Thunder, Sun, and Moon ceremonies in the spring and summer honor the Thunderers, sun, and moon respectively. Although other beings are also addressed in the Midwinter ceremonial, some parts of the ritual are in particular honor of the Creator. Handsome Lake is remembered in the fall gatherings, the "Six Nations meetings" at which the teachings of the Prophet are recalled.

Although not mentioned in the Thanksgiving Speech—it would be inappropriate to be thankful for death—the dead are honored in various ceremonies.[3] These include the wake and funeral, the Tenday feast (so-called as it is held ten days after a death), and the anniversary of the death held a year later. If the deceased was a chief, his name is transferred to his successor at the Condolence Ceremony. All the dead of the community are remembered at the ʔohki:we:h (Chafe's [1963] transcription of Seneca words will be followed throughout), or Feast of the Dead, still held in some longhouses once or twice a year.

Not all supernatural beings recognized by the Iroquois are mentioned in the Thanksgiving Speech. Important among these are the spirits associated with what are generally termed the medicine societies in the literature. These medicine societies, each of which has its own rituals and myths, include the False Face and Husk Face societies, both of which use masks in certain of their rituals; the Bear, Buffalo, Eagle, and Otter societies; the Society of Mystic Animals (yéiʔdo:s) and the order of this society charged with renewal of the medicine—the Little Water Society; as well as the Society of Charm Holders—also called the Pygmy Society after one important type of associated spirits or the Dark Dance after one of the important rituals of this society—and its associated groups that perform the Changing Ribs and Quavering dances. Membership in these groups is usually restricted to those who have been cured by members of the society, that is, to those who have had the ritual of the society performed for them as the symptoms of illness, a dream, or a seer indicated such ritual was necessary. Performance of the rituals of the society are the responsibility of its members. In contrast, the responsibility for the performance of the rituals addressed to those beings mentioned in the Thanksgiving Speech rests with the community.

In general, if the ceremony honoring any of these spirits is open to all, it is held in the longhouse; if the ceremony is open only to those invited, it is held in a private home. This means that most ceremonies in honor of those beings mentioned in the Thanksgiving Address are held in the longhouse, while those of the medicine societies are held in private homes, although on occasion certain ceremonies of the medicine societies are held in the longhouse.

The typical longhouse is a rectangular frame building with two stoves, one at or near each end. These stoves serve as a source of ashes and coals used for the False and Husk Faces when they blow ashes on their patients and on each other and as a place to hold tobacco invocations as well as a source of heat. Windows and electricity serve as a source of light. Around the walls are two rows of benches, the second row raised above the first on risers. This arrangement leaves the center of the longhouse open for the dances and games that constitute the major religious rites. Several benches that may be moved when necessary to the center of the room to provide seating for the musicians are the only other essential furnishings. The interior of a longhouse is typically plain, and what decorations may be present, since they have no religious relevance, seem incidental to the purposes for which the building is built. For example, on the walls of the Tonawanda Longhouse are two framed pictures—one of the "Seneca Council Tree" and the other of the council house in Letchworth State Park—and two unframed illustrations—one on "Wampum Making" and the other on "Iroquois Fortifications," issued by the Pontiac Motor Company. Instruments for the dances, such as the large turtle shell rattles used in the Feather Dance, may be temporarily hung on the walls.

The present-day longhouse, used solely as a building where people meet, developed out of the old longhouse whose primary function was to provide living quarters for a number of families. This old type of longhouse was a bark-covered structure from 18 to 24 feet wide and up to 200 feet in length, depending on the number of families living in it. The roof, originally arbor-shaped and later gabled, was some 20 feet high. Along both long walls were two benches approximately 6 feet wide, one about a foot off the ground and the other 5 to 6 feet from the floor. The lower benches provided both sleeping space near the fires in the winter and seating. The upper benches provided sleeping space in the summer and storage space in the winter. A row of fires down the center of the longhouse provided both heat and cooking facilities, the two families on either side of a fire sharing it. Holes in the roof served as chimneys and a door at either end as exit and entrance. One house in each village was built particularly long to serve as a meeting place for the community (Tooker 1964:42; Beauchamp 1916:74).

In the latter part of the seventeenth and in the eighteenth century, the average number of families occupying a single longhouse declined and many dwellings came to house a single nuclear family, although bark construction was still favored. However, the older type of longhouse was retained as a council house. John Bartram (1751:40–41) described such a council house at Onondaga in 1743:

We alighted at the council house, where the chiefs were already assembled to receive us, which they did with a grave chearful complaisance, according to their custom; they shew'd us where to lay our baggage, and repose ourselves during our stay with them; which was in the two end apartments of this large house. The *Indians* that came with us were placed over against us: this cabin is about 80 feet long, and 17 broad, the common passage 6 feet wide; and the apartments on each side 5 feet, raised a foot above the passage by a long sapling hewed square, and fitted with joists that go from it to the back of the house; on these joists they lay large pieces of bark, and on extraordinary occasions spread matts made of rushes, this favour we had; on these floors they set or lye down every one as he will, the apartments are divided from each other by boards or bark, 6 or 7 foot long, from the lower floor to the upper, on which they put their lumber, when they have eaten their homony, as they set in each apartment before the fire, they can put the bowel over head, having not about 5 foot to reach; they set on the floor sometimes at each end, but mostly at one: they have a shed to put their wood into in the winter, or in the summer, to set to converse or play, that has a door to the south; all the sides and roof of the cabin are made of bark, bound fast to poles set in the ground, and bent round on the top, or set aflatt, for the roof as we set our rafters; over each fire place they leave a hole to let out the smoak, which in rainy weather, they cover with a piece of bark, and this they can easily reach with a pole to push it on one side or quite over the hole, after this model are most of their cabins built.

In 1818, Timothy Alden (1827:54–55) described a similar council house at Tonawanda.[4] It was

fifty feet long and twenty wide. On each side of it, longitudinally is a platform, a little more than one foot high and four feet wide, covered with furs, which furnishes a convenient place for sitting, lounging, and sleeping. A rail across the centre separates the males from the females, who are constant attendants and listen, with silence, diligence, and interest, to whatever is delivered in council. Over the platform is a kind of galley, five or six feet from the floor, which is loaded with peltry, corn, implements of hunting, and a variety of other articles. At each end of the building is a door, and near each door, within, was the council fire. . . . Over each fire several large kettles of soup were hanging and boiling. The smoke was conveyed away through apertures in the roof and did not annoy. The chiefs and others, as many as could be accommodated, in their appropriate grotesque habiliments, were seated on the platform, smoking calumets, of various forms, sizes, and materials, several of which were tendered to me in token of friendship. Profound silence pervaded the crowded assembly.

At present, on most occasions, the men sit separately from the women and young children in the longhouse. One end of the longhouse becomes thus the men's end and the other, the women's end. The exception to this rule are those occasions where customary seating is by moiety rather than by sex. (Among all Iroquois tribes, the clans are grouped into moieties. See p. 23.) Then both men and women of the same moiety sit on the same end. In these instances, those entering the longhouse should use the door at the end where their moiety sits—if the doors of the longhouse are so placed that this may be done. Usually, however, the men enter and leave by the door on their end, and the women by the door on their end. If this rule is broken, it is probably more often broken by men than women. This may be a carryover from earlier experience: as children, the men would have entered the longhouse with their mothers through the women's door. The first men and women to arrive take seats at the far side of their respective ends. As more arrive, the space between the men and women gradually fills, the middle section filling up last. This seating arrangement presents some difficulty for white couples who attend the longhouse ceremonies. Frequently, they resolve a minor problem in culture conflict—in white society seating is usually by couples rather than by sex—by sitting in the middle section so that the wife is on the women's side and the man on the men's side. This is usually easy to do as this middle section is the last to be filled by the Indians.

The use of the two stoves in the longhouse is affected by this seating arrangement. Those rituals involving primarily women take place near the stove at the women's end, and those rituals involving primarily men take place near the men's stove. Dances begun by only the men thus begin around the men's stove, and women's dances and those dances begun by the women start near the women's stove. Since the cooking of food is ever women's work, food brought into the longhouse for distribution at the end of the ceremony is placed near the women's stove. Likewise, since only men perform tobacco invocations, these rites are most often made into the men's stove.

Anyone may take part in most of the dances, and all should for at least a time in certain of them. The dancing itself can be quite vigorous, and those who dance well are admired. But no stigma is attached to those who do not, for what is important is that one dances. Consequently some, particularly young children and old people, may be seen to be merely shuffling around. Some of the dancers amuse the others by displaying exaggerated steps; some tease other dancers as they dance.

There is no absolute ban on talking during the ritual, rather only the feeling that the talk should not be so loud as to prevent hearing the speech or the singing. If the level of noise becomes too high, efforts are made to reduce it. Smoking in the longhouse is not taboo. This smoking is not a sacred act, but purely a social, secular one. Although there are a few occasions on which tobacco is ritually smoked, often the ritual acts involving tobacco are the acts of giving, receiving, and burning loose tobacco. There is no ban on entering or leaving the longhouse whenever one wishes except on those very few occasions when the longhouse is "closed." Similarly, there is no ban on changing one's seat. Children are apt to do so, sitting first with one woman and then with another.

Although a few longhouses are "closed" to both Christian Indians and whites, many are not. In the latter instance, the longhouse ceremonials provide a means for those Christian Indians who do attend to renew their identification as Indians, as well as an opportunity for a pleasant evening's entertainment and a chance to see friends. Indians cannot forget—nor are they allowed to forget—that they are Indians, and as the ceremonials are visible evidence that Iroquois, in fact, are different from whites, some attend the doings at the longhouse to see "how we used to do it." Some potential conflict between beliefs of followers of the Longhouse religion and followers of Christ is eased by the feeling among certain people that the "Creator" of the Longhouse religion is the "God" of the Christian religion and that therefore the two religions are not irreconcilable.

Near the longhouse may be auxiliary buildings. For example, close by the New York Onondaga Longhouse is a building called the "Mudhouse." When the two moieties separate for certain rituals, one moiety holds its rituals in the longhouse, while the other holds its rituals in the Mudhouse. However, Onondaga is unique in this respect. Often near the longhouse is a small building known as a "cook house." This building contains a large fireplace for cooking the soups distributed at the end of certain ceremonies. Near the Tonawanda Longhouse [5] and the Newtown Longhouse are buildings which contain both kitchen and dining facilities where a number of people can be fed with relative ease. Most of the activity, however, takes place in the longhouse itself.

Those in charge of setting the dates of the ceremonials held in the longhouse and planning them are the "Faithkeepers" (probably a slight mistranslation of the term hono^{n}di:o^{n}t), or what are termed "Deacons" in English on the Six Nations Reserve. On those few reservations that still retain the ancient system of hereditary chieftainships, those chiefs who are followers of the Longhouse religion are expected to help the Faithkeepers carry out the ritual, most importantly by giving the speeches that form an integral part of all Iroquois ceremonials, as well as by discharging their responsibility of looking out for the well-being of the people in general. At Tonawanda, one of the chiefs is the principal speaker and consequently leader of the Longhouse ceremonies. In contrast, at the Coldspring and Newtown Longhouses, where the hereditary chieftainship system was abandoned in the middle of the nineteenth century in favor of an elected councilor system, each moiety has a head man and woman who are charged with some of the leadership duties that fall to the chief at Tonawanda. The longhouses on the Six Nations Reserve, where the hereditary chiefs ceased to have political powers in 1924, also have a head man and woman Faithkeepers from each moiety. But this seems to have been old custom (Shimony 1961 :85–87).

Both Faithkeepers and chiefs are selected on the basis of clan affiliation. Each clan owns a set of personal names. A child is given one of the names not "currently in use" from this stock of names at the Midwinter or Green Corn ceremonial, whichever occurs first after the child's birth. At least this is the ideal custom; those who are not followers of the Longhouse religion often do not get around to having their children so named for some years. When the child becomes an adult, this "baby" name is changed to an "adult" name, which is also chosen from the clan's stock of names not in use. One of the duties of the "clan mother"—the senior woman of the clan—is to keep track of the names not in use, that is, those names that either belonged to those now deceased or have been given up by those still living. Certain names are chief (League or Sachem) names and others are Faithkeeper names. These names are given to individuals when they assume these offices, and like other personal names are "owned" by the clan. Thus, when a chief or sub-chief dies, the clan mother in consultation with the other women of the clan suggests a successor, who, if approved by the chiefs,[6] is "raised up" at a special ceremony called the Condolence ceremony. At this ceremony, the deceased chief is "raised up," or "resuscitated" by having the name transferred to his successor. Faithkeeper names are similarly conferred except that the new Faithkeeper receives his or her new name at Midwinter or Green Corn. Faithkeeper names, it is said at least at Tonawanda, cannot be taken away because some people are "born" Faithkeepers, that is, are given a Faithkeeper name as a baby or adult name. A chief's name, however, may be taken away from him if the women of the clan so wish, a process known as "de-horning" the chief.

Iroquois clans are exogamous and matrilineal; that is, no one should marry someone of his own clan, and everyone takes the clan affiliation of his mother, an affiliation he retains throughout his life. (However, the rule of exogamy is now breaking down, especially among those who are not followers of the Longhouse religion.) Although Iroquois clans are totemically named, these names usually are not the common names of the animals referred to by the clan name (Chafe 1963:27). The western Iroquois—the Seneca, Cayuga, and Onondaga—have eight clans, but not exactly the same set is found in each of these tribes. The Mohawk and Oneida have three clans.

The clans in each Iroquois tribe are grouped into two moieties (i.e., two halves), or what the Iroquois call "sides" in English. However, the grouping of clans into the two moieties is not identical in all the Iroquois tribes. For example, among the Seneca, the Bear, Wolf, Turtle, and Beaver clans comprise one side, and the Deer, Hawk, Snipe, and Heron clans the other. Among the Cayuga, the Bear, Wolf, Turtle, Snipe, and Eel clans comprise one side, and the Deer, Hawk, and Beaver clans the other (Morgan 1901 [2]:225; present practice at Six Nations is different; see Shimony 1961:56–57). Among the Onondaga, the Wolf, Turtle, Beaver, Snipe, and Ball clans comprise one side, and the Deer, Bear, and Eel clans the other. Among the Oneida and Mohawk, the Wolf and Turtle clans comprise one side, and the Bear clan the other.

Tradition states that the moieties were once also exogamous, that a man was supposed to marry a woman of the other "side." Although moieties no longer have—in a sense—the reciprocal obligation of providing spouses for each other, they still have other reciprocal obligations. They ought to bury the other's dead, a custom now often not followed. On occasion, the moieties may play against each other, one team being made up of members of one moiety and the opposing team being made up of members of the other moiety. Further, the positions are often paired by moiety, one member of the pair belonging to one moiety and the other member to the other, or "opposite," moiety. For example, each of the eight Seneca chiefs is paired with one of the opposite moiety, each moiety having four chiefly names. When a Faithkeeper receives his name, a Faithkeeper of the same sex but of the opposite moiety receives his Faithkeeper name at the same time.

Many of the appointments of positions in the Midwinter ceremony are also paired ones: for example, the two Bigheads who announce the beginning of the Midwinter ceremonial through the
houses on the first day should be of opposite moieties, and the committee in charge of the Bowl Game, a game of chance played as part
of the ritual of the ceremonial, should be composed of a man and a
woman from each moiety.

Although now there is no set number of Faithkeepers, the number once may have been limited. Fenton (1936:6–7) reports that
theoretically at the Coldspring Longhouse each of the eight clans
should have two representatives—a man and a woman—but that
now there are more than sixteen Faithkeepers, names belonging to
the now defunct Cornplanter, Plank Road, and Horseshoe Longhouses coming to be used at Coldspring. At Tonawanda, the exact
number of Faithkeepers is not known as some are never seen in the
longhouse. Shimony (1961:70–87) reports that at the Sour Springs
Longhouse there are non-hereditary as well as hereditary Faithkeepers. It seems most likely that at one time the association of Faithkeepers with particular clans was more evident in all longhouses than
at present, and that with decreasing numbers of Longhouse religion
followers, and lessening importance of the clan in the organization of
the society, this association has become less evident with fewer
Faithkeepers bearing "Faithkeeper names." At present, also, the
flexibility of numbers of Faithkeepers assures that there will be
enough to carry out the duties assigned to them.

Although clan-owned chief and Faithkeeper names tend to be
transferred to those in the same lineage with the result that important names tend to be concentrated in certain lineages, it should be
noted that the position of chief, or speaker of the longhouse at Tonawanda is not held by a particular clan: the position may be held by
any chief. Thus, the present chief is a member of the Hawk clan,
though his predecessor was a member of the Snipe clan.

In Iroquois custom, two devices are used to recognize special
abilities: (1) occasionally, though rarely, a position belonging to one
clan may be temporarily loaned to another and the position filled by a
member of that clan; (2) certain chiefs, often called Pine Tree chiefs
to distinguish them from the League, or Sachem chiefs, are given a
special name and thus recognition by virtue of some distinguished
achievement. Such a position, however, is not hereditary.

Various lesser positions in the ritual are allotted on the basis of interest and talent. Thus, the lead dancers and musicians for the dance are selected among those known to have the appropriate abilities. But these are not formal positions. The division of people is into chiefs, Faithkeepers, and others. The term referring to these latter is usually translated "commoner" or "ordinary people," but as Chafe (1961:10–11) has suggested, the literal translation "those with no assigned responsibility" or, more loosely, "the people generally" is the better translation.

The principal rites of an Iroquois ceremony—that is, those rites that follow the opening Thanksgiving Speech and precede the closing Thanksgiving Speech—are drawn from the Iroquois repertoire of songs, dances, and games. In ceremonies addressed to certain spirits, the performance of these rites is preceded by a tobacco invocation, that is, a speech during which the speaker throws loose tobacco onto the fire at intervals. Such an invocation is most notably a part of various ceremonials of the medicine societies, but it also occurs in some others, as the Maple ceremony, Thunder ceremony, and certain ceremonies addressed to ghosts. It is omitted in such ceremonies as those addressed to Our Life Supporters and Strawberry, and sometimes Moon and Sun. The general rule governing the inclusion of the tobacco invocation as a part of the ceremonial seems to be: if the spirit addressed in the ceremonial is thought to live outside the village and its fields, a tobacco invocation is included; but if not, the tobacco invocation is omitted.

The tobacco invocation, then, greets those beings who live at a distance and hence are not always about. Prominent among such beings are those of the medicine societies, but also included are Maple who, like the False Faces, live in the woods, and the Thunderers who appear in the spring and leave in the fall. Not included in this type are such beings as corn, beans, and strawberries, since they are near at hand. In those ceremonies addressed to ghosts, a tobacco invocation is given if the dead are addressed collectively or if a ghost is being asked not to bother further an ill person, but is omitted in the funeral ceremonies, those rituals held before the ghost has left for the land of the dead in the West.

Some of these principal rites of the Iroquois ritual repertoire as ʔadɔⁿ:weʔ (the Personal Chants of the men) and thɔwi:sas (comparable songs of the women) belong to individuals and consequently are usually sung only by these individuals. By Iroquois custom, each man has his own song, ?adɔⁿ:we?, a song often belonging to his father or maternal line (Fenton 1936:16; 1942:18–19; 1953:103; Speck 1949:135–37), which he sings on certain occasions. Anciently, it was the last song sung by a warrior before his death and the song sung by him while boasting during the war feast.

Other rites, such as the songs of medicine societies, belong to particular groups, and still others belong to the people as a whole. Some of these latter, as the people themselves, are regarded as more important than others, and are regarded as "sacred" dances. Such sacred dances hold a special place in the ceremonial life of the Iroquois and consequently should not be performed on certain occasions as when an Indian dance troupe puts on a "show" for a group of whites.

The most "sacred" are the Feather Dance and the Thanksgiving, Drum, or Skin Dance—two of the "Four Sacred Rituals." Other sacred dances include the dances given a part of the Our Life Supporters series, which at Tonawanda are called the "Four Ceremonies," as well as others. They include: Women's Dance; Corn Dance; Stomp, Trotting, or Standing Quiver Dance; Hand-in-hand, Linking Arms, or Bean Dance; Striking-the-pole, or Striking-the-stick Dance; War (wasa:se?), that is, "Sioux" dance (Morgan 1901[1]: 258; Parker 1913:103 *n*; Fenton 1936:9 *n*; Chafe 1964:282).

The least sacred, the "social dances"—performed primarily "for fun" or sociability—include: Fish Dance, Raccoon Dance, Chicken Dance, Sharpening-a-stick Dance, Choose-a-partner Dance, Shake-the-pumpkin or Shaking-the-jug Dance, Garter Dance, Dove or Passenger Pigeon Dance, Duck Dance, Robin Dance, Skin-beating Dance, Fishing Dance, Cherokee Dance, Grinding-an-arrow Dance, Knee-rattle Dance, Alligator Dance, Rabbit Dance, and Women's Dance (or new Women's Dance as these songs are social rather that the sacred ones belonging to the "sacred" Women's Dance mentioned above) (Kurath 1964:23–26; Fenton 1941:165). The dances performed outside the longhouse for the entertainment of whites are drawn from this series.

The most prominent game in the ritual is the Bowl Game, also called the Peach Stone Game, one of the Four Sacred Rituals. (For description see pp. 31–32.) Other games include lacrosse, snow snake, tug of war, "football," hoop and javelin, and "bone" game.

That the major rites of Iroquois ceremonies are songs, dances, and games rather than prayers has led the Iroquois to refer to their ceremonies as "doings" in English rather than "services"; an Iroquois says that he is going to "the doings" in the longhouse not to "the services." The connotations of the word *service* probably seem inappropriate to them. The Iroquois do not serve the supernatural through the ceremony; they participate in the activities of the ceremony. It is this contrast between Christian and Iroquois ceremonialism that led one Iroquois woman to remark to me, "We do not pray; we dance."

Various of these rites require special implements which, though used in sacred contexts, are not regarded as sacred objects. They are not objects of special ritual attention either in use or decoration, being subject only to the care in manufacture and storage that any ordinary useful artifact might be given. For this reason, Conklin and Sturtevant aptly term those used in the songs "singing tools." The Seneca word for these singing tools means "those things used for propping up songs" (Conklin and Sturtevant 1953:262) or "people use them to sing with" (Chafe 1963:44).

With the exception of the rarely used flute, all Iroquois singing tools are percussion instruments, primarily rattles and drums. They serve not as substitutes for the human voice as in western music, but as instruments which are used to beat a simple, steady rhythm—perhaps a necessity for dancing since the meter of Iroquois songs is often complex (Kurath 1964:40). Most prominent in the rituals are the turtle and horn rattles. The turtle rattle is made from a snapping turtle, the neck of the turtle reinforced with a stick serving as the handle. In the Feather Dance, the two musicians sit straddling a wooden bench and pound the edge of the rattle on the bench in front of them. The sound produced is so loud it is often difficult to hear the song. Such turtle rattles, often smaller, are also often used by the False Faces in the performance of their rituals. When used by them as an accompaniment for their dancing, while walking, or while standing erect, the rattle is snapped, thus producing a simple rhythm characteristic of Iroquois musical accompaniments. However, on other occasions, as when entering or leaving a house or during some tobacco invocations when no dancing occurs, the rattle is scraped against a wooden surface, such as the door jamb or the floor; the

False Faces are beings of the forest and their masks are made out of the wood of the forests. If a turtle rattle is not available, a substitute made of bark or of a tin can may be used, or a wooden rattle. The bark rattle is made of a piece of bark folded over and tied to make a handle. At present, they are rarely used in the longhouse. Conklin and Sturtevant (1953:272) did not see these rattles in use in the Coldspring Longhouse at the 1952 Midwinter ceremonial, and I have not observed them at the ceremonies of the Tonawanda Longhouse. The tin rattle, however, is commonly used at Tonawanda. It is made of an average-size tin can to which a simple wooden handle is added. A simple whittled wooden stick, what Conklin and Sturtevant term a "tempo beater," is a common substitute for the rattle in the dances of the Beggar Faces. A box turtle rattle is used, at least at Coldspring, in the thɔwi:sas, or Women's Rite; a "stamping stick," a long wooden pole is also used in this rite.

Perhaps most prominent, though not the most valuable in the ceremonies, is the horn rattle. It is made of a section of cow, steer, or bull horn, closed at both ends with flat plugs of wood, and has a wooden handle. It is commonly played by hitting the rattle against the palm of an open left hand, and occasionally, if the musician is seated, against the left thigh. At times during the song, it may be twirled in a small circle above the hand. It is used either alone or with the water drum in a number of songs.

A gourd rattle is used in the songs of the Society of Mystic Animals. It is made of a gourd with a wooden handle attached.

The most frequently seen instrument is the water drum. A larger drum of the same construction is used in the ʔohki:we:h, "Chanters-for-the-Dead" songs. The water drum is made of a wooden keg with a leather head and a plug in the side which is removed when water is added to the drum. It seems likely that in ancient times these drums were made of pots, not wooden kegs. The tone of the drum is regulated by the amount of water added and the tightness of the drum head. When stored, the drum is placed head down so that the skin head is kept moist. Before it is played, the drum is also turned to moisten the head. A single, simply carved wooden stick is used as a drum beater. The drum is held in the left hand and beat with the stick held in the right (see Conklin and Sturtevant 1953 and Fenton

1942:9–11 for a description of the manufacture and use of Iroquois musical instruments).

Other means are used for percussion effects. For example, the Husk Faces on occasion carry long, slender poles which they tap on the ground in what may best be described as a nervous sort of tap. The ʔadɔⁿ:weʔ chants, the Personal Chants of the men, are customarily accompanied by rhythmic responses of the men he: he: and hi:goⁿye:: and by the rhythmic clapping of the women. The dancing itself also provides a percussion noise; and if many are dancing and the dance step is vigorous, the floor shakes. The seated musicians often keep time by pounding their heels, not their toes, on the floor.

Iroquois dances are typically round dances, in partial circles of men and of women, of men and women alternating, or of women alone, depending on the dance. The dance is always counterclockwise except for certain dances for the dead. Each dance has its proper step (see Kurath 1964 for descriptions), but not all the dancers are equally proficient. Everyone may take part and many do: infants may be carried by their fathers, young children just beginning to learn to dance, adults, and old women barely able to shuffle around take part in the dance.

Two of the dances—the Feather Dance and Thanksgiving Dance —are costume dances; that is, if possible "Indian costume" ought to be worn for them. Otherwise, present-day Iroquois dress is like that of whites, and the dress for other dances is ordinary street wear. The reaction of whites to this acculturation in dress as well as housing affords the Indians some amusement: they recount those occasions when whites touring the reservation have asked them, "Where are the Indians?"—the whites apparently expecting to see skin teepees inhabited by Indians wearing feather war bonnets, leather leggings, and moccasins.

Just before a Feather Dance is to begin, the men who have brought their costumes leave the longhouse to put them on and after the conclusion of the dance, or of the Thanksgiving Dance if that is also given, leave again to change back to ordinary dress. Women and small children, if they have chosen to wear a special costume, however, do not retire to change, but wear the same dress throughout the entire morning or evening as the case may be. For the costume dances, the men often now wear a Plains-type feathered headdress. This idea, which is the white notion of what Indians should wear, was adopted by the Iroquois after some had worked in "Indian shows" in various parts of the United States. The feather Sioux-type of bonnet now often worn by the Iroquois are made by them from feathers ordered from Oklahoma and decorated with beadwork they make themselves. Formerly, more men wore the Iroquois twirling-feather headdress, a cap with a single long feather set in a socket so that it rotates. Leggings, and occasionally trousers with fringes down both sides; two aprons, one in front and the other in back, attached to a belt or a breechcloth, decorated with beadwork; a shirt; and shoes, and sometimes moccasins complete the costume. Women, if costumed, usually wear leggings that are tied below the knee, a skirt that covers the knee, and a long overblouse—all made of cloth and often decorated with beadwork—and moccasins. This style of dress has changed less than that of the men during the past hundred years. Since colonial times, the principle change in Iroquois dress has been the substitution of cloth for skin, of shirts and overblouses for fur robes worn over the shoulders, and of glass beads and silver brooches for shell ornaments. On rare occasions, Indian costumes of other tribes are seen in the longhouse. Although "Indian costume" should be worn for the costume dances, some of the men dancers and most of the women wear ordinary dress.

The only other occasions on which special costume is worn are those on which the Bigheads are dressed in their distinctive dress at the opening of Midwinter and those on which the members of the two masked medicine societies—the False Face and Husk Face societies—wear their distinctive masks. Members of the False Face Society wear carved and painted wooden masks, often with long, horse tail hair attached, and members of the Husk Face Society wear masks made of braided corn husks.

In general, Iroquois ritualism is little concerned with the manipulation of objects, sacred or otherwise. This is reflected in the simplicity of the longhouse itself and the relatively few occasions for which special costume is worn in the ritual. It is also reflected in the paucity of sacred objects.

The longhouse owns "wampums" which validate its position as a ritual center but which are rarely brought out. Wampum occasionally figures in the ritual, such as the string of wampum used in the rite of confession. But the significance of wampum generally is that because it is a valuable object, it is used to indicate the significance of the event, either by giving it as a commemoration of the event or as being shown in remembrance of the event. Wampum belts, for example, were given at treaties to indicate good faith in the making of the treaty, and might be brought out to remind others of the treaty. In and of itself, wampum is not sacred.

Certain of the medicine societies hold sacred objects. For example, the Little Water medicine is a powerful curing material which is the object of a renewal ritual held by the Little Water Society at three stated times during the year. But such objects as these are relatively rare.

The implements used in playing the games in various rituals have, like the implements used in singing the songs, no special ritual significance; they are merely "tools" used in the play. The game most often played as part of the ritual is the "Bowl," or "Peach Stone Game." As these names suggest, six peach stones colored black on one side and a flat-bottomed bowl are used in the play. Before peach trees were introduced into the New World, wild fruit stones were used as dice (Tooker 1964:115). Before play begins, a blanket folded into a square is placed on the ground. This blanket acts as a kind of cushion against which the flat-bottomed bowl is rather sharply struck. Hitting the bowl against the ground causes the peach stones in the bowl to jump and constitutes the "throw of the dice." After the bowl has been struck against the ground, the number of peach stones with the same color up are counted.

The scoring throws are: all six stones with the same color up or five stones of the same color up. The player who has a scoring throw continues until he throws the stones so that no score is made. The opponent then takes the bowl and throws in the same manner until he makes no score. The bowl is then taken by the first player. This continues until one side has all the beans used as counters and is thus the winner.

Throughout the game, those on both sides shout loudly and gesture to drive luck toward them and away from their opponents. When one side has won all the beans, the game is ended and the bowl is turned over on the blanket to indicate it is finished. The winning side collects all that has been placed as bets, what it has placed and the matching bets of the other side. What is placed as a bet should be something valuable; there is some feeling that money, that is, small change, is not as acceptable a bet as the goods themselves, though money is often used.

The score is counted by one of several methods. An elaborate system is used at Onondaga when the Bowl Game is played in the beginning portion of the Midwinter ceremonial (see Blau 1967 for a description). A far less complicated system of scoring, however, is usual on other occasions. This latter version has two forms—a long and a short form of the game. The difference between these two forms is a difference in the number of beans used to tally the score —hence the length of time needed to finish the game—and a difference in the value of the highest scoring throw. In the long form of the game, 100 beans are used at Tonawanda and about the same number at other longhouses; in the short form of the game, each side has 5 or 7 beans. In the long form of the game, a throw of all black or all white sides up counts 5; in the short form, such throws count 2 points. In both forms of the game, a throw of five black or five white sides up counts 1 point. In the long form of the game, the 100 beans are divided between the sides by playing for them according to these scoring rules; in the short form of the game, the beans are given to each side before the game begins.

It is evident from a comparison of Iroquois ceremonials that the songs, dances, and games comprise a class of rites. Recognition that there is such a class of activities from which the rites of a particular ceremony are drawn takes some of the apparent confusion out of Iroquois ceremonialism. In Iroquois ritualism, there is no constant association between a rite and the being so honored by the performance of the rite. For example, the Feather Dance may be given in ceremonies addressed to the Creator as when it is performed as one of the Four Sacred Rituals at Green Corn and Midwinter, in ceremonies addressed to wild foods as in the Strawberry ceremony, in ceremonies addressed to cultivated foods as in the Our Life Supporters series of dances, in ceremonies addressed to celestial beings as in the Sun ceremony, or in ceremonies held to cure an individual. Comparably, the Bowl Game when played as one of the Four Sacred Rituals at Midwinter and Green Corn is addressed to the Creator; when played at the Sap ceremony, it is addressed to the spirit of the maple. It also may be played to cure an individual or at Midwinter to "renew" a friendship. In summary, the basic rule seems to be that any rite may be used in a ceremony addressed to any being, though certain rites are more often used than others.

What rite or rites are chosen to help cure an ill person—whether the rites belong to a medicine society or to all the people—depend on the dream of the patient. If he has not had a dream or cannot remember it, he consults a seer or "fortune-teller" who, using any one of a number of methods including now looking at cards or tea leaves, ascertains what ritual should be performed. Perhaps the fullest statement of the Iroquoian theory of disease, or more properly good and bad fortune in general, is contained in the seventeenth-century French accounts of Huron practice (see Tooker 1964:82–122 for a summary). As the French describe it, the Hurons believed that the soul of an individual had "desires" and that if these "desires," which could be for an object, a feast, or the performance of a dance or game, were not satisfied, the individual would become ill or otherwise suffer bad fortune. An individual learned of these desires through the dream or, failing that, by consultation with a medicine man. All the desires of the soul had to be fulfilled in order for the patient to become well again. More generally, the dream was "the god of the country," and various endeavors were entered into on the advice of the dream. Although the dream is probably of somewhat less importance to the Iroquois in the twentieth century than it was in the seventeenth and eighteenth centuries, something of the same system of beliefs remains (see, for example, Shimony 1961 and Fenton 1953).

It seems entirely possible that the rites now given as part of the calendric series of ceremonials were originally dictated by dreams, that is, tradition was established when someone dreamed that a particular rite ought to be given for a particular being on a particular occasion. The ritual of these ceremonies may still be changed on the advice of a dream (Fenton 1936:20–22). However, these changes apparently most often do not radically affect the basic form of the ceremonial as can be noted in a comparison of the calendric ceremonies of the various longhouses.

Perhaps the most variable of these ceremonies are those for the sun and moon. These two ceremonies are also the most infrequently performed, and in some longhouses so infrequently performed that they may be regarded as obsolete. The Sun ceremony is now very rarely performed at the Tonawanda and Newtown Longhouses. When given, it was composed of a rite of shooting at the sun, accompanied at least at the Newtown Longhouse with a tobacco invocation, and followed by a performance of the Feather Dance (Fenton 1941:159; Parker 1913:103). The Sun ceremony has not been given in recent years at the Sour Springs Longhouse, but the three other longhouses on the Six Nations Reserve hold it jointly. There the ritual consists of a performance of the Feather Dance, the Rite of Personal Chant, and the Thanksgiving Dance (Shimony 1961:157–58).

The Moon ceremony is even more rarely given. It is no longer given at the Sour Springs, Tonawanda, Coldspring, and Newtown Longhouses, although Parker (1913:103–104) mentions a Newtown Moon dance that might be given on the advice of a dream or a clairvoyant. This ceremony consisted of a tobacco invocation to the moon and the playing of the Bowl Game. At the Six Nations Reserve, the three longhouses down below precede their combined ceremony for the sun with the Moon ceremony. Its important features are the singing of the Women's Planting Song and a Bowl Game played between the sexes (Shimony 1961:157).

The Thunder ceremony is more frequently given, though in most longhouses it is held only in time of drought, and now only rarely given. At Newtown it is held in the spring when the thunder is first heard coming from the West (my informant). The basic features of the ceremony are a tobacco invocation and a performance of the War (wasa:se$^{?}$) Dance. At Sour Springs, the Thunder ceremony also included the playing of a lacrosse game between the performance of the tobacco invocation and the War Dance (Shimony 1961:162–65). At Tonawanda, a rite of confession of sins, Thanksgiving Dance, and Rite of Personal Chant followed the tobacco invocation and the War Dance (Fenton 1941:160). At Coldspring, the tobacco invocation for the Thunderers, the War Dance, and the related Striking-a-pole Dance was preceded by a tobacco invocation to the sun and a playing of the hoop and javelin game for the sun and moon (Fenton 1936:8–9). This addition to the Thunder ceremony may represent a vestige of an old ceremony to the sun and moon. At Newtown, the rites of the Thunder ceremony consist of a tobacco invocation and the War Dance (Parker 1913:104 [7]; my informant).

The Maple ceremony, or Sap Dance, at the Tonawanda Longhouse is composed of a tobacco invocation to the maple held outside the longhouse, followed by a Bowl Game played between the men and women, and concluding with a series of social dances. It is still held every year. The Newtown Maple ceremony is similar except that a Bone Game is played after the playing of the Bowl Game and preceding the social dances (my informant; see Parker 1913:101–103 for the tobacco invocation given at this ceremony). At Coldspring, the ceremony has lapsed. It consisted of returning thanks to the maple, sometimes followed by social dances. At dusk, songs from the Chanters-for-the-dead series were sung and the next day a tobacco invocation for the maple was given (Fenton 1936:8). The association of the Chanters-for-the-dead songs with maple at Coldspring is unique, and perhaps represents a vestige of the longer all-night Chanters-for-the-dead ceremony still held in some longhouses about this time. At Sour Springs, the Maple ceremony is no longer given. When it was, it had the general form of the other ceremonies for wild fruits—raspberry and strawberry. It consisted of a tobacco invocation, Feather Dance, distribution of maple sap to those present, and Feather Dance. At the Six Nations Onondaga and Seneca Longhouses, a short Bowl Game is also played (Shimony 1961:146–48).

The Strawberry ceremony is still held at the Sour Springs and other Six Nations Longhouses, Tonawanda, Newtown, and Coldspring Longhouses. The basic ritual consists of a performance of the Feather Dance, passing of the berry juice to those present, and another performance of the Feather Dance. Shimony (1961:158–61) reports that at the Sour Springs Longhouse the berry juice is passed before the first Feather Dance and a sermon follows the performance of this Feather Dance. This may, however, represent recent change. Speck (1949:36) reports that the berry juice was passed between the performances of the two Feather Dances.

The form of the ceremonies for the agricultural food spirits—Planting, Green Bean, and Harvest—are outlined in the next chapter.

As are the principal rites, the feast foods distributed at the end of a ceremony are indicated by the patient if the ceremony is a curing one and indicated by tradition in calendric ones. Thus, for example, at Tonawanda the food distributed at the end of the Maple ceremony is corn mush; at the end of the Strawberry ceremony, soup to which has been added berry juice; at the Planting ceremony, potato soup; and so on. It is entirely possible that the association of particular feast foods with a ceremony was originally indicated in a dream. In any case, information in the historical documents suggests that the feast has long been important in Iroquois ceremonialism, the earlier writers often using the word *feast* to refer to a ceremony.

In most Iroquois ceremonies, the feast is not eaten in the longhouse, but taken home and eaten there. Consequently, those attending the ceremony bring a "pail," such as a lard pail or a covered enamel pail, in which to carry home the soup distributed at the conclusion of the ritual; on certain occasions when much other food is distributed, they also bring a brown paper bag. In the distribution of the feast, those who had important roles in putting on the ceremony—the speaker, lead dancers, and musicians—are served first, and then the pails of all the others are collected and the remaining food distributed. Fenton (1953:153) suggests that this custom of bringing pails to a ceremony is an ancient one, and has antecedents in the old custom of guests bringing their own dishes to a feast.

The principal food distributed at the end of Longhouse religious ceremonies is usually a soup. In fact, it is tempting to call Iroquois and other eastern North American cultures "soup" cultures in contrast to the "wafer bread," or "tortilla" cultures of the American Southwest and Mexico, for it is the various soups that form the basic recipes of Iroquois culture. Even many of the breads that were made and are made are boiled, not baked breads. There is also a difference in favorite grinding techniques between the East and West which is probably, as Driver and Massey (1957:243) have pointed out, dependent on climatic conditions. They suggest that in the West the drier climate produced hard, dry seeds that required stone grinding techniques, while in the more humid East the seeds were softer and could be prepared in a wooden mortar and pestle. With the introduction of agriculture, these techniques persisted. Further, flint varieties of corn were preferred in the more humid East as they would keep better than the flour varieties preferred in the West. However, since flint corn cannot be ground in wooden mortars, it was soaked and then hulled in the mortar. The mortar and pestle are still used among the Iroquois in preparing corn for these soups. Although once the task of women, it is now the men who do the heavy work of pounding, at least at Tonawanda. But the women still rise early in the morning to begin cooking the soup in large kettles for the feast later in the day.

Other foods may be distributed in addition to the soup, particularly on such important occasions as the last night of Midwinter. These include such foods as "fry bread," beans, squash, potatoes, parched corn, and boiled corn bread.

Although some of the old Iroquois foods are still made for the ceremonies and occasionally for other events, the usual diet is that of other Americans, often that of lower class Americans. Potatoes are a staple along with bread. The old-timers, it is said, eat potatoes three times a day, and are unhappy if they do not; spaghetti and macaroni are not acceptable substitutes for potatoes. Pork and chicken are the preferred meats; salads and green vegetables are relatively unimportant. Tea and coffee are the usual beverages.

It remains now to show how these various principles of Iroquois ritualism apply to the long and complex ceremonial of Midwinter.

PART II

The Structure of the Midwinter Ceremonial

The data available on the Seneca Tonawanda, Newtown, and Cold-spring Longhouses, the New York Onondaga Longhouse, and the longhouses on the Canadian Six Nations Reserve indicate that the Midwinter ceremonial consists of two major segments. The first segment is devoted primarily to the rituals of dream fulfillment and renewal, and the second primarily to the performance of the Four Sacred Rituals: Feather Dance, Thanksgiving Dance, Rite of Personal Chant, and Bowl Game. It is preceded by a series of meetings to collect the money for the food distributed at various times during the ceremonial, to make various appointments necessary for carrying out the ritual, and to prepare the people generally for the ceremonial that is to come.

At the Tonawanda, Newtown, Coldspring, and Sour Springs Longhouses, the Midwinter ceremonial begins the fifth day, that is, the fourth night after the January new moon, a date now ascertained by referring to a drugstore calendar. If January has two new moons, as occasionally happens, the date of Midwinter, at least at Tonawanda, is calculated from the second. Formerly, the date was set by observation of the Pleiades: the moon which was new when the Pleiades were directly overhead at dusk was the moon of Midwinter and the moon after which the Midwinter ceremonial should be held. There were, however, so many arguments over the date ascertained by this method that the date is now decided by referring to the white man's calendar. The principal reason for these disagreements is, of course, the difficulty of reconciling the solar and lunar observations. In fact, using the January moon may set the date slightly early: Kenneth Yoss, formerly of the Mount Holyoke College Observatory, informed me that the Pleiades are in the meridian when the sun is approximately 6 degrees below the horizon—that is, at dusk—about the middle of February. There is also some evidence that the Midwinter ceremonial was formerly held more often in February than it is now.

The Iroquois are still aware that the various longhouses may decide that the Midwinter ceremonial should begin on different dates. In 1964 when all three New York Seneca Longhouses decided to begin Midwinter on the same day, one Indian woman remarked to me that "the moon is coming up the same time over all the reservations this year." Despite these differences, however, it seems highly probable that the Midwinter ceremonial was and is a winter solstice one.

At the New York Onondaga Longhouse, the date of Midwinter, although also a January date, is determined in a slightly different way. First, the date of the tenth day of Midwinter, or "Children's Day" when children are named, is determined by counting five nights after the January new moon. Then, nine days are counted back to determine the beginning day of the ceremonial, that is, the first day devoted to the confession of sins. Onondaga, however, is unique in counting the three days devoted to confession of sins as part of Midwinter proper; in other longhouses, it is an optional rite and not so counted. Onondaga is also unique in having a three-day Bowl Game included as part of Midwinter following those days devoted to confession of sins. The Onondaga Midwinter ceremonial actually begins four days before the January new moon.

Before Midwinter begins, the feast foods must be obtained. Formerly, a hunt was organized for this purpose, but now money is collected in order to buy the necessary food. As one Iroquois told Speck (1949:41), "In ancient times the men would go out and hunt deer to provide meat for the ceremony. Now there aren't any deer, so the men have to go out and 'hunt work' in order to secure funds with which to purchase the 350 pounds of beef required to feed the people during the ceremony." At the Six Nations Reserve, for example, men will seek work, offering, for example, to cut a cord of wood for $1.00 instead of the usual $2.00 rate, and turn the money so earned over to the longhouse (Shimony 1961:165). In fact, the association of the hunt with Midwinter seems to have been so strong that Tuscarora, which now has no longhouse, still retains the practice of having a hunt as the major activity of a New Year's celebration (Graymont 1969).

At Tonawanda, Midwinter is preceded by two series of meetings. The purpose of the first series is to collect the money, called "the head," necessary to buy the food for the ceremonial; the purpose of the second series is to ascertain who will act as "Our Uncles, the Bigheads," the two men who will go around the houses announcing the beginning of Midwinter. The first series of four meetings is held in private homes. The Faithkeepers attend, and any others who wish to may also come. At the first such meeting, two collectors are appointed, one from each moiety. These two collectors formerly looked for work and told others that such work was available. The money earned by those who did such work was given to the longhouse. At the second meeting, held at a house closer to the longhouse than the first, the collectors formerly reported how much money had been received, and two women were appointed to raise more by giving "socials" and selling food, soup, plate lunches, and the like. The second meeting used to be held a week or two after the first, but now is held two days later. If the money collected by the end of this second meeting was not sufficient, other meetings were held. Now, however, much of the money necessary to buy the feast has been raised in the summer at an annual Field Day. The Field Day, which features Indian games and dances, attracts a number of whites and Indians, and, though admission is free, money is raised for the longhouse by selling food, concessions for Indian jewelry, and chances on quilts. The third meeting of the series before Midwinter is held at a house still closer to the longhouse than the second. At this meeting, a final report of the finances is made and the date set on which the Faithkeepers will turn over the money they have collected to the chiefs. At the fourth and final meeing held at a house still closer to the longhouse than the third, the Faithkeepers give the money to the chiefs.

Two days after this meeting, the second series of four preliminary meetings begins at noon in the longhouse. The purpose of this series is to determine the two men who are to represent the Bigheads, and, formerly, who was to sacrifice the white dog—once a prominent feature of the Midwinter ceremonial. At this first meeting of the series, the chiefs are asked, "Who has an old dream? Who has

a new dream? Who has a white dog?" (Fenton 1941:161). They
also are asked if any have had a dream which should be fulfilled by
representing the Bigheads. At a second meeting two days later, the
chiefs reply to these questions. If two of them do not volunteer, then
the question is put to the sub-chiefs. If two still have not volunteered
to be Bigheads, the question is put to the Faithkeepers and then to
the people generally. If two days later at the fourth meeting no one
has replied and the positions still have not been filled, they are done
so by appointment. At this final meeting, the people sit so that the
members of one moiety sit opposite those belonging to the opposite
moiety, and the appointments for various positions are made. Four
young men, two from each side, are appointed to shoot the guns that
signal the Bigheads are beginning their round of the houses. Two
women, one from each side, are assigned the task of preparing the
food for the Bigheads and of dressing them. These appointments
made, Midwinter can begin two days later when the Bigheads go
around to each of the houses near the longhouse.

As has been noted, a rite of confession of sins may be held before
Midwinter begins. In some longhouses, this rite is customarily given
before Midwinter, but in other longhouses, such as Tonawanda, it is
held only if someone requests it. This rite, which is held one, two,
three days, or a week before the Uncles go around, consists of the recitation of part of the Code of Handsome Lake—the teachings of the
Prophet—and a confession of sins by all participating. A string of
wampum is placed on a bench, and each man and woman in turn
picks up the wampum string and states what he has done that he
ought not to have done, replacing the wampum on the bench when he
has finished.

Other less formal preparations are made before the Midwinter
ceremonial begins. Not all preparations are finished by the time the
ceremonial starts, but planning for them begins. Individuals begin to
think about the dances and other rituals they will ask to be performed in renewal of dreams and begin to make preparations for the
feast foods given to those who perform these rituals. Costumes, as
those to be worn in the Feather Dance and Thanksgiving Dance,
may be readied, and also the dress worn by the Beggars. Parents
begin thinking when they will take their children out of school, for
the local public school now regards Midwinter as a religious holiday.

A supply of tobacco is obtained, for tobacco is the important ritual commodity of the ceremonial. In fact, the entire Midwinter ceremonial could be described as revolving around the giving, receiving, and burning of tobacco. Collections of tobacco are made and tobacco invocations given at various points in the ceremonial. These include the collection of tobacco by the two women who are to dress the Bigheads on the day before the Bigheads go around, and subsequent collections of tobacco for the tobacco invocation that once was given over the white dog. Before the False Faces and the Husk Faces perform major dances in the longhouse, a collection of tobacco is taken from the members of the audience to be used in the invocation of these societies. The lesser masked figures, the Beggars, go around requesting tobacco and having received it, dance, much as the "big ones"—the more important False Faces impersonated by adults—are given tobacco before they dance. Participation in certain rituals is requested, and thanks to performers for their participation is given by gifts of loose tobacco. "Indian tobacco," given to the more important performers, is the tobacco burned in the tobacco invocations. Since some men still grow this tobacco, those who do not buy it from those who do. It dries a green color, and the quality of the tobacco is judged by its greenness. Ordinary store-bought pipe or chewing tobacco is given to lesser figures such as the Beggars, and sometimes to more important performers. Loose tobacco is usually distributed by the pinch, a large pinch given to each person. On certain occasions, it is wrapped in paper and the packet given to the collector. If tobacco is requested, cigarettes are usually acceptable. However, cigarettes are somewhat more expensive than chewing tobacco and consequently are not frequently given except by white and casual Indian spectators who find they have brought no other type of tobacco. Money is sometimes an acceptable substitute. If only Indian tobacco is acceptable, an announcement should be made of this fact before the collection is taken. These preliminaries finished, the Midwinter ceremonial proper can begin.

The first segment of Midwinter—that devoted to the rites of dream fulfillment—is undoubtedly the oldest (see next part). This segment in turn has three principal parts: a series of ashes-stirring rites, followed by a series of individually sponsored dream-renewal rites, and the concluding rite of the burning of the white dog.

Midwinter proper begins with the circuit of the two Uncles through the houses. They announce in each house visited that the New Year is to begin and then stir the ashes in the stove of each house. As has been noted, a man might dream that he should perform the role of one of the Uncles and thus volunteer to do so. The two Uncles represent each of the two moieties. In the New York Seneca Longhouses, the Uncles, specially costumed for their circuits of the houses, are termed the "Bigheads" in addition to "Our Uncles" —a practice not followed in the other longhouses where the Uncles are dressed in "Indian costume." In these three New York Seneca Longhouses, they also make the circuit through the houses three or four times. On the last circuit, they do not wear their distinctive costume and are accompanied by the two women—one from each moiety —who had dressed them for their previous rounds.

In the western longhouses, other ashes-stirring rites follow those of the Uncles. In the New York Seneca Longhouses, these include a party of Faithkeepers—a man and a woman from each moiety—and, at Tonawanda, a party composed of a chief from each moiety. At Coldspring and Sour Springs, parties representing the moieties also stir the ashes. Although at Sour Springs the ashes so stirred are now only those in the longhouse stove, older practice is represented by the New York Seneca custom where ashes in houses near the longhouse are stirred. Comparably, the individually sponsored rites of dream fulfillment are performed through the houses at the New York Seneca Longhouses, but not the Sour Springs Longhouse. The difference reflects a difference in settlement pattern, and a comparable change is occurring in the New York Seneca Longhouses. At Newtown, I was told, three houses used to be visited, but now only one is since this is the only remaining house belonging to a Longhouse follower which is near the longhouse. There only the Feather Dance, Thanksgiving Dance, Bowl Game, and Women's Dance go to this house. At Tonawanda, many more houses used to be visited, but the number of houses near the longhouse has declined within memory of the oldest Indians and the circuit decreased to include only those seven or eight houses nearest the longhouse. It seems destined to decline further; for example, the log house that was once included in the circuit recently burned to the ground, and if not rebuilt, the number of houses included in the circuit is reduced by one. The Six Nations Reserve, unlike the New York reservations, is laid out in sections. Consequently the houses of Longhouse followers are not clustered around the longhouses as at Tonawanda. Visiting the houses with individual dream-fulfillment rites is not so possible. At Coldspring, the building of new houses in the two relocation areas has also led to the abandonment of visiting the houses with dream-fulfillment rites (Fenton: personal communication).

The ashes-stirring rites seem to be the present remnant of a New Fire rite, and is sometimes so termed in the nineteenth-century accounts. Although now the fires are not extinguished and relit, it seems entirely possible that they once were and that the denomination of this part of the Midwinter ceremonial as a New Fire rite does not rest on the greater interest in New Fire rituals in the last century. The speech of the Bigheads may include a reference to the kindling of fires (Fenton: personal communication). Perhaps even better evidence is that given by Hewitt (1889). He reports that if an epidemic was thought to be the result of failure to rekindle the new fire at the time of Midwinter or of the failure to perform the new fire rite correctly, the fires in every house might be extinguished and the ashes removed to control the epidemic.

Following the ashes-stirring rites in the western longhouses are the days devoted to the individually sponsored rites of dream renewal. Rites that have been performed for the benefit of an individual should be periodically renewed by him at Midwinter; that is, he should sponsor a performance of that rite during this portion of Midwinter. In the New York Seneca Longhouses, these rites are performed through the circuit of houses, including the longhouse, in which the ashes have been stirred; in the Sour Springs Longhouse, these rites are held only in the longhouse. As any song, dance, or game may be performed in the fulfillment or renewal of a dream, the rites given on these days of dream fulfillment and renewal are many and various. Perhaps the most popular of these rites are those of the False Faces and Husk Faces. Also going around the houses on these days are the Beggars, children usually dressed in old clothing and wearing masks, who beg for tobacco, and on particular days, the Feather Dance, Thanksgiving Dance, Bowl Game, and Women's Dance also go around through the circuit.

At Tonawanda it is said that years ago many more dances went around through the houses and that many more people visited in the houses during these days. It is said that sometimes the houses were so crowded and the dances so numerous that a second troupe of dancers might arrive while the first was still dancing and could not get in the door. The decreasing numbers of persons participating probably reflects the declining number of followers of the Longhouse religion as does the declining number of houses visited. Still, however, relatives and friends come to watch the "doings" in the comfort of the homes near the longhouse.

The custom of holding a ceremony through the houses is probably an old one. Seventeenth-century documents not infrequently mention that the rite went through the houses (Tooker 1964:101 ff).

New York Onondaga practice on these first days of Midwinter differs in two important respects from that in the West: the rite of ashes-stirring is preceded by a three-day Bowl Game between the moieties played according to special rules, and the days devoted to dream fulfillment are cast in the form of a dream-guessing rite rather than in the form of a series of individually sponsored rites. In the western longhouses, the dream-guessing rite—a rite in which the dreams are indicated by a riddle that others attempt to guess—is an optional one; it is given only at the request of an individual, rather than being a stated part of the Midwinter ritual program as at Onondaga. It is now an infrequently given rite in the western longhouses, and was given up in the early part of the twentieth century in the New York Seneca Longhouses, though there is evidence that it was once more frequently given.

The concluding ritual of the dream-fulfillment segment of Midwinter was once the burning of a pure white dog that had previously been ritually strangled and decorated with ribbons, paint, and wampum. The last actual burning of a white dog occurred in the last quarter of the nineteenth century among the New York Seneca, and in the late 1930's among the Canadian Iroquois. The last sacrifice took place at the Seneca Longhouse on the Six Nations Reserve (Shimony 1961:185; see also Speck 1949:145). In the early part of the nineteenth century, two dogs were often sacrificed, probably one for each moiety. Although the white dog is no longer sacrificed, the place of the rite in the Midwinter ceremonial is still remembered, and the tobacco invocation once offered in conjunction with the burning

of the dog is still held on this day in some longhouses such as Tonawanda, Newtown, and New York Onondaga. In the longhouses that
no longer hold the tobacco invocation on the day the white dog was
once burned, the invocation is given on the day the Rite of Personal
Chant (performed as one of the Four Sacred Rituals) is given. Such
a combination was apparently suggested by the brief Rite of Personal
Chant which formerly concluded the rite of the white dog sacrifice
and now still concludes the tobacco invocation once held in conjunction with the white dog sacrifice in other longhouses.

A Husk Face rite often forms part of the ritual of the evening before the white dog was formerly burned. The prominence of this
Husk Face rite in the Midwinter ceremonial varies: for example, at
the Coldspring Longhouse it is a lengthy one, while at the Tonawanda Longhouse, it is merely a circuit of the Husk Faces as the last
such circuit of the houses. A Husk Face rite may form part of the
ritual of the second part of Midwinter and another Husk Face ritual
may be held not long after the conclusion of Midwinter.

The second segment of Midwinter—that in which the Four Sacred Rituals of Feather Dance, Thanksgiving Dance, Rite of Personal Chant, and Bowl Game are the major rites—was undoubtedly
added at the instigation of Handsome Lake in the beginning years of
the nineteenth century. The Four Sacred Rituals are old ones in Iroquois ritualism; it is only their addition to Midwinter as a unit that
is relatively recent. When given as a unit in Midwinter and Green
Corn, the Four Sacred Rituals should be performed in the morning
as they are rites in honor of the Creator and the "morning belongs to
the Creator." [1]

Also often included as part of this second segment of Midwinter
is a performance of the Our Life Supporter dances. This may well be
an old ritual, but the documentary evidence gives no weight either to
the suggestion that it is old or that it is new. Some early descriptions
of the white dog sacrifice do, however, mention that a women's dance
was given at the conclusion of that ceremony, and it might be that
this practice is retained in the Our Life Supporter dances—the
women's dance being the only dance which is part of the Our Life
Supporter series in all the longhouses.

Once the Four Sacred Rituals had been added, Midwinter came
to be composed of three ceremonies—the Dream-Fulfillment rites,

the Four Sacred Rituals, and the Our Life Supporter dances. In an important sense the rituals are built up in the following manner: take the Our Life Supporter dances that comprise the major rites of such ceremonies as Planting, Green Bean, and Harvest; add to them the Four Sacred Rituals to make the Green Corn ceremony; add to the Green Corn ceremony the Dream-Fulfillment rites to make the Midwinter ceremonial. These additions often precede the ceremony being added to, and may be longer than that ceremony. How the Midwinter ceremonial is built up is indicated in the following outlines of practice in each of the longhouses for which there is information. In these outlines, mention of the Thanksgiving Speech that begins and ends each ritual gathering has been omitted and should be assumed. Also omitted from all the outlines except that for Tonawanda is the distribution of the feast at the end of many of these gatherings.

The Tonawanda Midwinter Ceremonial

At Tonawanda, the Midwinter ceremonial is built up by taking the Our Life Supporters ceremony which is given as a separate ceremony three times a year, preceding this with the Four Sacred Rituals to make the Green Corn ceremony which is given separately once a year in the summer, and preceding this with the rituals distinctive to Midwinter and consequently performed only then. In other words, to make the Midwinter ceremonial, take the Our Life Supporters ceremony, that is, the "Four Sacred Ceremonies" that comprise the Tonawanda Planting, Green Bean, and Harvest ceremonials in their entirety: Women's Dance, Feather Dance (in costume), Stomp Dance, Corn Dance (before 1963, the Hand-in-hand Dance; in 1963, it was decided to substitute the Corn Dance as Handsome Lake had said the Hand-in-hand Dance was the dance of the devil), and Women's Dance.

Precede it with the Four Sacred Rituals—Feather Dance, Thanksgiving Dance, Rite of Personal Chant, and Bowl Game—to make the Green Corn ceremonial, dancing social dances in the evening if the Bowl Game has not been completed and announcing new names at the end of the ceremony on the first two days:

FIRST DAY

Morning in the longhouse: Thanksgiving Speech, Feather Dance (in costume), Thanksgiving Dance (in costume), Thanksgiving Speech and announcements of new names, and distribution of corn soup.

SECOND DAY

Morning in the longhouse: Thanksgiving Speech, Bowl Game between the moieties begun, Rite of Personal Chant, Thanksgiving Speech and announcements of new names, and distribution of corn soup.

Evening in the longhouse: social dances if the Bowl Game was not finished in the morning.

THIRD DAY

Morning in the longhouse: Bowl Game resumed and played until one side wins even though it must be played past noon.

Evening in the longhouse: Thanksgiving Speech; Our Life Supporters ceremony: Women's Dance, Feather Dance (in costume), Stomp Dance, Corn Dance (before 1963, the Hand-in-hand Dance), and Women's Dance; Thanksgiving Speech; and distribution of potato soup and other food.

Precede this with the three distinctive major rituals of Midwinter —the ashes-stirring circuits, individually sponsored dream-fulfillment rites, and tobacco invocation once said over the white dog to make the Midwinter ceremonial. Begin the days devoted to dream fulfillment with the singing of the Dawn Song in the longhouse, Perform four of the major rites of Green Corn—Feather Dance, Thanksgiving Dance, Bowl Game, and Women's Dance—through the circuit of houses on the last two days devoted to dream fulfillment, then dance of "all kinds of dances," that is, the social and medicine society dance in the evening on those days the Bowl Game is played, and add a Husk Face rite to the dances on the evening of the sixth day, and finally a speech recapitulating the year and announcement of new Faithkeepers to the rituals of the evening of the seventh day:

FIRST DAY

The two Uncles, or Bigheads go around the houses near the longhouse three times, about 9, 12, and 3 o'clock, stirring the ashes in each house, announcing the beginning of the New Year ceremonial, and telling the people what they should do, such as watch the fires so that they do not go out, watch the dogs, wash the floor, clean the house, and watch that the children do not get sick from the False Faces.

Before the Bigheads are to begin each circuit, a man goes outside the longhouse and fires one shot from a shotgun. This is the signal for the Bigheads to return to the longhouse. During Midwinter, a gun shot serves to announce to all those in the houses near the longhouse and in the longhouse itself that a group is on its way through the circuit of houses; the shots announcing the circuit of the Bigheads differ from these others only in number.

A little later, two men go out of the longhouse and each fires one shot; this is the signal that the Bigheads should prepare to get dressed, should go to the women's end of the longhouse. In practice, however, the men may not go to the women's end of the longhouse at this signal, but wait until three shots have been fired, the signal that the dressing of the Bigheads should begin. This signal is made by three men, each of whom fires one shot outside the longhouse; if three men are not present, two do the shooting, alternating shots. For the first circuit, a Thanksgiving Speech is given after the two shots have been fired and at the conclusion of the speech, three shots are fired.

Each Bighead is dressed by a woman. She turns the man she is dressing so that he faces the men's end of the longhouse and puts a blanket over his head and body, leaving his face uncovered. Formerly, buffalo robes were used instead of the store-bought blankets. The blanket has been tied and corn husks inserted into the top; it is placed so that this corn husk spray rests on the head rather like a crown. The dresser then ties the blanket in place with a cord wrapped around the Bighead's neck and around his waist, and inserts a corn cob in each of the two knots in back, one at the neck and the other at the waist, to hold them. Next, she ties a corn husk braid around the Bighead's waist, and puts shorter corn husk braids around each of his ankles, tying the ends in back, the result bearing some resemblance to a snowshoe frame, rounded in front and pointed in back. Finally, she puts charcoal on the Bighead's face and gives him a paddle. This special paddle has the shape of a corn pounder (that is, the shape of the pestle used to pound corn in the wooden mortar), but it is lighter.

The Bighead, now dressed, is led to the middle of the longhouse by the woman who dressed him. There a man standing at the men's end of the longhouse tells the Bigheads what they are to announce on that circuit of the houses. Four shots are fired from guns outside the longhouse, and the Bigheads chant this speech, beating their paddles on the floor and walking towards the men's stove. They finish the recitation of the speech when they reach the men's stove and go out of the longhouse by the men's door to visit each of the houses near the longhouse and repeat the speech in each. On the last round, they also stir the ashes in the stove of the household with their paddles, and one of them sings a thanksgiving song as they leave the house.

After each circuit of the houses, the Bigheads return to the long-house, repeating their ritual as they enter by the women's door. They are then divested of their special costume by the two women who dressed them in it. After the noon round, those taking part in this ritual are given lunch in the kitchen. Formerly, after the last round, the two Bigheads raced back to the longhouse; it was thought that the Bowl Game played on the closing days of Midwinter would be won by the moiety of the Bighead who was first uncostumed.

After the last circuit of the Bigheads, the speaker thanks the Big-heads and their dressers, and tells the people what they should do: that they should not travel, use firearms, or play games. They are also told what is going to take place next and to open their houses. For this speech, the Faithkeepers sit on benches along the southwest side of the longhouse, the men on the south, or men's end and the women on the north, or women's end. Someone is designated to start the fires in the stoves in the longhouse in the morning.

The day before the Bigheads circuit the houses, the two women dressers go around the houses and collect tobacco to be used in the tobacco invocation on the fifth day and gifts of food for the Big-heads. The "watch of the Bigheads" is held that night, that is, the night before the Bigheads go around the houses. Formerly, the Bigheads and their dressers stayed up all night in the longhouse and the dressers cooked a midnight meal for the Bigheads, the four men who were to shoot the guns that day, and any others who were there. It is said that many people used to come to this midnight "banquet."

This watch is now observed only by young people who stay awake all night some years playing games in the longhouse and shooting guns or setting off firecrackers or dynamite during the night. They used to shoot one shot at midnight, two about 3 o'clock in the morning, three before daybreak, and four at daybreak, and at least something of this pattern is still retained.

Anciently, the white dog was strangled on this first day of Midwinter.

SECOND DAY

Very early in the morning, long before dawn, the False Faces may go to various houses, even houses far distant from the longhouse, and wake up the occupants asking for tobacco. They may also appear early on other mornings. There is no round of houses visited, the selection being made by those who go around.

Morning: Dawn Song, the personal chant of Handsome Lake, is sung in the longhouse. Formerly, it was sung at dawn before the sun came up, but the rite now starts at 7:30, 8:00, or 8:30 in the morning. A Thanksgiving Speech by the speaker precedes and follows it. Anyone may attend, and those who do take seats on two benches facing each other along the west side of the longhouse near the men's stove, the men sitting on the south, or men's end of the longhouse and the women on the north, or women's end of these benches. The singer walks between these benches while singing the Dawn Song, a ritual that resembles the ordinary Personal Chant although the usual accompanying responses of the men and women are omitted.

The Bigheads, not in costume, and the two women who dressed them go around the houses, reminding the people of the important things they mentioned in their speeches the day before and stirring the ashes in the household stoves with the paddles they carry. These paddles are long, slender wooden sticks shaped so that one end forms a blade. One Bighead sings a thanksgiving song as they leave each house.

Four Faithkeepers, a man and a woman from each moiety, next

go around to each of the houses to give thanks that they are still alive and to stir the ashes using the same paddles the Bigheads and their dressers had used. The way is then open for the False Faces; they may go through the circuit of houses.

Afternoon and evening: various dances go around. Actually, little happens during the remainder of this day. In the evening, a few Beggars do go around. These Beggars are usually children. They wear wooden masks that usually lack the horse hair that frames the face of False Face masks and are dressed in old and often absurd clothing. The Beggars go around the houses in groups of two, three, or more. In the house, they go up to each person there requesting tobacco by extending a hand, open paper bag, ladies' handbag, or whatever they happen to be using as a container.

After they have been given tobacco, they dance. The accompaniment for their dance is provided by one of the men in the house, who sings while beating a stick against a bench. If the Beggars' performance has been particularly noteworthy, they may be asked to dance again; the request is made by giving them more tobacco. Ludicrous dancing and vigorous dancing is particularly admired. If tobacco had not been given to the Beggars, they would be free to take what they wanted.[2]

Although the Beggars are usually children, sometimes they are adult men and women. Sometimes, their dress is a parody of women's dress—very short skirts, out-size bras, girdles, and the like—and sometimes when so dressed their dance is a Women's Dance danced to the usual music of that dance rather than the customary Beggar's dance.

THIRD DAY

Morning: Dawn Song is sung in the longhouse.

Two chiefs, one from each moiety, go around to all the houses in the circuit. They tell the people that what has taken place the day before has ended, remind the people of what the Bigheads said, and stir the ashes of the household stoves.

Feather Dance is danced through the circuit of houses.

Thanksgiving Dance is danced through the circuit of houses.

Afternoon and evening: various groups of individuals go around the houses. Before a group starts out, a shot from a shotgun may be

fired to indicate that a group is starting out. The beginning of all
such circuits should be announced with the firing of a gun, but not
all are : some sponsors of the dance are bashful about asking someone
to do the shooting and as a result, it is omitted. No shots announce
the beginning of the circuits of the Beggars.

The groups that go around on this and the following day include
members of the medicine societies, such as False Face, Husk Face,
Bear, and Buffalo societies, and social dances, such as the Fish
Dance. In fact, virtually any ritual of the Iroquois repertoire may be
performed by a group going around. A circuit, now rarely done, may
also be made for reasons of friendship, the two people going around
the houses, giving thanks for having survived the year. A leader
goes with them to tell why they have come. In each house, the people
there may sing their Personal Chant, but if no one does, one of the
two friends sings.

In the past, many more groups of people made the circuit of the
houses. The decreased number of participants in Midwinter has limited the amount of such visiting, and much of the activity on these
two days now occurs in the late afternoon and evening after work
hours. Most in evidence are the False Faces and, of course, the Beggars. Children seem to have unlimited enthusiasm for impersonating
Beggars.

Before a False Face troupe enters a house, a False Face opens the
door, rubs his rattle—a turtle shell rattle or one made of a tin can
filled with stones and with a stick handle—against the wood, emits
the characteristic False Face cries, and closes the door. Finally, the
troupe enters crawling and goes to the stove. A member of the
household begins to beat a stick on a bench and sing, and the False
Faces dance. After the dance, they leave.

The Common Face dance is the most usual False Face dance.
The Common Faces are thought to be deformed, either hunchbacked
or crippled below the waist, and hence enter a door crawling. They
are underlings of the False Face leader, a large person-spirit, who
lives on the rim of the world. Their leader is not deformed and hence
stands erect.

His dance, the Doorkeepers' Society dance, is more rarely given
than that of the Common Faces. In this dance, the masked "Doorkeepers" make all those in the house dance in a circle (Fenton

1937:224–26, 234, 236–37; 1940:420, 427–28). The dance is for "all who belong'" to the False Face Society, but as all in the house are usually members of the False Face Society, all in the house dance. Those who are not members should give tobacco to the False Faces. Although this dance is called the Doorkeepers' Society Dance, those who are the dance leaders in it need not belong to that order of the False Face Society.

In the house where the dance started, the False Faces blow ashes on the person or persons who sponsored the dance. They rub their hands in the ashes and hot coals of the stove, place their hands on the person and blow, sending out a cloud of ashes. Various parts of the body are so treated. The power of the False Faces is believed to be such that they are not burned while handling these hot coals and ashes, although it is said that they will be burned if a menstruating woman is present. Some False Faces do not pass up the opportunity afforded by the ashing rite for a little fun and blow ashes in some absurd fashion, as, for example, exaggeratedly blowing ashes under the arm as if applying a deodorant.

In certain False Face rituals, the mask is held over the smoke of the open stove to purify it. The False Faces are said to like tobacco and corn mush, and for this reason False Faces who make the circuit of houses are given tobacco and corn mush by the person who asked that the ritual be performed. Each participant brings a pail in which to take home his corn mush. A tobacco invocation precedes the going around of the False Faces; a tobacco invocation always precedes the dance of a medicine society.

Also in evidence on these days are the Husk Faces. Members of this society wear masks made of braided corn husks. Their food is corn dumplings; at least, corn dumplings are supposed to be given them, but now the dumplings often are made of wheat flour rather than corn meal. Like the False Faces, the Husk Faces have several different rituals, and like them, they may ash individuals to cure them.

The committee in charge of the Bowl Game, a man and a woman from each moiety, appoints two women who go around the houses the evening of the third day collecting tobacco and gifts, including those of money, apples, and oranges. These gifts are used the next day to match the bets placed by the members of the household.[3]

FOURTH DAY

Morning: Dawn Song is sung in the longhouse.

Bowl Game is played through the circuit of houses. Before the circuit begins, the money and goods collected the night before are divided into four piles, and one pile given to each of the committee of four, a man and a woman from each moiety, who are to play the Bowl Game that morning.

Then preparations are made for playing the game first in the longhouse. Two benches are placed in the middle of the longhouse, a folded blanket is placed on them, and the bowl, beans, and peach stone dice set on the blanket. A couple of wrapped packages of tobacco are placed on the blanket; the committee takes this tobacco at the end of the game, and at the end of the circuit these and all other such packages collected in the houses are given to the speaker to be used in the tobacco invocation. Then, the bets are placed and matched. Each person who wishes to place a bet puts it on the blanket where it is covered by one of the committee from what has been given him earlier. Some may make side bets. The game is accompanied by much shouting and gesturing, all with the intent of driving luck away from one's opponents and to one's own side. As only five or seven beans are used, the game does not take long to finish.

When all the beans have been won by one side, the bowl is turned over and winnings are collected. The troupe then leaves the longhouse to play the game in each of the houses on the circuit. As they leave, a shot from a gun announces that they are beginning the circuit of houses. When the group playing the game arrives at a house, they place a folded blanket on the floor and put the bowl on it. A member of the household places a packet of tobacco on the blanket, and the members of the household then place their bets, coins, apples, oranges, and such, which are matched by the troupe representing the longhouse. Although in the past there were also many side bets, there are now few. The game is played in the houses as it was in the longhouse, and, as always, to accompaniment of much shouting, gesturing, and teasing.

After the game has been played in all the houses, it is played again in the longhouse. The bets in this final game may be many as the committee may choose to stake all of its winnings up to this point on the outcome of this final game. The winnings of the troupe at the end of the circuit go to the longhouse.

Women's Dance goes around after the circuit of the Bowl Game has been completed. The woman leader of this dance carries a basket containing a couple of ears of corn and a potato. The group of women dancers is accompanied by men musicians. In each house, chairs are placed in the middle of the room for the musicians, who use horn rattles and water drums to accompany the song, while the women dance in a circle around them. The dance is first danced in the longhouse. A gun shot announces as they leave the longhouse that they are beginning the circuit of the houses. After the dance has been performed in all the houses, it is repeated again in the longhouse. The dance ends about noon.

Afternoon and early evening: various groups go around through the circuit of the houses and the longhouse as they did the previous day. The last group to make the circuit in the early evening are the Husk Faces. They wear masks, are dressed in swimming trunks and sneakers, and carry long, slender sticks which they constantly tap on the ground in a nervous sort of manner. On entering the house, they go to the stove and stand in front of it, tapping until someone begins to play and sing for them, and they dance, and then leave. (This Husk Face appearance may be a vestige of a once longer Husk Face rite; at the Newtown and Coldspring Longhouses, a Husk Face rite is given at approximately this place in the ceremonial.)

Almost immediately—it is now about 8 o'clock in the evening—a man appointed by the speaker goes around to the houses to announce that all activities are now to take place in the longhouse, and those in the houses should come to the longhouse. Two women and two men have been appointed to take charge during the remainder of the evening's activities, which is devoted to social and society dances, that is, to what are called "all kinds of dances." Those who so wish sponsor a medicine society dance. Social dances are used to fill in the time between medicine society dances. Before each dance of a medicine society, a tobacco invocation is made into one of the stoves.

The most popular of the medicine society dances is that of the Bear Society. A pail of berry juice, often now made by mixing packaged frozen berries with water, and often also a basket of peanuts, or more rarely walnuts, are placed on a bench near the dancers. The rationale for these foods is that bears like nuts and berries. The dancers, while dancing, help themselves to the juice and nuts, affording an opportunity for much clowning. Some juice and nuts are also set aside for the musician.

The Buffalo Society dance is the next most popular dance. As for the Bear Society dance, a tobacco invocation is given first. The singer uses a water drum. The more out-going members of the society who dance this dance clown by butting each other in the manner of bulls. Sometimes, a pan of corn mush is placed on the bench for these dancers and eaten in much the same manner as the berries and nuts are by the Bear Society dancers.

In addition to various medicine society dances, the social dances given are many and varied, and the evening is full of activity. Two dances, a medicine society and a social one, may be on the floor at the same time, and jokingly compete with each other. Beggars may also appear during the evening, as usual begging for tobacco and dancing. Several False Faces may come in and perform their ritual of ashing one, two, or more individuals in front of the men's stove. One or two children wearing False Face masks may come in and crawl near one of the stoves and be given tobacco. To renew the ritual friendship of two men or two women, a Bowl Game may be played between the men and women, bets being collected from all those in the longhouse who wish to place such. The dancing in the longhouse ends in the late evening, often around 10:30 or 11 o'clock.

FIFTH DAY

Morning: Thanksgiving Speech in the longhouse.

Tobacco invocation in the cookhouse. Anciently, the white dog was burned with a tobacco invocation. The Thanksgiving Speech that now accompanies this tobacco invocation is essentially the same as that of the ordinary Thanksgiving Speech, but is repeated first in reverse order, that is, beginning with the Creator and ending with the people, and then in the normal order, that is, beginning with the people and ending with the Creator. In the first repetition, thanks are returned and, in the second, hope expressed that each will continue for another year (Chafe 1961:11).

Burning of tobacco accompanies the recitation of each section, the tobacco being thrown into the fire over which corn soup is cooking in large iron kettles. The tobacco used during this invocation is that which the various groups have collected earlier in the Midwinter ceremonial. As the tobacco invocation is being recited, the cooks, who have risen early in the morning to begin preparing this soup, occasionally stir the soup in the kettles on the fire. The number of people watching the tobacco invocation is small; the cook house is small and relatively few can stand in it to hear and watch the ritual. Also, in January it usually is too cold to stand outside the cook house to hear the invocation, which takes about one hour to complete.

A brief rite of Personal Chant follows the tobacco invocation in the cook house. The first men to sing their chant are the two who have impersonated the Bigheads. Then, the two male Faithkeepers who stirred the ashes on the second day and next those in charge of the Feather and Thanksgiving Dances sing theirs. Finally, anyone who wishes may sing his song. This ritual in the cook house ends about 10 o'clock, and all then go to the longhouse.

A brief tobacco invocation is made by the speaker into the men's stove in the longhouse. This ritual announces to the Creator the next events, the Feather and Thanksgiving Dances, to take place that day and the members of the committees in charge—the two men in charge of the Feather Dance and the two in charge of the Thanksgiving Dance; it also announces the events of the following day, the Bowl Game and Rite of Personal Chant, and the individuals in charge of these rites. During this tobacco invocation, the two singer-musicians for the Feather Dance appointed by the committee in charge of this dance sit in their places on the bench in the middle of the longhouse.

Feather Dance, Thanksgiving Dance, Thanksgiving Speech and announcements of new names, and the distribution of corn soup conclude the activities.

SIXTH DAY

Morning in the longhouse: Bowl Game between the moieties is begun. The game played is the long version of the game using one hundred beans. Sometime before the game starts, the members of the committee in charge of the Bowl Game, a man and a woman from each moiety, go around the houses to collect the bets for it. Each on the committee collects from members of his or her own moiety, but the man and woman of the same moiety do not go together; the man collects from certain houses, the woman from others.

Before beginning play, two benches are placed in the middle of the longhouse for the committee and others most concerned with the game. The folded blanket and bowl are placed on the floor between the benches, the players kneeling on the floor between these benches. Since one hundred beans are used as scoring counters, the game is rarely finished on this day.

The committee of four in charge of the game decide disputes over scoring such as those caused by one of the stones being thrown so that it stands on end. The man and woman who represent their moiety on the committee appoint a member of their moiety to designate the order in which that side's players will take their turns. Each player is given seven beans with which to play. When he has lost them, he retires and another member of his moiety takes his place. Bets of money placed on the game are recorded in a book so that the winners may be paid accurately. Other bets of articles such as yard goods, stockings, plates, food, and soap have been placed in baskets on one of the side benches.

People drift in and out of the longhouse during the morning to watch the game and to take part in it. The seating for this game is by moiety: members of the "animal" side—the Bear, Wolf, Turtle, and Beaver clans—should sit on the men's end of the longhouse, and members of the "bird" side—the Deer, Hawk, Snipe, and Heron clans—should sit on the women's end. They should also enter and leave by the appropriate door; that is, the members of the "animal" side should use the door normally used by the men and the members of the "bird" side, the door normally used by women.

The seating on the benches in the center of the longhouse is also by moiety, those on the bench closest to the men's stove being members of the animal side and those on the bench facing (that is, the bench closest to the women's end) being members of the bird side. Formerly, the members of one moiety stood on one end of the longhouse and the members of the other on the other end. If a member of the moiety crossed over the center line between them, he got his face blackened with charcoal. It is said that sometimes this is still done.[4]

The Bowl Game is stopped sometime between 11:00 and 11:30

so that the Rite of Personal Chant may be begun. The implements for playing the Bowl Game are picked up and the benches moved so that they are closer to the men's stove. The male Faithkeepers sit on the bench nearest the stove and the female Faithkeepers on that bench behind them. At least, the Faithkeepers are supposed to sit on these benches; not all do so now.

Rite of Personal Chant. The order in which each man takes his turn singing his song is counterclockwise: first those on the benches in front of the stove, beginning with the two men in charge of the Bowl Game and also the Rite of Personal Chant, then the Faithkeepers, and finally the other men sitting on the benches on the men's end of the longhouse. Each man, in turn, stands up, may briefly speak, and then walking forward and back, chants his song. As in the brief rite of Personal Chant following the tobacco invocation on the previous day, other men respond he: he: in rhythm and the women clap their hands to accompany the singer. A man who feels he cannot sing may request that another man sing for him and both walk together while his song is being sung for him. A man may also have another sing for him if he is absent, if, for example, he is in the army.

The last song sung is that of Handsome Lake. The Faithkeepers appoint from among those who know this song the man who will sing it on this occasion. The ritual ends at noon or a few minutes before.

Thanksgiving Speech and announcement of new names, distribution of the soup that has been brought in earlier. This soup used to be a sweet corn soup, made with sugar and no meat. The corn soup distributed the day before is made with meat and no sugar. Usually now, however, the same kind of soup is made on both days.

Evening in the longhouse: "all kinds of dances," that is, social dances and dances of the medicine societies. The events of the evening begin about seven o'clock when several men carrying False Face masks bound together and the Keeper of the False Faces enter the longhouse by the women's door. They are followed by some masked False Faces crawling in a single line. The procession proceeds along the west side of the men's stove, and a collection of tobacco is taken by the Keeper of the False Faces from the people sitting on this side. The collector then proceeds from the stove in a counterclockwise circuit around the longhouse, collecting tobacco from those sitting on the east side. Next, a tobacco invocation is made at the men's stove, and the False Faces, who are sitting on the floor near the men's stove, scrape their rattles against the floor whenever tobacco is thrown into the fire. After the invocation has been concluded, the False Faces ash each other. During this ashing rite, a man sitting on a bench hits a stick against it and sings, and the False Faces begin to dance, continuing to ash each other. This finished, the False Faces, led by the two men carrying the masks and the Keeper, file out the women's door in a single line. The entire circuit, in the women's door to the men's stove along the south side of the longhouse and back out the women's door along the north side of the longhouse, is a counterclockwise one around the longhouse.

Various social and medicine society dances and other events follow in no particular order. Either before these dances begin or after they have started, some False Faces may come back into the longhouse and monitor a dance for "all who belong," that is, all those who are members of the society. They drag reluctant members off the benches and make them dance this Doorkeeper's Dance. Almost all the people attending the ceremony join in this dance. The False Faces may also ash some individuals in front of the men's stove. Such a ritual begins with a tobacco invocation. Husk Faces may also appear in the longhouse to ash various individuals in the same manner as the False Faces.

Other social and medicine society dances may be given as on the fourth night of Midwinter. Also, as on the fourth night, the Beggars appear throughout the evening, collecting tobacco and dancing, but their efforts are incidental to the main events. As on the fourth night, many in the longhouse do not give them tobacco, and they usually are told to dance in a corner of the longhouse. In addition to the medicine society and social dances, one of the Four Sacred Rituals, such as a brief uncostumed Feather Dance or a short Bowl Game played between the men and women, may be given for reasons of friendship on this night.

The Husk Faces are scheduled to appear in the longhouse in the latter part of the evening, the time they will appear having been announced in the longhouse on the previous day. First, two Husk

Faces run through the longhouse, one entering by the men's door and going out the women's door, and one entering by the women's door and leaving by the men's door. The longhouse is then closed; the Husk Faces stationed outside the longhouse prevent the usual coming and going unless given a gift of tobacco.

Social dances continue until the Husk Faces return and break up the dance then going on, quite violently but in good fun, knocking the instruments from the musicians' hands and dispersing the musicians and dancers. This done, they leave.

Shortly after, one Husk Face returns and takes one man outside. As the choice of the Husk Faces is different each year, there is some interest in whom the Husk Faces will choose and how well he will repeat the speech they teach him.[5] Outside the Husk Faces teach the man a speech and one brings him back into the longhouse to repeat it. He relates the message of the old woman, leader of the Husk Faces, to the effect that they are hurrying westward to hoe their crops, that they grow huge squashes, corn, and beans in the fields around their houses, and that some of their women have remained home to tend crying babies. He then relates that they request the privilege of dancing with the people (Fenton 1937:220; 1940:416).

After the speaker has finished, tobacco is collected in the longhouse for the Husk Faces and taken outside for them. A bench is placed crosswise across the longhouse near the men's stove, and a man sits on the bench and beats a stick against it. Two Husk Faces come into the longhouse and dance briefly. This concludes the evening's events. No food is distributed.

SEVENTH DAY

Morning in the longhouse: the Bowl Game is resumed in the longhouse and concluded, usually sometime during the afternoon. Since the Bowl Game is one of the ceremonies dedicated to the Creator and hence should be performed only before noon, in former times it was always adjourned at noon, begun again the next morning, and so continued until it was finished. Social dances were given the evenings of the days on which the Bowl Game was played. Now the Bowl Game is played until it is finished even though it must be played past noon in order to conclude it.

Evening in the longhouse: Thanksgiving Speech. As the ritual of this evening is a long one, it usually now begins relatively early, about 6 o'clock.

Our Life Supporters ceremony: Women's Dance, Feather Dance (in costume), Stomp Dance, Corn Dance (before 1963, the Hand-in-hand dance), and Women's Dance. At the end of this dance, women dance around the food that has been brought into the longhouse earlier and placed near the women's stove. It is uncovered for this dance.

Announcement of new names between the dances and at the conclusion of the Our Life Supporters ceremony.[6]

Induction of new Faithkeepers (optional). The new Faithkeepers sit on benches in the middle of the longhouse while the speaker delivers a speech. This concluded, the new Faithkeepers stand near the men's stove and are congratulated by the older Faithkeepers, who come up and shake their hands.

Long speech by the speaker that recounts what has been done during New Year's and what should be done during New Year's. It lasts about an hour and a half. For this speech, two benches are moved to the southeast part of the longhouse, much as they were placed for the Dawn Song. The women Faithkeepers sit on the end of these benches toward the women's end, the men on the end towards the men's end of the longhouse, the Faithkeepers on the east bench, and the chiefs on the west. The speaker stands in the middle between the two benches to deliver the speech.

Distribution of the feast. This includes distribution of various kinds of food, such as bread, biscuits, pounded parched corn, cooked squash, mashed potatoes, corn soup, and other foods that have been brought by individuals. These are distributed by women, the women in charge consulting with each other and written lists to be sure all those who hold important positions are given food. Finally, the potato soup, which has been cooked in the large cast iron pots used to cook soup for the longhouse, is distributed by men. After the pails have been filled, all leave. The Midwinter ceremonial has ended.

MEDICINE SOCIETY RITUALS FOLLOWING MIDWINTER

On the weekend following the end of Midwinter, the False Faces and the Husk Faces hold their final dances. The False Face Society holds its ceremony in the morning, usually Sunday morning, but occasionally on Saturday morning. The Husk Face Society holds its ceremony on Saturday evening. Both ceremonies are essentially like the respective False Face and Husk Face parts of the evening ceremony on the sixth day of Midwinter.

The False Face ceremony begins with a procession into the longhouse from the women's door. The first men in the line are those carrying False Face masks bound together and the Keeper of the False Faces, and behind them are those wearing such masks. All masks are supposed to be present for this ceremony; those not being worn are carried.

The line proceeds to the men's stove, a collection of tobacco being taken from those sitting on the west side and then the east side of the longhouse. Next follows a tobacco invocation into the open men's stove. Then, the False Faces ash each other.

Although these rituals are similar to those on the sixth night of Midwinter, the next is not. The False Faces sit on the benches in the southwest corner of the longhouse and a woman goes counterclockwise around the women's section of the longhouse indicating in turn each woman beginning with those sitting in the southeast section. When so designated, each woman goes to the center of the longhouse and dances, facing a False Face that has been chosen to dance with her. They dance between the benches in the middle of the longhouse and the south side, dancing toward the men's end and back. Then, another woman and another False Face dance in the same manner until all the False Faces have danced with a woman. If there are more False Faces than women in the longhouse, the counterclockwise designation of women is begun again.

Finally, the woman who has been choosing the women to dance and the man who has been choosing the False Faces dance facing two False Faces. This finished, there is a dance for "all who belong," that is, those who belong to the False Face Society. After several individuals have been ashed by the False Faces, the False Faces leave, completing the counterclockwise circuit of their entrance. They come back unmasked into the longhouse for the distribution of corn soup and corn mush. During this ceremony and that of the sixth day of Midwinter, several men who have chosen to wear clown masks may sit on the benches near the False Faces and engage in humorous antics. They are not False Faces proper, and their masks are unlike those of the False Faces as they do not have horsehair.

The first part of the evening of the Husk Face ceremony is devoted to social dances. After a number of these social dances have been given, the longhouse is closed in the same manner as on the sixth evening of Midwinter. Social dancing is continued, and the Husk Faces appear in the doors and windows and occasionally run through the longhouse. They also may run along the sides of the longhouse, making an eerie sound by running their sticks along the shingles. Finally, they enter and break up the social dance being given in the longhouse and dance themselves. This dance, a longer one involving more Husk Faces than that on the sixth night of Midwinter, is a satire on the way women behave, the Husk Faces wearing appropriate costumes for their fun. This dance finished, the Husk Faces leave. Finally, the food—corn dumplings or flour dumplings or both—is distributed. Corn dumplings are the food of the Husk Faces, although now flour dumplings may also be made for them. This distribution of food concludes the ceremony.

THE NEWTOWN MIDWINTER CEREMONIAL

The longhouse nearest to Tonawanda is the Newtown Longhouse, the only remaining longhouse on the Cattaraugus Reservation. It is not surprising, then, that the Tonawanda Midwinter ceremonial most closely resembles that at Newtown. (The following description of the Newtown Midwinter ceremonial is based on Parker 1913:81–85; Brush 1901:67 ff; and information supplied by William C. Sturtevant and two Tonawanda Senecas.)

To make the Newtown Midwinter ceremonial, take the Our Life Supporters ceremony, which at Newtown has the form: thɔwi:sas (women's songs), Women's Dance, Stomp Dance, Women's Dance, Shake-the-pumpkin Dance, Women's Dance, Corn Dance, Women's Dance, and Feather Dance (not in costume). Precede it with the Four Sacred Rituals—Feather Dance, Thanksgiving Dance, Rite of Personal Chant, and Bowl Game—to make the Green Corn ceremony, dancing social dances in the evening if the Bowl Game has not been completed, and announcing new names at the end of the ceremony on the first two days:

FIRST DAY

Morning in the longhouse: Feather Dance, Thanksgiving Dance, and announcements of new names.

Evening in the longhouse: social dances.

SECOND DAY

Morning in the longhouse: Bowl Game between the moieties begun, and Rite of Personal Chant.

Evening in the longhouse: social dances.

THIRD DAY

Morning in the longhouse: Bowl Game.

Evening in the longhouse: Our Life Supporters ceremony: thɔwi:sas, Women's Dance, Stomp Dance, Women's Dance, Shake-the-pumpkin Dance, Women's Dance, Corn Dance, Women's Dance, and Feather Dance (not in costume).

Precede this with the distinctive major rituals of Midwinter—the ashes-stirring circuits, individually sponsored dream-fulfillment rites, and tobacco invocation once said over the white dog—to make the Midwinter ceremonial, beginning the days devoted to dream fulfillment with the singing of the Dawn Song, performing four of the major rites of Green Corn—Feather Dance, Thanksgiving Dance, Bowl Game, and Women's Dance on the last three days devoted to dream fulfillment, adding a Husk Face rite on the fifth and eighth nights, and a speech recapitulating the year into the rituals of the last evening:

FIRST DAY

The two Uncles, or Bigheads, go around the houses three times, about 9, 12, and 3 o'clock.

SECOND DAY

Morning: Bigheads (undressed) go around stirring ashes in the houses, and four Faithkeepers, a man and a woman from each moiety, go around stirring the ashes in the houses.

THIRD DAY

Morning: Dawn Song in the longhouse; Feather Dance goes around the houses.

Afternoon in the longhouse: various dances.

FOURTH DAY

Morning: Dawn Song in the longhouse; Thanksgiving Dance goes around the houses. (Note that the Feather Dance and Thanksgiving Dance are given on separate days in the first part of Midwinter, but on the same day in the second part.)

Afternoon and evening in the longhouse: various dances.

FIFTH DAY

Morning: Dawn Song in the longhouse; Bowl Game goes around; Women's Dance goes around.

Afternoon and evening in the longhouse: various dances ending with a Husk Face rite in the late evening.

SIXTH DAY

Morning: Tobacco invocation (formerly, white dog also burned), Rite of Personal Chant (note that the short rite of Personal Chant that follows the tobacco invocation at Tonawanda is elevated at Newtown into a major rite and the Rite of Personal Chant in the Four Sacred Rituals sequence of the Green Corn ceremony is omitted), and scrub the longhouse.

SEVENTH DAY

Morning in the longhouse: Feather Dance, Thanksgiving Dance, and announcements of new names.

Evening in the longhouse: social dances.

EIGHTH DAY

Morning in the longhouse: Bowl Game between the moieties; announcements of new names.

Evening: social dances ending with a Husk Face rite.

NINTH DAY

Morning in the longhouse: Bowl Game.

Evening: Our Life Supporters ceremony with speech recapitulating year's events inserted: thɔwi :sas, Women's Dance, Stomp Dance, Women's Dance, Shake-the-pumpkin Dance, Women's Dance, Corn Dance, Women's Dance, inserted message, and Feather Dance.

The Coldspring Midwinter Ceremonial

The Coldspring Longhouse is the only remaining longhouse on the Allegany Reservation. In 1935, the Horseshoe Longhouse, which took its name from the great bend of the Allegheny River east of Salamanca, was torn down and the lumber given to the Coldspring Longhouse for a cook house. The Coldspring group is an old one; Handsome Lake went to Coldspring in 1804 with about ten families and insisted that a longhouse be built there (Deardorff and Snyderman 1956:593). In 1965, the frame longhouse that had served this community for many years was torn down along with the houses in the take area of the Kinzua Dam, which was built some twelve miles south of the New York–Pennsylvania line. A new longhouse—slightly larger, but in the same architectural style as the old one—was built in the Steamburg Relocation center, one of the two communities of new houses built for those whose homes had to be abandoned as the result of building the Kinzua Dam Reservoir. The "fire was moved" to this new longhouse on June 12, 1965. (For a description of this ritual see Abrams 1967.)

The Coldspring Midwinter ceremonial is built up in much the same manner as those at the Tonawanda and Newtown Longhouses. (For the following, I have used Fenton's 1936: 10–13 and 1963 descriptions.) To make the Coldspring Midwinter ceremonial, take the Our Life Supporters ceremony, which at Coldspring comprises the Planting, Strawberry, and Harvest ceremonies and which has the form: Feather Dance for the Faithkeepers (not in costume), Women's Dance, and Feather Dance. Add to it the Four Sacred Rituals —Feather Dance, Thanksgiving Dance, Rite of Personal Chant, and Bowl Game—to make the Green Corn ceremony, combining the Our Life Supporters ceremony with the first of the Four Sacred Rituals and precede it with a rite of naming of the children:

FIRST DAY

Feather Dance for the Faithkeepers; naming of the children born since Midwinter; and Feather Dance for all.

SECOND DAY

Feather Dance for the Faithkeepers (not in costume); Women's Dance; announcements, including change of names and installation of Faithkeepers; and Feather Dance for all.

THIRD DAY

Morning: collection of tobacco and food through the houses; tobacco invocation in the longhouse (Coldspring practice differs from that of other longhouses by including this tobacco invocation as part of Green Corn as well as Midwinter, and in turn, this difference may reflect an older difference: it is reported that the Allegheny Seneca sacrificed a white dog at both Green Corn and Midwinter, a practice not recorded for other Iroquois groups); Rite of Personal Chant; and Thanksgiving Dance.

Afternoon: thɔwi:sas.

Evening: social dances.

FOURTH AND SUCCEEDING DAYS

Begin the Bowl Game, and hold social dances in the evening.

Precede this with the distinctive major rituals of Midwinter, combining the tobacco invocation and its succeeding Rite of Personal Chant with the Rite of Personal Chant given as one of the Four Sacred Rituals and preceding the whole with a rite of naming of the children (preliminary confession should be held two mornings during the week before the ceremonial):

FIRST DAY

Morning: Feather Dance for the Faithkeepers, naming of children born since Green Corn, and Feather Dance for all.

SECOND DAY

Morning: Bigheads go around the houses three times before noon. On the first circuit, at dawn, they wake the people and notify them of the New Year; on the second, they stir the ashes and hail the occupants of the houses as nephews, instruct them to put everything aside, and summon them to the longhouse to reveal their dreams; on the third circuit, the two men who represented the Bigheads and their dressers stir the ashes in the houses.

The two head male longhouse officers, one from each moiety, go around and stir the ashes in the houses. Then the two women officers, one from each moiety, go around and stir the ashes.

Anciently, the white dog was strangled on this day.

THIRD DAY

Morning: parties representing each moiety go around and stir the ashes, the rite ending with the singing of Handsome Lake's own song. Various dances and other rites go around the rest of the day.

FOURTH DAY

Morning: a troupe dancing the Feather Dance goes around the houses, preceded by a leader who announces that the time has come to sponsor rites revealed through dreams. In each house, they receive two ears of corn.

Women's Dance is danced through the circuit of houses. (Note that at the Coldspring Longhouse the Women's Dance follows the Feather Dance on both the fourth and seventh days, that is, in both the first and second parts of Midwinter, while at the Tonawanda and Newtown Longhouses the Women's Dance follows the Bowl Game in both the first and second parts. This difference reflects the difference of where the Our Life Supporters ceremony is inserted into the sequence of the Four Sacred Rituals.)

Medicine society rituals as requested by individuals are performed the rest of the day; anciently, this was the first day of dream-guessing. In the evening, the Beggars go about the houses begging for tobacco.

FIFTH DAY

Morning: Thanksgiving Dance is danced through the circuit of houses. Various dances and other rites go around the rest of the day.

SIXTH DAY

Morning: Bowl Game is played through the circuit of houses. Before leaving the longhouse, the players play against the men and on returning, play against the women. Various dances and rites go around the rest of the day.

Evening in the longhouse: social, medicine society, and Beggar dances.

Husk Face rite (see also Skinner 1925:194–96 for a description of this rite). The appearance of the Husk Faces has previously been announced by two sets of masked runners. They indicate that their company is approaching the village by racing through the longhouse. Finally, they arrive with a great din, beating and rubbing the outside of the longhouse with staves and wooden shovels. The two heralds burst into the longhouse, break up the dances, and take some elderly man, usually one with a sense of humor, outside—supposedly to talk with their leader whom he says is a woman. He returns in their custody and delivers her supposed message, but in the middle of it simulates forgetfulness and makes some absurd excuse for going outside again to see the woman, whom he says he has not seen for a year. He returns and conducts both sides of a conversation with the masked company.

Through him, the Husk Faces reveal that they are a race of agriculturists who dwell on the other side of the earth, where it is summer and where they are now hurrying westward to till their crops which grow in fields amid high stumps. They describe ears of corn growing to prodigious lengths. They sometimes say they can linger to dance but a few songs with the people of the longhouse, since their women must hasten home to tend to crying babies. Such statements are interpreted as prophecies of good crops and many births.

The Husk Faces are dressed to represent both men and women, a few of the latter carrying corn husk dolls wearing miniature husk masks. (The masked actors are usually men.) Their "women" request the privilege of dancing the Women's Dance. Then the male Husk Faces dance the Fish Dance with the Seneca men; and their "wives," who are also men, join in couples like Seneca women and employ women's dance steps. Meanwhile, the Seneca women also enter in couples and dance opposite the Seneca men, or the male Husk Faces.

SEVENTH DAY

Morning in the longhouse: Feather Dance for the Faithkeepers (not in costume), Women's Dance, announcements including change of name and installation of Faithkeepers, and Feather Dance for all.

EIGHTH DAY

Morning: collection of tobacco and food throughout the houses.

Tobacco invocation once used over the white dog in the longhouse. (No one now living at Coldspring has seen the white dog sacrifice, and there is disagreement over when it was given. Some say the white dog was burned on the fifth morning of Midwinter, others on the sixth morning. If Coldspring practice was like that of other longhouses, the white dog would have been burned on the seventh morning, that is, after the conclusion of the dream-fulfillment rites and the Husk Face rite on the sixth evening and before the Feather Dance, the beginning of the Four Sacred Rituals on the seventh day. The confusion at Coldspring regarding the day on which the white dog was burned seems to be the result of the moving of the tobacco invocation to the eighth day—a change that combined the rite of Personal Chant following the tobacco invocation with the Rite of Personal Chant given as one of the Four Sacred Rituals and perhaps suggested by it.)

Rite of Personal Chant, beginning with the Personal Chants of the chiefs and officials and ending with Handsome Lake's own song.

Thanksgiving Dance. At Coldspring, the dance leader carries a miniature bow and arrow which he hands to the speaker before each prayer and takes it back after each prayer. This commemorates Handsome Lake's conversation with the Four Beings or Messengers when their speaker had a bow in his hand.

Evening in the longhouse: social dances. The evening's activities are opened and concluded with a brief Feather Dance. Between the social dances, which invariably start with the "Quiver" or "Stomp Dance," the people are divided into moieties for the game the next day. Collectors to match the wagers and referees to watch the pits and score the beans are appointed. The Bowl Game symbolizes the struggle between the Creator and his twin evil brother for control of the earth, and the moieties exchange the role of playing for the Creator at Green Corn and Midwinter.

This night once marked the last appearance of the Husk Faces and ends the public celebration of dreams. However, the Husk Faces no longer appear a second night at Coldspring, as Hiram Jacobs decided some years ago that it was illogical for them to return when they had already said on the first night that they were hurrying westward. (The former appearance of the Husk Faces on this day is paralleled in Tonawanda practice of giving a Husk Face rite on this day, the sixth day of the Tonawanda Midwinter ceremonial, and at Newtown, the comparable Husk Face rite on the eighth day of the Newtown Midwinter ceremonial.)

NINTH DAY

Morning in the longhouse: Bowl Game is begun.

Afternoon: thɔwi :sas.

Evening: social dances, beginning and ending with a Feather Dance.

TENTH AND SUCCEEDING DAYS

Mornings in the longhouse: Bowl Game is resumed until one moiety wins all 102 beans.

Evenings: social dances, beginning and ending with a Feather Dance.

THE SOUR SPRINGS MIDWINTER CEREMONIAL

Although the four longhouses on the Six Nations Reserve—the Seneca, Onondaga, Lower Cayuga, and Upper Cayuga (or Sour Springs) Longhouses—take their names from the dominant group that founded them, membership is not limited to the tribe after which the longhouse takes its name; actual membership in each longhouse crosscuts tribal lines. It seems likely that this crosscutting affiliation as well as the proximity of the longhouses has blurred whatever tribal differences may have once existed in the ritual of these four groups. At least, the available data suggest that practice in the four longhouses on the Six Nations Reserve is similar in many respects.

Of the four groups, practice at the Upper Cayuga Longhouse is best documented in the anthropological literature (see especially Shimony 1961:140–91; Speck 1949 [7]; see also Witthoft 1946). And, as will be seen, the Sour Springs Midwinter ceremonial resembles in its major features those of the three New York Seneca Longhouses.

At the Sour Springs Longhouse, the Our Life Supporters ceremony, which comprises the major rites of the Raspberry, Green Bean, and Harvest ceremonies, has the form: Feather Dance, Women's Dance, Stomp Dance (Standing Quiver Dance), Corn Dance, Bean Dance, and Squash (Pumpkin) Dance.

To make the Green Corn ceremony, take the Our Life Supporters ceremony and precede it with the Four Sacred Rituals—Feather Dance, Thanksgiving Dance, Rite of Personal Chant, and Bowl Game:

FIRST DAY

Feather Dance.

SECOND DAY

Rite of Personal Chant, announcements of new names, Thanksgiving Dance, and installation of Faithkeepers.

THIRD DAY

Begin the Bowl Game.

Immediately after or one week after the Bowl Game is finished, give the Our Life Supporters ceremony: Feather Dance, Women's Dance, Stomp Dance, Corn Dance, Bean Dance, and Squash Dance.

To make the Sour Springs Midwinter ceremonial, take the Green Corn ceremony, substituting for the Our Life Supporters ceremony the Bush ceremony (but also designated by some informants as Our Life Supporters ceremony according to Shimony 1961:142): Feather Dance, False Face Dance (unmasked), Stomp Dance, Eagle Dance, and Women's Dance. Precede it with the three distinctive major rituals of Midwinter—the ashes-stirring rites, dream-fulfillment rituals, and tobacco invocation once said over the white dog, combining the tobacco invocation and its succeeding rite of Personal Chant with the Rite of Personal Chant given as one of the Four Sacred Rituals (a rite of confession may be held before Midwinter proper begins) :

FIRST DAY

The two Uncles now stir the ashes in the longhouse stoves, although at the other three longhouses on the reserve and until recently at the Sour Springs Longhouse, the Uncles stir the ashes in the houses. The Uncles are dressed in "Indian costume" not in special costume, nor are they called "Bigheads" as they are in the New York Seneca Longhouses.

Small parties, each composed of members of the same moiety, stir the ashes in the longhouse stoves. The way is open for dream fulfillment and renewal.

Various dances, games, and other rituals including optionally the dream-guessing rite are given in the longhouse.

SECOND DAY

Ashes-stirring in the longhouse by groups of each moiety, the two Uncles, and the Faithkeepers.

Various dances, games, and other rituals of dream fulfillment and renewal.

THIRD DAY

Various dances, games, and other rituals of dream fulfillment and renewal.

FOURTH DAY

Longhouse scrubbed.[8] (Anciently, white dog burned, names given, and Our Life Supporters dances danced.)

FIFTH DAY

Feather Dance.

SIXTH DAY

Tobacco invocation once said over the white dog, Rite of Personal Chant, announcements of names, and Thanksgiving Dance.

SEVENTH DAY

Bowl Game begun. If Bowl Game ends quickly, immediately following, or if not, within six to ten days later, the Bush or Forest ceremony is given: Ashes-stirring Song (usually), Feather Dance, False Face Dance (unmasked), Stomp Dance (Standing Quiver Dance, unmasked dance of the Husk Faces), Eagle Dance, and Women's Dance.

THE SIX NATIONS ONONDAGA MIDWINTER CEREMONIAL

As Shimony (1961:173–91) indicates, the Midwinter ceremonials held at the three longhouses "down below" on the Six Nations Reserve are much like that given at the Sour Springs Longhouse.[9] Hewitt (1910b:940–44) described the ceremonial at the Onondaga Longhouse as follows. The first day the heralds (the Uncles), one a federal chief of the Deer clan (holder of the chiefly title of the Deer clan) and the other a federal chief of the Wolf clan (holder of the chiefly title of the Wolf clan), stir ashes around the houses and announce the beginning of the New Year. (Hewitt states the fires were actually rekindled by the Uncles.) Having visited the houses, they return to the longhouse and turn the ceremony over to the people. A speaker from the "Deer" moiety (on the Six Nations Reserve the moieties are often identified by the name of the "leading" clan of the moiety; see Shimony 1961:46 ff) gives the Thanksgiving Speech. Then, small parties, each party being composed of members of the same moiety, stir the ashes. Following this ritual, the dances and other rituals concerned with dream fulfillment, including dream-guessing, are given. The period of dream fulfillment lasts three days. At sunrise the following morning, the white dog was burned with tobacco thrown into the fire during the speech. (Hale 1885 describes the white dog sacrifice at the Onondaga Longhouse, but unfortunately limits his description to include only this rite of Midwinter.)

On the four or five days following the sacrifice of the white dog, the Four Sacred Rituals—Feather Dance, Thanksgiving Dance, Rite of Personal Chant, and Bowl Game—are given.

In 1966, I obtained from an informant of the Onondaga Longhouse an outline of Midwinter practice there. This agrees with Hewitt's earlier description.

FIRST DAY

The Uncles go around the houses dressed in Indian costume.

SECOND DAY

Ashes-stirring rite in the longhouse.

THIRD DAY

Dream-fulfillment rites in the longhouse in the afternoon.

FOURTH DAY

Dream-fulfillment rites in the longhouse in the afternoon and evening. The dream-guessing rite is not given.

FIFTH DAY

Clean longhouse and cook food. Formerly, white dog sacrificed.

SIXTH DAY

Feather Dance.

SEVENTH DAY

Thanksgiving Dance.

EIGHTH DAY

Bowl Game and Rite of Personal Chant. At the conclusion of the Bowl Game, the Feather Dance and Thanksgiving Dance are performed. A week or two later, the Bush, or Forest ceremony is held.

THE NEW YORK ONONDAGA MIDWINTER CEREMONIAL

Of the practice in the six longhouses here considered, that of the New York Onondaga Longhouse is the most variant. Yet, some of the same patterns that underlie the Midwinter ceremonial in the more western longhouses are to be ascertained in that of the New York Onondaga Longhouse.

At the New York Onondaga Longhouse, the Planting and Harvest ceremonials do not consist solely of a single day's ritual devoted to the Our Life Supporters ceremony, but of the Four Sacred Rituals in which the Our Life Supporters ceremony has been inserted between the day on which the Rite of Personal Chant is given and the day on which the Bowl Game is played, and the whole preceded by a day devoted to the confession of sins:

FIRST DAY
Confession of sins.

SECOND DAY ("Children's Day")
Children named and Feather Dance.

THIRD DAY ("Four Beings," that is, messengers to Handsome Lake, Day)
Thanksgiving Dance and Feather Dance.

FOURTH DAY ("Creator's Day")
Tobacco invocation to the Creator, Feather Dance, Rite of Personal Chant, and Feather Dance.

FIFTH DAY ("Our Life Supporters Day")
War Dance, Feather Dance, Women's Dance, Bean Dance, Women's Dance, and Corn Dance.

SIXTH DAY
Bowl Game between the sexes. The Green Corn Ceremonial is identical with the exception that three days rather than one should be devoted to confession of sins.

Like the western Iroquois longhouses, the New York Onondaga Longhouse constructs the Midwinter ceremonial by preceding the Green Corn ceremony with the rituals distinctive of Midwinter: the ashes-stirring rites, dream-fulfillment rituals (which among the New

York Onondaga take the form of an elaborate dream-guessing rite),
and a tobacco invocation which was once said over the white dogs.
But unlike the western Iroquois Longhouses, the New York Onondaga Longhouse practice includes a Bowl Game between the moieties
inserted between the rite of confession—which is a mandatory rite,
not an optional one as in the West—and the circuit of the Uncles.
The False Face rite held a week after the final Bowl Game is counted
as the final day of Midwinter. (Nineteenth-century descriptions of
the Onondaga ceremony include those of Beauchamp 1885, 1888,
and 1895; E. Smith 1883; and DeC. Smith 1888. Parts of the ceremonial have been described recently in Blau 1963, 1964, 1966, 1967,
and 1969; and Kurath 1954.)

FIRST DAY

Rite of confession in the morning.

SECOND DAY

Rite of confession in the morning.

THIRD DAY

Rite of confession in the morning.

FOURTH DAY

Bowl Game between the moieties is begun. The scoring system is
different from that customarily used among the Iroquois (see Blau
1967 for a description).

FIFTH DAY

Bowl Game between the moieties is continued.

SIXTH DAY

Bowl Game between the moieties is concluded. Two Uncles accompanied by two associates go around the houses stirring the ashes.
At each house they are given food and sometimes money.

Dream-guessing rite begins in the evening. For this rite, the
moieties separate, the members of the Wolf, Turtle, Beaver, and
Snipe clans going to the longhouse and the members of the Deer,

Bear, Hawk, and Eel clans going to the adjacent Mudhouse. In the dream-guessing rite, a representative is sent to the ritual house of the opposite moiety, a gun shot announcing his departure. There he mentions the name of the dreamer and presents the matter of the dream in the form of a riddle. Those assembled in the house attempt to guess the answer to the riddle. When someone does, or, more accurately, guesses *part* of the dream, the representative returns to his own ritual house and asks for another guess. Having obtained a second correct answer, he sings a Personal Chant if the dreamer is a man. The correct answers secured, he announces them and the names of those who correctly guessed the dream. The person who guesses the dream correctly is obliged to give the item guessed to the dreamer; these gifts are those of food and miniature objects such as False Face masks, lacrosse sticks, and animal figures. The guessers are thanked with tobacco and small presents (Blau 1963:234–43; see also Beauchamp 1888:198–99; 1895:209; DeC. Smith 1888: 190–91).

SEVENTH DAY

Evening: dream-guessing rite is continued. False Faces accompanied by the Husk Faces appear to amuse the people.

EIGHTH DAY

Evening: dream-guessing rite is concluded. Rites of the False and Husk Faces. (Note that in the New York Seneca Longhouses a Husk Rite is given at this point in Midwinter.)

NINTH DAY

Anciently, white dogs burned. Now, two baskets of ribbons and two baskets of tobacco, one for each moiety, are burned in place of the two dogs.

Rite of Personal Chant.

TENTH ("Children's") DAY

Children named and Feather Dance.

ELEVENTH ("Four Beings") DAY

Thanksgiving Dance and Feather Dance.

TWELFTH ("Creator's") DAY

Tobacco invocation to the Creator, Feather Dance, Rite of Personal Chant, ending with Handsome Lake's chant, and Feather Dance.

THIRTEENTH ("Our Life Supporters") DAY

War Dance, Feather Dance, Women's Dance, Bean Dance, Women's Dance, and Corn Dance.

FOURTEENTH DAY

Bowl Game between the sexes.

FIFTEENTH DAY (one week later)

False Face rite.

PART III

The Midwinter Ceremonial in
Historical Perspective

Although much changed over the centuries, the Midwinter ceremonial is undoubtedly an old one in Iroquois ritual. One important line
of evidence for its antiquity is linguistic and is based on the idea that
if the word for ceremonial is ancient, the ceremonial itself is probably
also old. As Edward Sapir pointed out, unless there is evidence that
they are words introduced from another language, words that are
unanalyzable into more simple forms are probably older than those
that are so analyzable. Using this method, Wallace L. Chafe (1964)
suggests that the Midwinter ceremonial as well as certain rituals associated with shamanistic (curing) ceremonies are old ones in Iroquois religion, while the ceremonies associated with agriculture are
relatively recent additions.

Another line of evidence indicating the antiquity of the Midwinter ceremonial is its general resemblance to various New Fire rites in
other parts of the continent, perhaps the most well-known of which is
the Aztec New Fire ceremony (see especially Prescott 1843[1]:
125–27). But unfortunately the descriptions of these ceremonials
are so sketchy that it is impossible at this time to do more than suggest that in some important respects they resemble each other and
are historically related.

In its ancient form, the New Fire rite seems to have been a winter solstice rite, one of whose purposes was to turn back the sun. The
ritual involved: (1) the extinguishing of old fires and the rekindling
of new ones (which survives in the Iroquois ceremonial as the ashes-stirring rites), (2) renewal by performance of the important rituals of the religion (which survives in the Iroquois ceremonial as the
renewal of dreams), and (3) often a sacrifice of either a human or a

dog. In addition, New Fire rites apparently often had war associations, which evidently rested on the association of the sun with war. In the Iroquois ceremonial, the dog sacrifice apparently had such war connotations and the ceremonial once included a war dance. Although the War Dance is no longer a part of many Iroquois ceremonials, the Thanksgiving Dance, a war dance transformed into its present form by Handsome Lake, is still performed. The Rite of Personal Chant also has war connotations, the chants once being sung by a captive during his torture and by warriors before going to war.

THE MIDWINTER CEREMONIAL IN THE SEVENTEENTH CENTURY

Although some information on northern Iroquoian religion is to be found in Samuel de Champlain's account of his travels in Huronia in 1615–16, Gabriel Sagard's account of his visit in 1623–24, and Johannes Megapolensis' account of the Mohawk, our knowledge of the seventeenth-century Midwinter ceremonial comes principally from the great collections of the Jesuit Relations (cited as JR). The Jesuits began their intensive work among the Iroquoian speakers in 1634, living among the Hurons. Their work among these Indians in their homeland ended in 1650 when the Iroquois defeated the Hurons and dispersed them. Following this defeat, the Jesuits turned their attention to the Five Nations Iroquois, withdrawing from the Iroquois field early in the eighteenth century.

The most explicit statement indicating the Iroquois had a Midwinter ceremonial in the seventeenth century was made by the Jesuits living at Onondaga in 1670–71. They said that the dream-guessing ceremony was held annually about February as well as being given to cure a sick individual, before going on hunting expeditions, and before adopting some important war plans (JR 55:61). As the Jesuits wrote:

They have a certain ceremony—one of the most important of their superstitious observances—which they hold at least once a year, toward the month of February, with great solemnity, in honor of their dreams, through which they claim to know all the decrees of a certain Taronhiaouagon respecting their good or evil fortune. This spirit, they declare, is the mightiest of all spirits, and the Master of our lives. The ceremony is held either for the cure of some person of wealth and station; or before their hunting expedition, to obtain good success therein; or when they are about to adopt some important war plans. It will sometimes last four or five days, during which all is disorder, and no one does more than snatch a hasty meal. All are at liberty to run through the cabins in grotesque attire, both men and women, indicating—by songs, or by singing in enigmatical and obscure terms— what they have wished for in their dreams; and this each person tries to divine, offering the thing guessed, however precious it may be, and making a boast of appearing generous on this occasion. The head-man of the Village is the prime mover in this whole affair, and to him it belongs to determine the time and conditions of the ceremony.

The name of this dream-guessing ceremony (variously spelled by the Jesuits *Honnonouaria, onoharoia, ononhouaroia,* etc.) in the seventeenth-century documents on the Iroquois and the Hurons is cognate to one of the names now used by the Iroquois to refer to the Midwinter ceremonial (Beauchamp 1891:41–42; 1895:188; Fenton 1941:158–59; 1942:15; Blau 1963:233; cf. Hewitt 1910b:940; Chafe 1963:29; Tooker 1964:110). But the use of the name *onoharoia* to refer to the Midwinter ceremonial does not mean that every ceremony so referred to was the Midwinter ceremonial. As noted above, the Jesuits state that the dream-guessing ceremony could be given to cure a sick individual, before going on hunting expeditions, and before adopting important war plans.

Such practice is confirmed in specific instances mentioned by the Jesuits. For example, in 1677 a girl at Onondaga dreamed that in order to be cured, nine feasts, the first two being the dream-guessing ceremony, would have to be given for her (JR 60:187 ff). However, the recorded use of the term *ononharoia* in the seventeenth century as well as in the nineteenth and twentieth centuries to refer to the Midwinter ceremonial does suggest that the dream-guessing rite was an important one in the seventeenth century, at least among the Onondaga. In time the name of an important rite of the Midwinter ceremonial may have come to refer to the entire ceremonial.

The deity *Taronhiaouagon* mentioned in the Jesuit Relation of 1670–71 is the same as *Taronhiaouagui* (he-who-holds-up-the-Sky) mentioned by Dablon (JR 42:197). This deity is also mentioned by other seventeenth-century writers as being the most important spirit among the Iroquois. For example, Father Carheil (JR 54:65–67) said:

The first is, that it is not, properly speaking, the Dream that they worship as the Master of their lives, but a certain one of the Spirits called by them Agatkonchoria [1]—who, as they think, sometimes speak to them in sleep, and command them to obey their dreams exactly. The principal of these Spirits is Taronhiaouagon, whom they acknowledge as a Divinity, and obey as the great Master of their lives; and when they speak of dreams as of a God, they mean nothing else than that it is by this means that they gain knowledge of the will of God, and of what is needful for the preservation of their lives, and that the doing of what they have seen in dreams is a means which contributes to the establishment of their health and of their good fortune. Sometimes, too, they gave this same name of "Master of their lives" to the subject of their dream—for example, to a bearskin or deerskin, or to other like objects that they have seen in their sleep, because they regard them as remedies to which God has attached to good fortune of a long life. And, in fact, they take marvelous pains to preserve these things, with this in view, and, when they are ill, they cover themselves with these, or put them near at hand, as a defense against the attacks of the disease.

Johannes Megapolensis (1644; 1909:177), a Dutch missionary among the Mohawks, also mentions this deity:

They are entire strangers to all religion, but they have a *Tharonhijouaagon* (whom they also otherwise call *Athzoockkuatoriaho*), that is, a Genius, whom they esteem in the place of God; but they do not serve him or make offerings to him. They worship and present offerings to the Devil, whom they call *Otskon,* or *Aireskuoni.* If they have any bad luck in war, they catch a bear, which they cut in pieces, and roast, and that they offer up to their *Aireskuoni,* saying in substance, the following words: "Oh! great and mighty Aireskuoni, we confess that we have offended against thee, inasmuch as we have not killed and eaten our captive enemies; forgive us this. We promise that we will kill and eat all the captives we shall hereafter take as certainly as we have killed, and now eat this bear." Also when the weather is very hot, and there comes a cooling breeze, they cry out directly, *Asoronusi, asoronusi, Otskon aworouhsi reinnuha;* that is, "I thank thee, I thank thee, devil, I thank thee, little uncle!"

The *Aireskuoni* mentioned by Megapolensis are *Agreskoué*

(*Agriskoué, Aireskoi*, etc.) frequently mentioned by the Jesuits in Iroquois country (JR 39:207–209, 215; 53:225, 229, 235, 239, 265, 267, 281, 295; 57:97, 123, 147, 157; 58:205) and rather less frequently by the Jesuits in Huronia (JR 33:225; Bressani in JR 39:13 may be thinking of Iroquois rather than Huron usage). It seems to mean "spirits."

Various authors have identified *Taronhiaouagon* with *Agreskoué* and *Agriskoué* as the God of War and the Sun (e.g., JR 5:286; Charlevoix 1870[2]:109 *n*, 143 *n*, [3]:157 *n;* Parkman 1867:73). Such identifications seem to be in error, as Hewitt (1910a:719; 1928:468) has suggested.

However, *Taronhiaouagon* seems to have had war associations. Dablon (JR 42:197) says that when this being appeared to a warrior in 1656, he said that he had given the Iroquois many victories. A few years later, a woman at Oneida said that *Taronhiaouagon* had revealed to her that the Susquehanna would come to attack the village in the spring and that one of their most powerful enemies would be captured and burned by the Oneida (JR 53:253). The Mohawk prophet in 1798 also indicated that this deity provided success in war among other things. However, *Taronhiaouagon* seems not to have been simply a god of war, but rather he gave success in war as he gave success in other endeavors.

This deity's name is now used only at the Onondaga Midwinter ceremonial (Beauchamp 1892:348; 1907:411; Hewitt 1928:467–69; Blau 1964:106; Chief George Thomas also told me this). It is apparently not used by the Senecas.

There is some evidence that this name is one of the names of the elder of the Twin Brothers in Iroquois mythology (Hewitt 1910a:718–19; Fenton 1962:292; for a summary of this myth and references see Tooker 1964:151–55). The Creator or Great Spirit is identified with this Elder Brother among the Seneca (Morgan 1901[1]:147–48; Seaver 1824:171–72). Among the Hurons in the seventeenth century, this Elder Brother was called *Iouskeha (Jouskeha, Yoscaha)* (Tooker 1964:146–48). The Jesuits (JR 10:133) said that the Huron believed that *Iouskeha* was the sun and his grandmother the moon. The Iroquois today call the sun "elder brother" and the moon "grandmother" (see, for example, Chafe 1961:35, 37; Speck 1949:33).

Some years before the 1670–71 description of the dream-guessing ceremony, Claude Dablon had described it in greater detail as it was given at Onondaga in 1656. Following the ceremonial that year, ten dogs were sacrificed to the Holder-of-Heavens as a consequence of a dream of a returning warrior. Dablon's description is as follows (JR 42:155–65):

Not only do they believe in their dreams, but they also hold a special festival to the Demon of dreams. This festival might be called the festival of fools, or the Carnival of wicked Christians; for, in both, the devil plays almost the same part, and at the same season.[2] They call this celebration HONNONOUARORIA, and the Elders announce it through the Village streets. We witnessed the ceremony on the twenty-second of February, of this year, 1656. Immediately upon the announcement of the festival by these public cries, nothing was seen but men, women, and children, running like maniacs through the streets and cabins—this, however, in a far different manner from that of Masqueraders in Europe, the greater number being nearly naked, and apparently insensible to the cold, which is well-nigh unbearable to those who are most warmly clothed. Some, indeed, give no farther evidence of their folly than to run thus half naked through all the cabins; but others are mischievous. Some carry water, or something worse, and throw it at those whom they meet; others take the fire-brands, coals, and ashes from the fire, and scatter them in all directions, without heeding on whom they fall; others break the kettles, dishes, and all the little domestic outfit that they find in their path. Some go about armed with javelins, bayonets, knives, hatchets, and sticks, threatening to strike the first one they meet; and all this continues until each has attained his object and fulfilled his dream. In this connection, two things are worthy of note.

First, it sometimes happens that one is not bright enought to guess their thoughts; for they are not clearly put forth, but are expressed in riddles, phrases of covert meaning, songs, and occasionally in gestures alone. Consequently, a good Œdipus is not always to be found. Yet, they will not leave a place until their thought is divined; and, if they meet with delay, or a disinclination or inability to guess it, they threaten to burn up everything. . . . [There follows mention of an Indian who had dreamed that he killed a Frenchman; the Jesuits gave him a French coat and two dogs, and after the second was given to him, he left.]

Our host's brother, like all the rest, wished to play his part. Dressing himself somewhat like a Satyr, and decking his person from top to toe with the husks of Indian corn—he had two women disguise themselves as veritable Megeras—their hair flying, their faces coal-black, their persons clothed with a couple of Wolfskins, and each armed with a handspike or large stake. The Satyr, seeing them well fitted out, marched about our cabin, singing and howling at the top of his voice. Then, climbing on to the roof, he went through a thousand antics, with an outcry as if the day of destruction had come. After that, he came down, and proceeded solemnly through the entire Village, the two Megeras walking before him, and striking with their stakes whatever chanced to come under their hands. . . .

Scarcely had our Satyr and Megeras passed out of our sight, when a woman, armed with an arquebus which she had obtained through her dream, rushed into our cabin. She was shouting, howling, and singing, saying that she was going to war against the Cat Nation, that she would fight them, and bring back some prisoners—with a thousand imprecations and curses on herself, if what she had dreamed should not take place.

This Amazon was followed by a warrior, who came in carrying his bow and arrow and a bayonet. He danced and sang, shouted and threatened; and then suddenly rushed at a woman who had entered to view this comedy. He leveled the bayonet at her throat, then seized her by the hair, but was satisfied with cutting off a few locks; after this, he retired, to give place to a Diviner who had dreamed that he could guess the location of any concealed article. He was ridiculously attired, and bore in his hand a sort of divining-rod, which he used for pointing out the place of concealment. Still, his companion, who carried a vase filled with some kind of liquor, was obliged to take a mouthful and blow it out upon the head, face, hands, and wand of the Diviner, before the latter could find the object in question. I leave the solution of the mystery to the reader.

A woman came in with a mat, which she spread out, and arranged as if she wished to catch some fish; she thus indicated that some must be given her, to satisfy her dream.

Another simply laid a mattock on the ground. It was guessed that she wanted a field or a piece of ground, which was exactly her desire. She was content with five furrows for planting Indian corn.

After that, a little grotesque figure was put in front of us. We rejected it, and it was placed before other persons; after the mumbling of some words, it was carried off without further ceremony.

One of the Village chiefs appeared in wretched attire, and all covered with ashes. Because his dream, which called for two human hearts, was not guessed, he caused the ceremony to be protracted one day, never ceasing his foolish actions during that time. Entering our cabin, in which there are several fireplaces, he went to the first, and tossed ashes and coals into the air; he repeated the performance at the second and third, but did nothing at ours, out of respect.

Some come entirely armed, and behaved as if they were engaging the enemy. They assume the attitudes, shout the battle-cries, and join in the scramble of two armies in action.

Others march about in companies, and perform dances with contortions of body that resemble those of men possessed. In short, one would never end if he tried to relate all that is done during the three days and three nights in which this nonsense lasts, such a din prevailing the while that scarcely a moment's quiet is to be had. . . .

It would be cruelty, nay, murder, not to give a man the subject of his dream; for such a refusal might cause his death. Hence, some see themselves stripped of their all, without any hope of retribution; for, whatever they thus give away will never be restored to them, unless they themselves dream, or pretend to dream, of the same thing. But they are, in general, too scrupulous to employ simulation, which would, in their opinion, cause all sorts of misfortunes. Yet there are some who overcome their scruples, and enrich themselves by a shrewd piece of deception.

Later Dablon appends the following (JR 42:195–97):

On the twenty-fourth, while the Honnaouaroia—of which we spoke above, in connection with dreams—was being held, there arrived three Warriors, returning, after more than a year's absence, from the war against the Cat Nation. One of them announced, on his arrival, that he had a matter of very great importance to communicate to the Elders. These having assembled, he told them that, while seeking the enemy, he met a Tortoise of incredible size; and, some time after, he saw a Demon in the guise of a little Dwarf, who is said to have already appeared to others. They call him Taronhiaouagui, which means "he who holds up the Sky." This Dwarf or Demon spoke as follows: "I am he who holds up the Sky, and the guardian of the earth; I preserve men, and give victories to warriors. I have made you masters of the earth and victors over so many Nations; I made you conquer the Hurons, the Tobacco Nation, the Ahondihronnons, Atiraguenrek, Atiaorek, Takoulguehronnons, and Gentaguetehronnons; in short, I have made you what you are; and, if you wish me to continue my protection over you, hear my words, and execute my orders.

"First, you will find three Frenchmen in your Village when you arrive there. Secondly, you will enter during the celebration of the Honnaouaroria. Thirdly, after your arrival, let there be sacrificed to me ten dogs, ten porcelain beads from each cabin, a collar ten rows wide, four measures of sunflower seed, and as many of beans. And, as for thee, let two married women be given thee, to be at thy disposal for five days. If that be not executed item by item I will make thy Nation a prey to all sorts of disasters; and, after it is all done, I will declare to thee my orders for the future." So saying, the Dwarf vanished. This vision the man immediately related to his companions, who witnessed, as they affirmed its verification that very day. Seeing by chance a Stag, he called it from a distance, and bade it come to him. The Stag obeyed, approaching and coming up to receive its death-stroke from our Visionary.

Hewitt (1910b:940) interprets this latter passage as referring to the white dog sacrifice given as part of Midwinter and notes that "In early times the number of dogs to be sacrificed was apparently not ritually limited." This interpretation assumes that this dog sacrifice was part of Midwinter and also suggests that the dream of the returning warrior indicated some detail of the ritual, since dreams in more recent times may indicate how ritual ought to be performed. For example, in the nineteenth century, when the white dog was still being sacrificed as a part of the Midwinter ceremonial, an individual might dream that he or she should provide the dog.

Harold Blau (1964:108) has offered another interpretation of Dablon's account. He suggests that this description may be a description of the origin of the dog sacrifice as part of Midwinter. In part, this interpretation is based on the fact that Dablon does not mention the sacrifice of dogs as being part of the *Honnaouaroia* in 1656, but that a warrior had had a dream that indicated the Holder-of-the-Heavens wished to have ten dogs sacrificed to him, among other things. It may have been this dream or a similar one that led to the addition of the dog sacrifice to the Midwinter ceremonial. In part, also, Blau is led to this conclusion because there is a belief (at least in some longhouses) that the dog was sacrificed in fulfillment of the dream of the Creator (Blau 1964:99, 102; Shimony 1961:186; Fenton 1942:16–18) and thus ought to be renewed just as the dreams of individuals ought to be renewed at Midwinter.

There is a third interpretation of Dablon's description. It may be that in the seventeenth and eighteenth centuries *Teharonhiawagon* (Holder-of-the-Heavens) might indicate through the dream of an individual that he wished to have a sacrifice of dogs made to him and that such a sacrifice need not have been part of the Midwinter ceremonial. Dablon states merely that the dream of the Onondaga warrior indicated that he would arrive back in the Onondaga village at the time of *Honnaouaroia* and that after he had returned the ten dogs and other objects should be sacrificed. It might have been that the sacrifice of the dogs was performed quite independently of the Midwinter ceremonial. Such a separate ceremonial seems also indicated in Kirkland's account of the revival of the white dog sacrifice at Six Nations and among the Oneida. Further, although now the white dog sacrifice is associated with dream fulfillment and also with dream-guessing, it might not have had only this association in the past.

The problem of interpretation of this passage is confounded by the nature of Iroquoian ritual practice: many rituals can be performed as part of a calendric rite or for curing or for success in such activities as war. The dream-guessing rite, for example, could be given as part of Midwinter or at other times to cure a sick person or to gain success in war—as the Jesuit Relation of 1670–71 states. Similarly, dog sacrifices have been reported as being performed as part of Midwinter (at least so reported as being customary at the end of the eighteenth century and during much of the nineteenth century) and as being performed for success in war (at least about the time of the American Revolution). In the Jesuit Relations, there are frequent references to dogs being eaten at feasts and of sick individuals dreaming that dogs be eaten at feasts to cure them. In fact, some writers (Waugh 1916:133) have suggested that the white dog sacrifice was a survival of these seventeenth-century dog feasts.

Although the Jesuits at Onondaga report the dream-guessing rite was given as a calendric ceremonial as well as a curing ceremony, the Jesuits among the Hurons only report its use as a curing ceremonial. There are two long descriptions of such Huron ceremonies.

The first is contained in Le Jeune's Relation of 1636 (JR 10:175–77):

I do not undertake to mention in detail everything our Savages are accustomed to do in virtue of their dreams; I should be compelled to display on this paper too many absurdities. I shall content myself with saying that their dreams usually relate either to a feast, or to a song, or to a dance, or to a game—or, lastly, to a certain sort of mania that they in fact call *Ononharoia,* or "turning the brain upside down." If therefore it happens that some one of some consideration falls sick, the Captain goes to inquire so often, on behalf of the Old Men, what he has dreamed, that at last he draws from him what he desires for his health, and then they all put themselves to trouble to find it for him; if it does not exist, it must be found. From this mode of acting, and from the fact that they exercise hospitality among themselves gratuitously, taking nothing except from us, from whom they always expect something, I entertain the hope that they will one day become susceptible of Christian charity.

The *Ononharoia* is for the sake of mad persons, when some one says that they must go through the Cabins to tell what they have dreamed. Then, as soon as it is evening, a band of maniacs goes about among the Cabins and upsets everything; on the morrow they return, crying in a loud voice, "We have dreamed," without saying what. Those of the Cabin guess what it is, and present it to the band, who refuse nothing until the right thing is guessed. You see them come out with Hatchets, Kettles, Porcelain, and like presents hung around their necks, after their fashion. When they have found what they sought, they thank him who has given it to them; and, after having received further additions to this mysterious present—as some leather or a shoemaker's awl, if it were a shoe—they go away in a body to the woods, and there, outside the Village, cast out, they say, their madness; and the sick man begins to get better.

The second description is to be found in Le Jeune's Relation of 1639 (JR 17:165–87):

A woman, born in this village, but married in another, near by, named Angoutenc, going out one night from her cabin with one of her little daughters in her arms, at the time when they were celebrating in the village a feast like that I have just described [the referent here is unclear; it may refer simply to feasts in response to dreams], saw in an instant, she said, the Moon stoop down from above, forthwith appearing to her like a beautiful tall woman, holding in her arms a little girl like her own.

"I am," quote this specter to her, "the immortal seignior general of these countries, and of those who inhabit them; in testimony whereof I desire and order that in all quarters of my domain, those who dwell therein shall offer thee presents which must be the product of their own country—from the Khionontaterons or tobacco Nation, some tobacco; from the Attiwandarons or neutral Nation, some robes of outay; from the Askicwaneronons, or Sorcerers, a belt and leggings, with their porcupine ornaments; from the Ehonkeronons or Islanders, a deer skin." Thus it continued to name to her certain other nations, each one of which it ordered to make her some present, and, among others, named the French who dwelt in this country, as we shall soon relate.

"The feast which is now being solemnized in the town" (adds this Demon) "is very acceptable to me, and I desire that many like it be held in all the other quarters and villages of the country. Besides," it informs her, "I love thee, and on that account I wish that thou shouldst henceforth be like me; and, as I am wholly of fire, I desire that thou be also at least of the color of fire"; and thereupon it ordains for her a red cap, a red plume, a belt, leggings, shoes, and the rest of her clothes with red ornaments; this is, indeed, the garb in which she appeared at the ceremony that afterward was solemnized for her benefit.

This poor creature returned to her cabin, and no sooner had she reached it than behold her prostrated with a giddiness in the head and a contraction of the muscles, which made them conclude that she was sick of a disease of which the remedy is a ceremony, which is called, in the language of our barbarians, Ononhwaroia, or turning round the head—a name taken from the first symptom of this disease, or rather, this pretty superstition. The sick woman was confirmed in this belief by seeing in her dreams only goings and comings and outcries through her cabin; this made her resolve to demand in public that they should celebrate this feast for her.

Her devotion—or rather the purpose of the devil to spite us, and to thwart the affairs of Christianity, which were in their first splendor and glory—prompted her to address herself to this village where we are, Ossosane, or residence of la Conception, of which, as we have said, she was a native. They came, then, in her behalf, to make the proposition to its Captains, who immediately summoned the council. There it was declared that this affair was one of those most important to the welfare of the country, and that they certainly ought to avoid any failure, on such an occasion, to give every pleasure and satisfaction to the sick woman.

The next morning, the matter was published throughout the village, and people were vigorously exhorted to go promptly to bring the sick woman, and to prepare themselves for the feast. They ran thither, rather than walked, so that towards noon she arrived—or, rather, she was carried upon their shoulders in some kind of basket, with an escort of twenty-five or thirty persons who were killing themselves with singing.

A little while before she arrived, the general council was assembled, to which we were invited. Three of our Fathers went to it without knowing the subject for discussion. At the outset, we were informed that they desired to see us at this council in order to get our advice upon the proposition that such a sick woman had made, and to know what we thought of it. The substance of the response was, that they could not do a worse thing for the country—that they were continuing to render homage to evil spirits, whose empire, consequently, they were more and more confirming over themselves and over the country; and that only misfortune could happen to them if they continued to serve so bad a master.

The principal Captain, who secretly directed the whole affair—an adroit and crafty man, if ever the earth bore one—instead of speaking in reference to what we had said, addressed the entire assembly, and began to exclaim, "Courage, then, young men; courage, women; courage, my brothers; let us render to our country this service, so necessary and important, according to the customs of our ancestors!" Now followed a great speech in the same strain and tone; then, in a somewhat lower voice, he said, addressing himself to those who were around him, "This is the advice I gave to my nephews, the French, last Autumn. 'You will see this Winter,' I said to them, 'many things that will displease you—the Ononhwaroia, the Outaerohi, and similar ceremonies; do not say a word, I pray you,' I said to them; 'pretend not to see what shall take place; with time, it may change.' We were formerly told at the three Rivers and Quebec," he added, "that, provided we believed in four years, it was enough."

As he continued the like discourse, the deputies entered on the part of the patient, who came to announce her arrival to the council, and to say for her that they should send her two men and two girls arrayed in robes and collars of such and such a fashion, with certain fish and presents in his hands—and this, in order to learn from her own lips her desires and what was necessary for her recovery. No sooner proposed, than executed.

Two men, therefore, and two girls went, loaded with all that the sick woman had desired, and immediately returned—for one thing, as naked as the hand, except their clouts, all they had carried having been left with the sick woman; and, for another, charged with demands which were the essential ones, and those the fulfillment of which should begin the recovery of her health, what had been carried her being accepted only as a compliment, and a token of their pleasure at her arrival. Accordingly, the deputies announced twenty-two presents that she desired they should give her, which were those the devil had specified to her in the apparition, as we related a little earlier. One was six dogs of a certain form and color; another was fifty cakes of tobacco; another, a large canoe; and so on—among other things was named a blue blanket, but with this condition, that it must belong to a Frenchman.

The report having been made by the deputies, the Captains began to exhort every one to satisfy promptly the desires of the sick woman, constantly representing and inculcating upon them the importance of such a matter. They became so excited over it that, before our Fathers went out of the assembly, fifteen of these presents had already been furnished.

Meanwhile, our Fathers were repeatedly attacked, on various occasions, and exhorted not to spare what at least concerned them, and depended upon them. Our Fathers answered to this that they were making sport of us, and that, if it were for this purpose that we had been called to the council, the sick woman might as well return, if, without our contribution and our homage rendered to the devil and to his ordinances, she could not recover.

Notwithstanding this, a half-hour after our Fathers had returned to the cabin, a Captain came there on behalf of the council, to tell us that everything was furnished except the blanket they were expecting from us, according to the desire of the sick woman. This second charge received no answer except that, in case they would go no further in this ceremony, which was still only in its beginning, and if they would send the sick woman back to the place whence she came, we would, in such case, willingly make to the public a present of a blanket, or of some other article of greater value.

Such was the first ceremony of the feast. I would prefer to call it the first act, if I could be sure of the catastrophe of the whole affair, that I might accurately characterize it; this term, however, will serve us henceforward.

The second act, then, or the second ceremony of this feast, was that—all the presents being furnished and carried to the patient, with the customary forms of which we have spoken above—towards evening public notice was given, warning all the cabins and all the families to keep their fires lighted, and the places on both sides of them all ready for the first visit which the sick woman was to make there, in the evening.

Accordingly, the Sun having set, upon hearing the voices of the Captains, who redoubled their cries, all stirred up their fires, and maintained them with great care—the patient having caused it to be recommended everywhere that these should be made as large and bright as possible, and that this would avail much for her relief.

The hour having come when she was to set out, her muscles, it was said relaxed, and the freedom to walk, even better than before, was restored to her; but it seems more certain that this did not occur until after she had passed through several fires, which usually results thus. Be that as it may, two Savages remained beside her all the time during her promenade, each one holding up one of her hands; and, thus supported, she walked between the two, and went through all the cabins of the village.

In the cabins of the Savages, which are in length and form like garden arbors, the fires are in the every middle of their breadth, and there are several fires along its length, according to the number of families and the size of the cabin, usually two or three paces apart. It was through the middle of the cabins, and consequently through the very middle of the fires, that the sick woman marched, her feet and legs bare—that is to say, through two or three hundred fires—without doing herself any harm, even complaining all the time how little heat she felt, which did not relieve her of the cold she felt in her feet and legs. Those who held up her hands passed on either side of the fires; and, having led her thus through all the cabins, they took her back to the place whence she had departed, namely, to the cabin where she was sheltered; and thus ended the second Act.

The third followed, which, according to forms and customs, consists in a general mania of all the people of the village, who—except, perhaps, a few Old Men—undertake to run wherever the sick woman has passed, adorned or daubed in their fashion, vying with one another in the frightful contortions of their faces—making everywhere such a din, and indulging in such extravagances, that, to explain them and make them better understood, I do not know if I ought not to compare them, either to the most extravagant of our maskers that one has ever heard of, or to the bacchantes of the ancients, or rather to the furies of Hell. They enter, then, everywhere, and have during the time of the feast, in all the evenings and nights of the three days that it lasts, liberty to do anything, and no one dares say a word to them. If they find kettles over the fire, they upset them; they break the earthen pots, knock down the dogs, throw fire and ashes everywhere, so thoroughly that often the cabins and entire villages burn down. But the point being that, the more noise and uproar one makes, the more relief the sick person will experience, they have no concern for anything, and each one kills himself to do worse than his companion.

Our cabins that are in the villages are not exempt from the results of such a feast. The door of the cabin of the residence of Saint Joseph was broken down three times in a like ceremony. As for this residence here where I am, that of la Conception, we have been more quiet during such storms, because we are about a musket-shot from the village. This, then, is the third act; let us come to the fourth.

The next day's Sun having risen, every one prepares to go again through all the cabins where the sick woman has passed, and particularly to that one in which she is harbored. This is for the purpose of proposing at each fire each person's own and special desire or "Ondinonc"—according as he is able to get information and enlightenment by dreams—not openly, however, but through Riddles. For example, some one will say, "What I desire and what I am seeking is that which bears a lake within itself"; and by this is intended a pumpkin or calabash. Another will say, "What I ask for is seen in my eyes—it will be marked with various colors"; and because the same Huron word that signifies "eye" also signifies "glass bead," this is a clue to divine what he desires—namely, some kind of beads of this material, and of different colors. Another will intimate that he desires an Andacwandet feast—that is to say, many fornications and adulteries. His Riddle being guessed, there is no lack of persons to satisfy his desire.

I am no longer surprised that Satan is so greatly pleased with this feast and solemnity—as he declared to the poor, wretched creature concerned therein—since in it all the internal and external faculties apparently strive to render him a sort of homage and acknowledgment. And it would seem that, of all the ceremonies of the feast, he especially values this one, where even the mind so labors in his behalf, as may be seen in what follows.

As soon, then, as the Riddle is proposed, they immediately strive to guess it; and saying, "It is that," they at the same time throw the object to the person who demands and announces his desires. If this is really his thought, he exclaims that it has been found, and thereupon there is rejoicing by all those in the cabin, who manifest their delight by striking against the pieces of bark that form the walls of their cabins; at the same time the patient feels relieved; and this happens as often as they find the desires of those who have proposed them in Riddles. It was found in the council that was held as the conclusion of this present ceremony—where this matter was examined, according to their forms and customs—that a hundred Riddles had been guessed this time.

But if what is guessed is not the answer of him who has proposed the Riddle, he says that they are near it, but that that is not it; he does not refrain, for all that, from carrying away what has been given him, in order to show it through the other cabins, and thus make them see and understand better that it is not that—so that, by the exclusion of many things, one is better prepared to tell what it is. True, he afterward brings back what was given him—either because his desire has finally been ascertained, or because it has not, only reserving what was really his thought. Some observe the whole ceremony very religiously; but I do not doubt that many tricks and cheats also creep into it. At all events, behold the 4th act—which, with the preceding, is repeated on each of the three nights and the three days that the feast lasts.

The fifth or last is begun on the 3rd day. This consists of a second journey or promenade by the sick woman through the cabins, which closes the whole feast, this being done to propose her last and principal desire—not openly, as she did when she first arrived, but in a Riddle, as the others had done on the preceding days. It is here that the devil triumphs, and acts the master and lord in earnest. For first, when this poor unhappy woman goes out from her cabin she is attended by a number of persons, some following her, and some going before; all filing along, one by one, without saying a word, with the faces, appearance, and attitudes of persons afflicted and penitent—and especially the sick woman, who appears alone in their midst, all the others, before and behind, being at some distance from her. Seeing them, then, walk as they do, it is impossible to form any other opinion than that they are persons who desire to inspire with compassion, and bend to mercy, some powerful sovereign whom they recognize as the origin and cause of the trouble of the person in question, and on whose will depends, in their opinion, its continuation or its cure; and, in fact, such is precisely the case.

Now it is necessary that while this sort of procession lasts, not one Savage should appear outside of the cabins—so that, as far away as one can see them, those who are escorting the sick person nearly kill themselves making signs and gestures that all must retreat and go indoors.

The sick woman having returned to the cabins, she begins to relate her troubles in a plaintive and languishing voice, giving the rest to understand that her recovery depends upon the satisfaction of her last desire, of which she proposes the Riddle. Each one straightway applies himself to ascertain its solution, and at the same time they throw to the sick woman whatever they imagine it may be, as we have just stated.

Those who are attending the sick woman collect all these things and go out burdened with kettles, pots, skins, robes, blankets, cloaks, necklaces, belts, leggings, shoes, corn, fish—in short, everything that is used by the Savages, and which they have been able to think of, to attain the satisfaction of the sick woman's desire.

These appear, and not without good cause, to eyes illumined by the light of faith, a veritable trophies of Satan—or, rather, a thorough ceremony of faith and homage that these peoples render to him whom they recognize as their sovereign master and Lord, upon whom they consider that all their happiness or unhappiness depends.

Finally, the patient does so much, and gives so many and such hints as to the explanation of her Riddle, that her answer is found; and at once there is a general outcry and rejoicing of all the people, who everywhere strike against the bark walls—which is only by way of congratulations offered her, and, on her part, of thanks for the health she has recovered. She returns, for this purpose, a third time through all the cabins, after which the last general council is held, where a report is made of all that has taken place, and, among other things, of the number of Riddles solved. Then follows the last present, on the part of the public, which consists in completing and crowning the last desire of the sick woman, over and above what that individual who has guessed it has been able to give; and there ends the ceremony.

It is to be presumed that the true end of this Act, and its catastrophe, will be nothing else but a Tragedy, the devil not being accustomed to behave otherwise. Nevertheless, this poor unhappy creature found herself much better after the feast than before, although she was not entirely free from, or cured of her trouble. This is ordinarily attributed by the Savages to the lack or failure of some detail, or to some imperfection in the ceremony—which keeps these peoples in continual feats, and is so exact observance of the forms and details of their ceremonies.

I do not know whether the devil—according to his common practice of never abstaining from one evil act, except to commit another—intended, in exchange, to kill the little daughter of this woman, of whom we spoke at the beginning of this account.

At all events, she became very ill after the feast, which induced that one of our Fathers who had charge of the cabin where she was to baptize her, when in a critical condition, without the knowledge of her mother; after this, the little girl grew better. We do not know with certainty, however, what has happened since then, either to the mother or the daughter, who have returned to their own village.

The reference to the Moon saying "The feast which is now being solemnized in the town is very acceptable to me" in this account may refer to the Midwinter ceremonial, but this is conjecture. The ceremonial described seems to have been given primarily for the purpose of curing the woman.

The lack of any certain mention of the dream-guessing rite as a calendric ceremonial among the seventeenth-century Hurons does not mean that it was not given at the time. The French could have simply forgotten to mention it or they may not have realized that all the performances of the dream-guessing rite were not curing rituals. The winter was and is a time of much ritual activity. In fact, the Jesuits in Huronia in the seventeenth century complained that their missionary work was impeded by these many ceremonies. The Hurons were so engaged in them they had no time for the Jesuits. It may be that the Jesuits failed to note the Midwinter ceremonial in the midst of this religious activity.

Although there is some evidence that in the seventeenth century the dream renewal and fulfillment rituals—or at least the dream-guessing rite—were a part of Midwinter, there is less evidence for the ashes-stirring or New Fire rites. Hewitt (1910b:941–42) interprets the passage quoted above describing the passage through 200 or 300 fires by the woman for whom the dream-guessing rite was performed as an earlier form of the ashes-stirring ritual. He also identifies this passage through the fires with the *Aoutaenhrohi*. Both of these identifications may be in error. There is no reason to assume that walking through the fires is equivalent to stirring the ashes, though it may be. Even less certain is Hewitt's identification of this rite with the *Aoutaenhrohi* (*Awataerohi,* etc.) rite. The *Aoutaenhrohi* rite was a curing rite which involved much play with fire (see, for example, Tooker 1964:103–106). These actions seem closest to those of the False Faces and Husk Faces (see Speck 1949:92 and Fenton 1941:413), though in the seventeenth century those performing the ritual were not always masked. However, before metal tools became easily available, it seems likely that fewer members of the False Face society would have masks than at present. Blau (1966:573) has suggested that the name *Awataerohi* is cognate with the Onondaga word wnatainu?ni:, a now-archaic name for the False Face curing rite.

Although Hewitt's suggestion that the *Awataerohi* rite was an early form of the ashes-stirring rite seems untenable, his (Hewitt 1910c:87; Swanton 1910:405) suggestion that the white dog sacrifice was a substitute for the sacrifice of a human being may be correct. In the seventeenth century, feasts of dogs, which seem to have been common, seem also to lack the distinctive characteristics of the white dog sacrifice in the nineteenth and twentieth centuries, such as the decoration of the dog with paint and wampum, the hanging of the dog on a pole, and the burning at dawn. Among the seventeenth-century Hurons, at least, the torture and sacrifice of a captive was a ceremonial in honor of "the sun and god of war." Although the prisoner might be tortured for some days prior to his actual death, care was exercised that he would not actually die before the time appointed: daybreak. The prisoner was put on a scaffold for his last torture. The captive wore a wampum collar that designated him as a victim. If he had been particularly brave during his torture, the captive's heart and other parts of his body might be eaten (for a summary see Tooker 1964:31–39). All this resembles the sacrifice of the white dog. Also, although the Jesuits do not mention men singing their Personal Chants at the torture, the prisoner was expected to sing his while being tortured.

It seems possible that with the decreasing availability of captives to torture the Iroquois substituted a dog—perhaps in part stimulated by contact with more westerly Indians who apparently had a dog sacrifice. If this was the case, such a substitution was foreshadowed in an instance reported by the Jesuits (JR 23:171–73). A Huron man had dreamt that the Iroquois had captured and burned him. In order to prevent this from actually happening, the man who had had the dream was burned as if he was a captive, but a dog was killed, roasted, and eaten instead.

Beauchamp (1885:235; 1888:198; 1895:211) has also suggested on somewhat different grounds that the white dog sacrifice was a relatively recent addition to the Midwinter ceremonial. As he said, "the original feast was simply the great dream feast; the white dog sacrifice was grafted upon this in recent times, and has been the first to give way."

A Huron myth recorded by the Jesuits gives some confirmation to the association of war feasts with the dream-guessing rite recorded for the Onondaga in their custom of holding the dream-guessing rite before going to war. The Jesuits state that Hurons attributed the origin of the war feasts, the response *wiiiiii* (probably a war cry and response to the Personal Chants), and dream-guessing rite to a certain giant. The Hurons said that when they lived on the shore of the sea (the Jesuits do not indicate what body of water is being referred to), a Huron had wounded this giant in the forehead because he had not given the usual response to the Huron's greeting. In punishment, the giant sowed the seeds of discord among the Hurons and after recommending to them the war feast, the *ononharoia,* and the response, *wiiiiii,* disappeared into the earth (JR 10:183).

Despite the lack of information in the seventeenth-century documents, it seems likely that there was a Midwinter ceremonial at the time. It is uncertain, however, exactly what rituals comprised it. The best evidence, coming from the Onondaga, indicates that the Midwinter ceremonial there, then as now, involved the dream-guessing ceremony in honor of *Teharonhiawagon.*

TRADITIONAL CHANGES INTRODUCED BY HANDSOME LAKE

Iroquois religion as practiced today is the reform religion introduced by the prophet Handsome Lake in the early years of the nineteenth century. The basis of this New Religion was a series of visions in which messengers from the Creator appeared to Handsome Lake telling him that his people were not doing what they should be and what they should do. Handsome Lake's first vision occurred on June 15, 1799; the second on August 8, 1799; the third on February 5, 1800; subsequently he had others.[3] The messages given to Handsome Lake in these visions were of several sorts. Some were concerned with the moral behavior of the Iroquois, conveying the Creator's displeasure with the then current moral behavior of the Iroquois and setting forth what standards they should follow. Others were concerned with ritual practice, indicating what rituals should be kept up and what rituals should not. In time, these messages were codified into the "Code of Handsome Lake," the recitation of which takes three or four mornings. The "Code" is recited at the "Six Nations meetings," a biennial circuit of the longhouses that begins each year in September at the Tonawanda Longhouse and includes Tonawanda, Caughnawaga, St. Regis, New York Onondaga, Coldspring, and Canadian Onondaga one year, and Tonawanda, Newtown, Oneidatown (Muncie), Six Nations Reserve Seneca, and Lower Cayuga the next. The Sour Springs Longhouse elects each year whether or not it will participate that year (Shimony 1961:202). The "Code of Handsome Lake" may also be recited in whole or in part at other times as is deemed necessary by custom or inclination.

All the evidence indicates that at the time of Handsome Lake the Midwinter ceremonial was a well-established and important Iroquois ceremony. Handsome Lake only suggested certain changes in it; he did not introduce the ceremonial. The changes he advocated—some of which were accepted and others not—apparently did not alter the basic purpose or nature of the ceremonial, but confirmed it. But, at the same time, the changes he suggested did add a new dimension to the ceremonial.

That Handsome Lake confirmed the Midwinter ceremonial is recorded in the "Code." As Arthur Parker (1913:51) has recorded the relevant section of the Code:

There is a certain ceremony in the midwinter. It is said it is most important to uphold the customs of midwinter and that any one having a part should fulfil it. It is said that to fulfill the customs they must go about the neighborhood holding dances. It is said that the Creator has sanctioned certain dances for thanksgiving.

Now the messengers said that Ganio'dai'io' [Handsome Lake] must sing early in the morning on three mornings and give the cheer-cries of the Gai'wiio' [Good Message].

Although Handsome Lake sanctioned the continued performance of the Midwinter ceremonial, he did not sanction all the rituals that comprised it. There is a tradition among some Iroquois (Fenton 1936:12; Shimony 1961:185) that Handsome Lake condemned the burning of the white dog. Nevertheless, the reason given by the Iroquois themselves for the demise of this ritual was, and is, not the denouncement of the ritual by Handsome Lake, but the dying out of a special breed of dogs used for the sacrifice. Handsome Lake's condemnation of the white dog sacrifice seems to have been a result of a later vision, since in his vision of August 8, 1799, the messengers said that a white dog should be sacrificed. As Henry Simmons (Wallace 1952:54; see also 31, 49) reported it:

Guide mentioned one circumstance which he was Sorry for, that was, there would be Shortly great sickness in their Village, unless they did amend their way, and think more upon the great Spirit, who might then perhaps see cause to remove it. And that his people must collect together in Worship, and Cook a white Dog and every one eat thereof, as a preventative against the Sickness. . . .

After his Brother [i.e., Cornplanter] heard those Sayings he called a Council the same evening. . . .

The afternoon of the same day they prepar'd a white Dog to eat, and burnt his Skin to ashes During which time it was burning a number of them Circled around the Fire, Singing Shouting & dancing greatly; after which they all partook of their Delicious dish, of Dog Meat Etc.

It is also said—and this is recorded in part of the "Code of Handsome Lake" (Parker 1913:40)—that Handsome Lake condemned the medicine societies. But, although the medicine societies were declared disbanded at a council of chiefs and others, the tobacco-burning ceremony that Handsome Lake had directed should accompany this dissolution was not performed. Members of the medicine societies consequently declared that the societies had not been disbanded and they continued to perform their ceremonies (Parker 1913:114). The medicine societies continue to influence the lives of the Iroquois, and reflecting this influence, they continue to perform some of their rituals as part of the Midwinter ceremonial.

Another tradition states that Handsome Lake added the Four Sacred Rituals—Feather Dance, Thanksgiving Dance, Personal Chant, and the Bowl Game—to the Midwinter ceremonial (Fenton 1936:12). But, although Handsome Lake probably was instrumental in adding the Four Sacred Rituals to the Midwinter ceremonial, the rituals themselves are old ones in Iroquois culture. Personal chants and the Bowl Game are mentioned in the seventeenth-century documents (see for example Tooker 1964:39, 114–16, 129). The

Feather Dance is probably old also. The Thanksgiving Dance, another Iroquois tradition states, was once a war dance that Handsome Lake transformed into the Thanksgiving Dance by substituting the measured sections of the Thanksgiving Speech for the boasts of the warriors in the war dance (my informant; see also Fenton 1941:155 n; 1953:103–104; Speck 1949:138; Shimony 1961:190).

In sum, Handsome Lake attempted to reform or revise the Midwinter ceremonial as he attempted to reform Iroquois religion in general. But not all of his admonitions were accepted by the Iroquois, either in their religion in general or in the ceremonial in particular.

Late Eighteenth- and Nineteenth-Century Descriptions of the Iroquois Midwinter Ceremonial

There are five important descriptions of the Iroquois Midwinter ceremonial that date from the very end of the eighteenth century and from the first half of the nineteenth century: Halliday Jackson's (1830b:23–26) description of a Seneca ceremonial, probably that held at the Cornplanter settlement in 1799; Mary Jemison's (Seaver 1824:173–77) description of Seneca practice, probably of that in the Genesee Valley in the first quarter of the nineteenth century or earlier; Thaddeus Osgood's (Dwight 1822[4]:213–14) 1812 description of Seneca practice; Doty's (1876:53–56) summary of practice at Squakie Hill in the Genesee Valley as seen by Jerediah Horsford in 1816 and George W. Patterson in 1819[4]; and Lewis Henry Morgan's (1901[1]:199–213) description, probably of practice at the Sand Hill Longhouse on the Tonawanda Reservation in the 1840's. Taken together, these descriptions indicate the form of the Midwinter ceremonial at the time of Handsome Lake and in the years immediately following his death.

Although the white dog sacrifice was a feature of the Midwinter ceremonial at this time, not all descriptions of this rite are apparently descriptions of part of the Midwinter ceremonial. These include a handful of references to white dog sacrifices at the time of the American Revolution, the Reverend Samuel Kirkland's description of the ritual as revived among the Oneida in 1799, and Samuel Crowell's description of a white dog sacrifice performed by the Sandusky "Senecas" in 1830. These descriptions are considered below before those that describe the Midwinter ceremonial itself.

Many other nineteenth-century descriptions are not so useful because they are an obvious copying of either Mary Jemison's account or Morgan's account with some additional information included. These include the Reverend Joshua V. H. Clark's description, supposedly of the 1841 ceremonial at Onondaga; Harriet Caswell's description of the ceremonial on the Cattaraugus Reservation, supposedly from an Indian named Old Silverheels; and Harriet Converse's description, supposedly of practice at Cattaraugus. Although all three of these authors did talk with Indians themselves and seem to have included some of the data they learned by so doing, much of their descriptions apparently was taken from other sources. A fourth source is William O'Reilly (1838:275–77). Unfortunately, O'Reilly, after noting that the description of the last white dog ceremony held at Rochester in 1813 given him by Edwin Scrantom corresponded to those by Kirkland (probably meaning Thaddeus Osgood) and by Mary Jemison, merely repeats Mrs. Jemison's account.[5]

The Reverend Joshua V. H. Clark described a New Year's ceremonial (Clark 1849[1]:55–66; see Appendix, this volume) he said he saw in January, 1841, at Onondaga Castle. Apparently, however, he did not see the entire ceremonial, but only a portion of it. Clark describes in detail only the rituals of the last two days: the sacrifice of the white dogs on the next-to-last day of the ceremonial and the performance of the War Dance and Peace Dance on the last day. Much of his description of the earlier part of Midwinter is an obvious copy of Mary Jemison's account of Seneca practice. Clark has added to this some additional information which could have been obtained through interviews with Onondagas or with whites who had seen the ceremonial. If Clark had seen this portion of the ceremonial, it seems likely that he would not have copied Mrs. Jemison's description. Further, it seems likely that if he had seen this portion he would have recognized some difference between what he saw and Mary Jemison's description.

Probably Onondaga and Seneca practice was different at this time. The Onondaga Midwinter ceremonial as described in the 1880's and later differs in several important respects from Seneca practice from the 1840's and later. These differences probably reflect still older differences in practice between these two groups. Mary Jemison's account differs in some respects from those describing Seneca practice in the 1840's and later, but essentially agrees with other descriptions of Seneca practice in the later eighteenth and early nineteenth century and is a description of early Seneca practice. If Clark had seen the entire Onondaga ceremonial, it seems likely that he would have noted differences between it and the Seneca ceremonial. It is possible, of course, that Onondaga practice in 1841 was identical to Seneca practice described by Mrs. Jemison, and that Clark is describing actual Onondaga practice. The weight of the evidence, however, suggests that Clark made the error of assuming that the Midwinter ceremonial was identical in all Iroquois longhouses—a common error of nineteenth-century writers on the Iroquois.

In 1892 Harriet Caswell published a description that she said was given to her by an Indian named Old Silverheels. However, this description for the most part seems to have been taken from Morgan's "League of the Iroquois." Most striking are the parallels in the description of the Bigheads and the white dog sacrifice. The speech of the Bigheads given by Caswell and attributed to Silverheels is virtually identical to Morgan's as is the description of the costume of the Bigheads. The description of the white dog sacrifice is also similar. Further, Silverheels stresses and elaborates on the same parts of the ceremonial that Morgan does. There are, however, some differences which may be additions by Silverheels. These include the Thanksgiving Speech held over the white dog and a description of the War Dance held at the conclusion of the ceremonial.

About 1895 Harriet Converse published in a newspaper an account of the Midwinter ceremonial that would appear to be a description of practice at the Newtown Longhouse. This was later republished by the Heye Foundation. The description is brief, but much of it also apparently was copied from Morgan's description. Her account of the ceremonial differs from Morgan's in only two important respects: she mentions that a "dancing band . . . costumed and equipped with symbols of the harvest fruits" visited each house on the third day and that on the second day the Bigheads "freshen the old, or build a new fire—the first fire of the new year, as they plead for good to come to the family and dwell by the hearth-stone" (Converse 1930:74–75).

There are some accounts of the New York Onondaga ceremonial as performed in the last quarter of the nineteenth century. These include two fairly complete descriptions of Onondaga practice in the 1880's: Erminnie Smith's account, published in 1883, and Beauchamp's 1888 description obtained from Albert Cusick. Two shorter notes on certain parts of the ceremonial—DeCost Smith's 1888 account of the False Face rite in the dream-guessing part of Midwinter and Beauchamp's (1895:209–11) description of the white dog sacrifice he saw in January of 1894—provide supplementary and confirming data (see also Beauchamp 1885). These accounts indicate that the ceremonial as performed at the Onondaga Longhouse in the 1880's very closely resembled the ceremonial as performed at that Longhouse at the present time. For this reason, they will not be considered separately here.

The White Dog
Sacrifice at the Time
of the American Revolution

Certain eighteenth-century sources indicate that the white dog sacrifice was a ceremonial with war connotations. These are descriptions dating from 1778–79—those years of the American Revolution in which the Iroquois were at war with whites. Therefore opportunities for holding war ceremonies and the chance for whites to learn of these were somewhat greater than in previous years.

The most detailed of these accounts is that of Mrs. Jane Campbell. Mrs. Campbell, the wife of Colonel Samuel Campbell, and her four children had been taken captive during the Cherry Valley Massacre in 1779. She said that after they had arrived at Canadeseago, the principle village of the Senecas, the Indians killed, roasted, and ate a white dog in honor of their successes (Campbell 1831:178–79):

Early in the winter, the nation assembled at Canadaseago to hold a general council, and to celebrate their late successes. This village was laid out with some regularity, and in almost circular form, enclosing a large green. The houses were generally built of bark, after the rude style of the Indians. A few were of hewn logs. The ceremony was commenced by a sacrifice. A white dog was killed and borne along in procession to a large fire kindled in the centre of the village. In the mean time others went round to every house with a basket, in which each individual was required to deposit something. This basket, with all its contents, was first cast into the fire. Afterward the dog was laid on and thoroughly roasted, and was then eaten. This was followed by eating, drinking, and dancing, which continued for several days.

Another captive, a Mrs. Jane Whittaker (1930:244–45), also said that she had heard the Indians killed, roasted, and ate white dogs before and after the Wyoming Battle in 1778 and that the ritual was seldom not observed on return from a war expedition.

Various members of the Sullivan Expedition (1779) recorded in their diaries seeing white dogs hanging on poles in certain Seneca villages.[6] The earliest of these references is that for Friday, September 10, in Lieutenant-Colonel Adam Hubley's journal (Cook 1887:160):

In this town [Canandiagua] a dog was hung up, with a string of wampum round his neck, on a tree, curiously decorated and trimmed. On inquiry, I was informed that it was a custom among the savages before they went to war to offer this as a sacrifice to Mars, the God of War, and praying that he might strengthen them. In return for those favours, they promise to present him with the skin for a tobacco pouch.

In an entry dated three days later, Major Jeremiah Fogg (Cook 1887:99) records finding two dogs hanging on a pole in another Seneca village:

Here [at the village of Gohseolahulee] appeared the heathenish custom of offering sacrifices. Two dogs were found suspended on a pole, which signified that evil spirit was to be pacified by their skins, which would serve to make him a tobacco pouch and waistcoat.

The entries of September 19 in both the diaries of Lieutenant-Colonel Henry Dearborn (Cook 1887:76) and Major James Norris (Cook 1887:236) mention that white dogs had been found in several towns. As these entries (as well as others in these diaries) are virtually identical, one diary is apparently a copy of the other or both are copies of some other diary. This entry (in modern spelling and punctuation) reads:

At several towns that our army has destroyed, we found dogs hung up on poles about 12 or 15 feet high which we are told is done by way of sacrifice. When they are unfortunate in war, they sacrifice two dogs in the manner above mentioned to appease their imaginary gods. One of these dog skins they suppose is converted into a jacket and the other into a tobacco pouch for their god. The woman who came to us at Chenesee [the principle village of the Senecas on the Genesee River] says the savages hung up dogs immediately after the Battle of Newtown.

(The Battle of Newtown was fought on August 29, 1779, near Elmira, New York. The Indians under the leadership of Joseph Brant were defeated.)

The woman mentioned in the diaries of Dearborn and Norris was a Mrs. Lester who had been found at Genesee on September 15. She had been captured at Wyoming, had seen her husband and one of her children (she had five) killed before her eyes. At the time of her release, she had with her a child about 7 or 8 months old who died shortly after. She later married Captain Roswell Franklin, one of the first settlers of Aurora in Cayuga County (Cook 1887:75, 91, 99, 112, 131 n, 175, 371, and passim).

A similar entry is to be found in Sergeant Moses Fellows' journal (Cook 1887:91) for September 19:

We marched to Kannadasegea the 13th in this town we found hung up about 10 or 12 feet from the Ground on a Pole Set up we Supposed, two dogs Which is their method of Sacrificing to their Imaginary Gods of war in time of Danger.

The following to Be added to the 15th. This woman [i.e., the white woman found on the 15th at Genesee] informs us that the Dogs spoke of yesterday were Sacrificed on hearing of the Battle of Newton and of Desolation of their Country as we march through it.

The reference "the 13th in this town" is obscure. Fellows apparently confused the dogs found at Gohseolahulee on September 13 (mentioned by Fogg) with the dog found at Canandaigua on September 10 (mentioned by Hubley), attributing both occurrences to Kannadasegea. This may have come about in the following manner: on September 13, while at Canandaigua after having left this village on the way to Kannadasegea, someone may have mentioned the dog found earlier at Canandaigua. Mrs. Lester, the white captive, then mentioned the dog sacrifice she had seen. (This would account for the mention of the dog sacrifices in Dearborn's and Norris' Journals on September 19. There may have followed discussions of dogs in other villages, and Fellows may have simply misunderstood some of this discussion, thus wrongly identifying the village in which the dogs were found.

Another reference that has some bearing on the white dog sacrifice in 1779 is to be found in Colonel Daniel Brodhead's letter to General Washington (Cook 1887:308). Brodhead is reporting on his expedition up the Allegheny River:

At the upper Seneca Towns we found a painted image or War post, clothed in Dog skin, and John Montour told me this Town was called Yoghroonwago,[7] besides this we found seven[8] other Towns, consisting in the whole of one hundred and thirty Houses, some of which were large enough for the accommodation of three or four Indian families.

The "image or War post" mentioned by Brodhead is probably the same one later described by Halliday Jackson (see below and Wallace 1952:26). In his "Civilization of the Indian Natives," Jackson (1830a:29) says that near the house of Cornplanter

stood a wooden image of a man, round which at stated times they performed their religious ceremonies and sacrifices.

The image was about seven feet in height, elevated on a pedestal, of the same block, and being painted a variety of colours, it altogether exhibited a wild appearance.

Jackson (1830b:25 n) also noted that this image decayed, fell down about 1802, and was put by a son of Cornplanter into the river where it floated downstream.

This idol and its fate is described in some greater detail in Lewis Henry Morgan's manuscript journals (n.d., Vol. 2, No. 5) now owned by the University of Rochester.[9]

Mr. William Parker tells me that when he lived at Allegany about 50 years ago he saw the wooden Idol of the Senecas at that place. He was born there and how long they had had it before he was born he does not know. About 6 miles below Cold Spring the Idol was made. It was about 7 feet high standing up in position. It was cut out of a pine tree. It [had] two legs & two arms. It was a human figure, standing upon a pedestal of the same tree. This pedestal was sunk in the ground, but was so high above it that you could not touch his feet. It was about 14 feet high from top to bottom. One arm [*left* inserted here] was akimbo, the other down and a little forward. He looked to the south or was placed with his face to the south. His face bent down a little to see those at the foot. The people kept him dressed in costume. Over his head was a silk handkerchief & feathers. Around his neck was another silk handkerchief. His cheeks were painted. Rings of silver in his ears. Over his arms the tails of Buffalo were tied around both arms above the Elbow. Around the wrist was a dog skin wrist Band of white. . . . The arms were striped with red paint winding around. Around the waist he had a Belt. Over the left shoulder was an Indian Belt. Over the right was a belt of wampum (sea shell) three inches wide. His body was painted with red paint in stripes. He Had on the Breech Cloth of Cloth, lined around the Edges with red ribbon. An Indian Belt or Band was wound around his legs below the Knees . . . like the wrist belt. Around or above his ankle he had a White dog Skin Band. The body was striped in [?] lines whenever it was exposed. When Mr. Parker first saw it on growing up to take notice of it was at the Indian Village at Allegany called Gä-num-dä-gä-yose-hă on the Allegany Reserve on the north side upon the river bank. About 6 miles below Cold Spring. It stood up by the side of a large tree, on a flat upon the river bank. It was on the right side of the tree about 16 feet from the tree. [Diagram sketch inserted here.] He stood on a flat, about 15 rods from the river. About 30 rods from the river in the rear rose a hill covered with pine, & in the rear of that a range of hills parallel with the river. He stood in the midst of the settlement. The people were in the habit of dancing around him in the summer, at the green Corn Dance. When they gathered the corn also. Also this Standing dance. The tree out of which the idol was made was from 3½ to four feet in diameter—a pine. The idol was considerably larger than this large man. They knew there was a Great Spirit above, but they wished to bring him down to look over the people especially when they were dancing. The figurine was well proportioned. They dressed him up everytime they danced, & then took off his ornaments & left him exposed to the weather. . . . About 25 years after it was made this Idol was moved to Deo-no-sä-da-ga or the Burnt House or Cornplanter's village in Pennsylvania. When Handsome Lake became a prophet about 1802, Parker thinks they threw this idol into the river or destroyed it. He having a revelation direct from heaven this idol became unnecessary. Handsome Lake's license to preach as Johnson calls it is a letter to the Senecas from the Secretary of War Gen. Dearborn & is dated in 1802. Blacksmith has it and I saw it yesterday. It merely commends the plan to the people. The log had begun to rot before it was removed, and while at Cornplanter's village it rotted down until the feet came down to the ground

as the pedestal was set further in the Earth. Mr. Parker saw it last at
Cornplanter's village about 50 years ago. He . . . never saw it there.
He was born at Cornplanter's village. Handsome Lake . . . lived about
a mile & a half below Cornplanter's village. A few years before the idol
was destroyed the Senecas moved about a mile down the river & left
the idol above. It was in a year or so thrown into the river or otherwise
destroyed. The idol had been at the place first described about 25
years before it was taken to Cornplanter's village. It was there when
he was born, and was destroyed about 7 or 8 years after he was born.
Mr. Parker says he is now 55 (Dec. 1849). Mr. Parker saw this idol
among the flood wood of the Allegany River about 6 miles below
Cornplanter's village for the last time when he was about 7 years old.
This idol was made by two Senecas. One of them was Gä-she-o-ä
(Jacob Minister) a Seneca Chief. Mr. Parker knew him. He died about
25 years ago aged about 70. This is also the very man who caught
Horatio Jones and carried him into captivity.

THE WHITE DOG SACRIFICE IN THE LATTER PART
OF THE EIGHTEENTH CENTURY

Perhaps the most important description of a white dog sacrifice
in the eighteenth century is that by the Reverend Samuel Kirkland.
As young man, Kirkland traveled to Seneca country, arriving there
in February of 1765 and returning in May of 1766. Finding the
Oneida more responsive to his efforts, he served as a missionary to
them until his death in 1808.

However, the description of the Seneca white dog ceremonial
usually attributed to Kirkland by Beauchamp (1885:236) and subsequently by others and thought to be a description of Seneca practice
in the eighteenth century is actually the Reverend Thaddeus Osgood's description of the Seneca ceremony published by Timothy
Dwight (1882[4]:213–14) in his "Travels; in New-England and
New-York." Apparently Beauchamp consulted not Dwight's "Travels," but William Campbell's "Annals of Tryon County"
(1831:Appendix pp. 75–76) where Campbell, quoting Osgood's description, mistakenly attributes it to Kirkland. Dwight (1882[4]:
188) elsewhere says that he obtained from Kirkland information on
the Iroquois contained in his "Travels." However, Dwight states ex-

plicitly that the description of the white dog ceremony was given to him by Osgood, not Kirkland. (See also Tooker 1965 for a more detailed discussion of this confusion.)

Kirkland's own description of the white dog sacrifice is more significant than the one usually attributed to him. This description is contained in some copies of his 1800 journal, added to the end. It describes the white dog sacrifice as it had been performed among the Oneida in the fall of 1799. Kirkland wrote that the Oneida had not given the ceremony for at least thirty years, but that it was revived in 1799. A young Mohawk living at Grand River had had a vision in 1798 in which the Upholder of the Heavens appeared to him and said that with the exception of the Seneca, the Iroquois had been neglecting him by not holding the white dog sacrifice. As a consequence of this vision, the ceremony was revived at Grand River.

The Oneida learned of this revival and also decided to hold it. In the Oneida ceremony three dogs were strangled (not the two dogs mentioned for the Seneca by such writers as Osgood).[10] One dog was hung on a 12-foot pole to be left there until the next annual sacrifice or until it decayed. The other two dogs were thrown into the fire followed by a basket of tobacco. Then the speaker gave a speech, and the dogs were taken off the fire, cut into pieces, and given to those taking part in the ceremony to eat. There followed a War Dance and a social dance that lasted all night. The Bowl Game was played the next day, and the ceremony ended with a feast.

Kirkland's [11] description is as follows:

It will be expected that I should give some account of the ancient pagan sacrifice and religious festivals of their forefathers performed here last fall, and what occasioned their revival after a total neglect of them for more than thirty years. This must be only a general account, as want of time will not admit of going into particulars. In the autumn of 1798, a young Mohawk Indian of Grand River fell into a kind of trance for 24 hours or more, had dreamed a dream and had many visions in which he had a particular interview and conference with *Thauloonghyauwángoon,* which signifies *Upholder of the Skies or Heavens,* who from time immemorial or before the formation of this Island (or America) existed, and who placed it upon the back of a great tortoise, chief of the Turtle tribe. In the conference which this young Indian had with the *Upholder of the Skies,* the latter made grievous complaints, of the base and ungrateful neglect of the Five

Nations (the Senecas excepted) in withholding the homage due to him and the offerings he was wont to receive from their fathers as an acknowledgment for his guardianship. Many were the evils which had come upon them in consequence of this neglect: sickness, epidemic disorders, losses in war, unfruitful seasons, scanty crops, unpleasant days. The character of this young man was so unblemished, and remarkable for a sedate and reflecting mind, that when he declared his vision, in a serious and affecting manner, it immediately gained almost universal credit in the settlement. Brant from political reasons found himself obliged to give his consent to a sacrifice and offering to the *Upholder of the Skies,* with this condition, that it should not be considered as setting aside the Christian religion. The sacrifice with all its appendages was performed. Christian and Pagan all attended, though none but the Pagans partook of the feast. It seemed to diffuse new and general joy throughout the whole settlement. This transaction, its rise, and happy effects was last spring communicated to *Aughweehstanis* (alias Blacksmith) of Oneida, the only remaining old pagan chief or priest of the nation. He soon conferred with his nephew Pagan Peter (natural son of Good Peter who died some years since). They joined forces, and addressed one and another on the subject—urging a variety of arguments—and finally the old priest ventured to prophesy evil and denounce judgments against those who should refuse to celebrate the religious feast of the fathers which was instituted by their Guardian God and wickedly neglected for many years. It was at length agreed upon by about one-sixth part of the nation in addition to those who had professed no other religion than paganism. These consisted of several persons who had apostatized from the Christian faith, together with a number to whom I can give no better title than Nothingarians [12] who chiefly belonged to the class of drunkards. The requisites and preparations for the offering, feast, and subsequent amusements are three dogs, a basket of tobacco, and a bowl—curiously wrought—with a dozen dice with which the game of chance is performed at the close of the ceremonies. The dogs are previously strangled or choked without breaking any part of the body, the fire kindled, and at a small distance, perhaps 20 or 30 yards, a hole is dug in the ground for supporting the pole (answering to an altar) upon the top of which one of the dogs is to be hung up, tied by the neck fast to the end of the pole with a new and well-wrought mattump line, the head curiously painted with vermillion, two small belts of the choicest wampum round his neck— one of unmarred white, denoting the sachems or counsellors, who are always for peace; the other of black wampum, with red streaks of paint, characteristic of warriors, who ever stand ready to defend their liberties and resent any injuries offered them. The pole is then raised up about twelve feet long with great caution and solemnity and fixed in the ground and well-fastened and secured against any blasts which might overset it for it must stand with the dog (or offering) tied or laced on the top of the pole till the next annual sacrifice, or till it moulders away to atoms. The other two dogs are thrown into the fire, and shortly after, the basket of tobacco. The priest or old sachem then elevates his eyes toward the heavens and calls out with an audible voice and with a very distinct solemn and deliberate tone, "Come! Come! Thou *Upholder of the Skies gyànse* (i.e.) fellow citizen, or cousin by the mother's side, and all the holy inhabitants of Heaven, who are your assitants—Come! Descend even to the offering, which is elevated (upon the top of the pole). With this (meaning the dog), you will make your vest or garment, and from the fire you will have a sweet savor, the seed of the plant of which you gave our forefathers in the beginning. We thank thee that we yet live by thy guardianship. We now by this offering intreat thee to continue this protection to us. Give us a fruitful season, a plentiful harvest; defend us from pestilence, from hurricanes, thunder and lightning, from all serpents. Give us success in hunting, and if our liberties should be invaded, we depend upon you (*gyànse*), fellow citizen, to animate and inspire our warriors with skill and courage to drive the enemy from our country with shame and loss. Do you, our Great Captain, march in the front of our warriors, that aided by our prowess and skill they may always conquer their enemies." Next a dog is taken out of the fire. The priest cuts a small piece and eats and by the assistance of his aides the multitude are all served with a piece and profess themselves to be the dutiful subjects of the *Upholder of the Skies,* expecting to enjoy his protection and favor. Lastly, the war dance, with a rehearsal of military achievements, a social dance by males and females through the night, a game of chance and a generous repast the next day closes the scene. On this occasion, the use of ardent spirits was forbidden for the term of ten days, but was not observed more than ten hours.

This ceremony was apparently not the Midwinter ceremonial. Kirkland describes the activities as lasting only two days, not as five or more days as do other descriptions of the Midwinter ceremonial. More importantly, Kirkland states that the ceremony was held in the *fall* of 1799 not during January or February; winter is the time the Midwinter ceremonial is held. It may, however, have been a Green

Corn ceremony; the Allegheny Seneca at least at one time sacrificed a white dog at both the Green Corn and Midwinter ceremonials (Jackson 1830b:23; Wallace 1952:19, 26; Fenton 1936:16).

Also of some interest is that Kirkland states that the ceremony was revived as a consequence of a vision of a Mohawk on Grand River. This gives confirmation to what must be the suspicion of many students of this period of Iroquois history: that Handsome Lake was not the only Iroquois attempting to introduce reforms in Iroquois religious practice. In fact, although Handsome Lake is often, though somewhat inaccurately, regarded as preaching a nativistic religion, the religious practice advocated by the Mohawk prophet was more nativistic than that preached by Handsome Lake.

It is also of some interest that Kirkland reports in a later journal (1806–1807) that Handsome Lake condemned the sacrifice of the dogs, and said that deer or other game should be substituted for the dogs. This confirms the twentieth-century tradition that Handsome Lake did condemn the sacrifice of the white dog and a tradition contained in a version of the "Code of Handsome Lake" obtained by William Beauchamp from a Seneca chief called Hoh-shair-honh ("Stopper of the Crowd") at a council (i.e., "Six Nations meeting") at Onondaga Castle in August of 1894. According to Hoh-shair-honh (Beauchamp 1897:175; my emphasis), the messengers said to Handsome Lake:

You [i.e., the Iroquois] shall worship the Great Spirit by dancing the turtle dance [Feather Dance] at the new moon when the strawberry ripens. At the new moon of the green corn time you shall give a thanksgiving dance. In the midwinter, at the new moon, you shall give another thanksgiving dance. It shall be the New Year's dance, *but you must not burn the dog as you have been doing.* You shall have a thanksgiving dance at the new moon of the time of the making of sugar. You shall dance at the new moon of the harvest time, and give thanks for what the Great Spirit has given you. You shall make your prayers and dance in the forenoon, for at midday the Great Spirit goes to rest, and will not hear your worship.

THE WHITE DOG SACRIFICE OF THE SANDUSKY "SENECAS"

In 1830, Samuel Crowell saw a white dog ceremonial given by some Iroquois living near Sandusky, Ohio. Although the ceremony he describes was given in early February (a normal time at which to hold the Midwinter ceremonial) and although a False Face appeared during it, the description, by its lack of mention of the other rituals of Midwinter and by the statement that the ceremony was given in consequence of a dream of a particular Indian, suggests that it was not a performance of Midwinter, but simply a white dog rite of the type discussed in the previous section. On the other hand, it is possible that Crowell misconstrued Hard Hickory's comments: that Hard Hickory had merely dreamed that he should provide the dogs for the Midwinter ceremony—as once was Iroquois practice, not dreamed that the ceremony itself should be held.

Crowell's (1877) description follows:

On the second day of February, 1830, I witnessed an interesting, and to me, novel religious ceremony of the Seneca tribe of Indians, then occupying that portion of territory now comprising a part of the counties of Seneca, and Sandusky, Ohio, familiarly known to the inhabitants of this region as the Seneca reservation.

Shortly after our arrival at the house of this chief, Mr. D. retired; not so with our friendly host and myself—while sitting near a clean, brick hearth, before a cheerful fire, Hard Hickory unbosomed himself to me unreservedly. Mr. D. was asleep and the chief and I were the only persons then awake in the house.

Hard Hickory told me, among other things, that it was owing chiefly to him that this feast was now celebrated; that it was in part to appease the anger of the *Good Spirit,* in consequence of a dream he lately had; and as an explanation he gave me the following narration:

"He dreamed he was fleeing from an enemy, it was, he supposed, something supernatural; perhaps, an evil spirit; that, after it had pursued him a long time, and for a great distance, and every effort to escape from it seemed impossible as it was just at his heels, and he almost exhausted; at this perilous juncture, he saw a large water, toward which he made with all his remaining strength, and at the very instant when he expected each bound to be his last, he beheld, to his joy, a canoe near the shore; this appeared as his last hope; breathless and faint, he threw himself into it, and, of its own accord, quick as an arrow from the bow, it shot from the shore leaving his pursuer on the beach!"

While relating this circumstance to me, which he did with earnestness, trepidation and alarm, strongly expressed in his countenance, he took from his bosom something neatly and very carefully enclosed in several distinct folds of buckskin. This he began to unroll, laying each piece by itself, and on opening the last, there was enclosed therein, a canoe in miniature! On handing it to me to look at, he remarked that no other person save himself and me, had ever seen it, and that, as a memento, he would wear it, as "long as he lived." It was a piece of light wood, resembling cork, about six inches long, and, as intended, so it was, a perfect model of a canoe.

This chief being now in a communicative mood, I took the liberty to inquire of him "when they intended to burn their dogs?" for I began to fear I should miss the express object which I came to witness. After giving me to understand that "the red men did not care about the pale faces being present at, nor, if they chose, joining in the dance, but burning their dogs was another thing—this was offering sacrifice to, and worshipping the Great Spirit; and while engaged in their devotions they objected to the presence and interference of the whites; yet, as I had never been present, and coming as the friend of Mr. Dickinson, who was a good man, he would tell me they would burn their dogs soon tomorrow morning." The night being now far advanced, he pointed to the bed and told me to sleep there; but that he must go to the council house, to the dance, for his people would not like it if he would stay away, and wishing me good night, he withdrew.

Anxiety to witness the burnt offering almost deprived me of sleep. Mr. D and I, therefore, rose early and proceeded directly to the council house, and though we supposed we were early, the Indians were already in advance of us. The first object which arrested our attention was a pair of the canine species, one of each gender suspended on a *cross!* one on either side thereof. These animals had been recently *strangled— not a bone was broken* nor could a distorted hair be seen? They were of a beautiful cream color, except a few dark spots on one, naturally, while the same spots had been put on the other, artificially, by the devotees. The Indians are very partial in the selection of dogs entirely white, for this occasion; and for which they will give almost any price.

Now for part of the decorations to which I have already alluded, and a description of one will suffice for both, for they were *par similes.* A scarlet ribbon was tastefully tied just above the nose; and near the eyes another; next round the neck was a white ribbon, to which was attached something bulbous, concealed in another white ribbon; this was placed directly under the right ear, and I suppose it was intended as an amulet or charm. Then ribbons were bound round the forelegs, at the knees, and near the feet—these were red and white alternately. Round the body was a profuse decoration—then the hind legs were decorated as the fore ones. Thus were the victims prepared and thus ornamented for the burnt offering.

While minutely making this examination, I was almost unconscious of the collection of a large number of the Indians who were there assembled to offer their sacrifices.

Adjacent to the cross was a large fire built on a few logs; and though the snow was several inches deep, they had prepared a sufficient quantity of combustible material, removed the snow from the logs, and placed thereon their fire.

It was a clear, beautiful morning, and just as the first rays of the sun were seen in the tops of the towering forest, and its reflections from the snowy surface, the Indians simultaneously formed a semicircle enclosing the cross, each flank resting on the aforesaid pile of logs. Good Hunter, who officiated as high priest, now appeared and approached the cross; arrayed in his pontifical robes, he looked quite respectable. The Indians being all assembled—I say Indians (for there was not a squaw present during all this ceremony—I saw two or three outside of the semicircle, but they moved as if desirous of being unobserved), at a private signal given by Good Hunter, two young chiefs sprang up at the cross, and each taking off one of the victims, brought it down, and presented it on his arms to Good Hunter, who, receiving it with great reverence, in like manner advanced to the fire, and with a very grave and solemn air, laid it thereon—and this he did with the other—but to which, whether male or female, he gave the preference I did not learn. This done, he retired to the cross.

In a devout manner, he now commenced an oration. The tone of his voice was audible and somewhat chanting. At every pause in his discourse, he took from a white cloth he held in his left hand a portion of dried, odoriferous herbs, which he threw on the fire; this was intended as incense. In the meanwhile his auditory, their eyes on the ground, with grave aspect, and in solemn silence, stood motionless, listening attentively to every word he uttered. Thus he proceeded until the victims were entirely consumed and the incense exhausted, when he concluded his service; their oblation now made, and the wrath of the Great Spirit, as they believed, appeased, they again assembled in the council house, for the purpose of performing a part in their festival, different from any I yet had witnessed. Each Indian as he entered, seated himself on the floor, thus forming a large circle; then one of the old chiefs rose, and with that native dignity which some Indians possess in a great degree, recounted his exploits as a warrior; told in how many fights he had been the victor; the number of scalps he had taken from his enemies; and what, at the head of his braves, he yet intended to do at the Rocky mountains; accompanying his narration with energy, warmth, and strong gesticulations; when he ended, he received the unanimous applause of the assembled tribe.

This meed of praise was awarded to the chief by three times three articulations, which were properly neither nasal, oral, nor guttural, but rather abdominal. Indeed I am as unable to describe this kind of utterance, as I am the step in the dance. I have seen some whites attempt to imitate the step, and heard them affect the groan or grunt, but it was a mere aping thereof. Thus many others in the circle, old and young, rose in order, and *proforma,* delivered themselves of a speech. Among those was Good Hunter; but he "Had laid his robes away, / His mitre and his vest." His remarks were not filled with such bombast as some others; but brief, modest, and appropriate; in fine, they were such as became a priest of one of the lost ten tribes of Israel!

After all had spoken who wished to speak, the floor was cleared, and the dance renewed, in which Indian and squaw united, with their wonted hilarity and zeal.

Just as this dance ended, an Indian boy ran to me, and with fear strongly depicted in his countenance, caught me by the arm, and drew me to the door, pointing with his other hand towards something he wished me to observe. I looked in that direction, and saw the appearance of an Indian running at full speed to the council house; in an instant he was in the house, and literally in the fire, which he took in his hands, and threw coals of fire and hot ashes in various directions, through the house, and apparently all over himself! At his entrance, the young Indians, much alarmed, had all fled to the further end of the house, where they remained crowded, in great dread of this personification of the evil spirit! After diverting himself with the fire a few moments, at the expense of the young ones, to their no small joy he disappeared. This was an Indian disguised with an hideous false face, having horns of his head, and his hands and feet protected from the effects of the fire. And though not a professed fire king, he certainly performed his part to admiration.

During the continuance of this festival, the hospitality of the Senecas was unbounded. In the council house, and at the residence of Tall Chief, were a number of large fat bucks and fat hogs hanging up, and neatly dressed. Bread, also, of both corn and wheat in great abundance. Large kettles of soup ready prepared, in which maple sugar, profusely added, made a prominent ingredient, thus forming a very agreeable saccharine coalescence, and what contributed still more to heighten the zest

—it was all *impune* (scot free). All were invited, and all were made welcome; indeed a refusal to partake of their bounty was deemed disrespectful, if not unfriendly.

In the afternoon I left them enjoying themselves to the fullest extent: and so far as I could perceive, their pleasure was without alloy. They were eating and drinking (on this occasion, no ardent spirits were permitted), dancing and rejoicing—caring not, and, probably, thinking not of tomorrow.

HALLIDAY JACKSON'S DESCRIPTION OF THE MIDWINTER CEREMONIAL AT THE TIME OF HANDSOME LAKE

By one of those fortunate accidents of history, there are available some good data on the rituals of Midwinter as performed in the settlement where Handsome Lake lived just prior to the date of his vision. Handsome Lake had his first vision on June 15, 1799. Earlier that same year, Halliday Jackson witnessed the Midwinter ceremonial—or at least part of it—at the Cornplanter settlement (Wallace 1952:26–27) and later wrote a description of it.

Halliday Jackson had gone with two other young Quakers, Joel Swayne and Henry Simmons, Jr., to the Allegheny Senecas in 1798 on a mission to teach them agriculture and other crafts, and reading and writing. They were sent under the auspices of the Philadelphia Yearly Meeting of Friends. Accompanying them on their journey to Seneca country were two older men, John Pierce and Joshua Sharpless, members of the Indian Committee of the Philadelphia Yearly Meeting. After surveying the situation among the Senecas, the two older men returned to Philadelphia, and the three younger men remained among the Allegheny Senecas. Simmons established a school at the Cornplanter settlement and Jackson and Swayne settled upriver at Genesinguhta (Old Town), establishing a kind of demonstration project in white agricultural methods and attempting to teach Senecas these techniques. In January or February of 1799, Jackson visited Simmons at the Cornplanter settlement, witnessing the Midwinter ceremonial there. A brief account of the ceremonial is given in his journal (Wallace 1952:26–27) and a longer description in his "Sketch of the Manners, Customs, Religion and Government of the Seneca Indians." It is the latter that is quoted below.

Jackson returned to Philadelphia in June, 1800. And, though he did not again live with the Indians for any extended period of time, he did visit them in 1806 and 1814.

Halliday Jackson begins his description by noting that the Senecas at the Cornplanter settlement had two ceremonials—those now called Green Corn and Midwinter. The latter was held after the Indians had returned from their hunting expeditions.

Twice in the year, arranged in their best clothing, and decked with ornaments, they assemble at the town where their Chief [Cornplanter] lives, in order to render thanks to the Great Spirit for the favours which he hath conferred upon them. Their stated periods for these ceremonies are in the beginning of autumn, when their new corn, beans, squashes, potatoes, &c. are fit for use, and again about the middle of winter, when they generally return to their villages with the produce of their hunting expeditions.

The ceremonial began with a rite of confession. Then the men and women danced around a wooden image that stood a short distance from Cornplanter's house. Although it is not possible to identify with any certainty what dance Jackson is describing, it seems likely that the dance was the War Dance. A water drum, a wooden keg containing some water and covered with a head of skin (perhaps anciently a pottery vessel with a skin head), as well as a rattle are used in the old War Dance (called the Striking-the-stick, Pole Dance, or the Sun Dance), the Thanksgiving Dance (the Drum or Skin Dance, the War Dance transformed into the Thanksgiving Dance by Handsome Lake), and the dance now called the War Dance (or wasa:seʔ, a dance of Siouan origin). It may be that at one time only drums were used. At one time also, the War Dance was danced around a pole, the men striking the pole before reciting their war exploits.

After they are generally collected, both men and women, with the children, an examination takes place, whether any uneasiness or dissatisfaction exists among them, and whether any have committed offenses or evil acts. Of these it is often the case that the offender makes confession, the design of which is that all wrong things may be done away and reconciliation take place, where any differences have occurred, and a promise on the part of the aggressor to try to do better for the future; which done, the council then assembled forgive them.

Tonawanda Longhouse, January, 1970. *Photographs by Clarence Blueye*

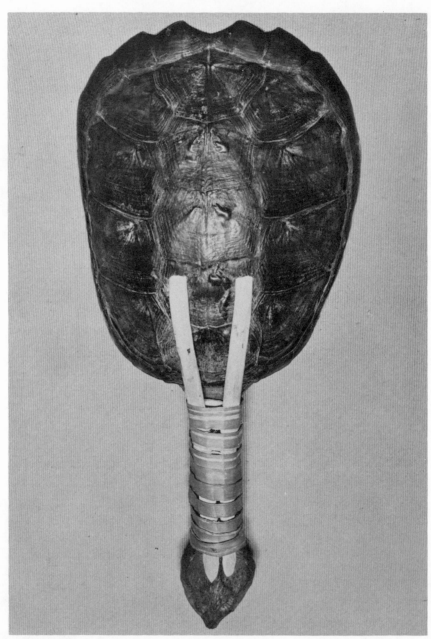

Singing Tool: Turtle Rattle.   *Rochester Museum and Science Center*

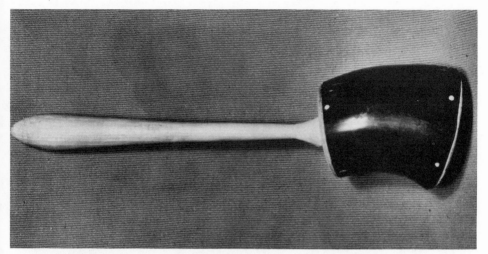

Singing Tool: Horn Rattle.   *Rochester Museum and Science Center*

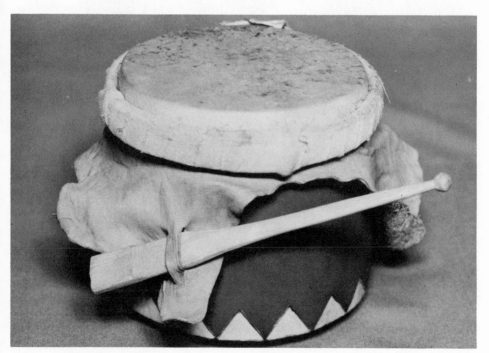

Singing Tool: Water Drum.   *Rochester Museum and Science Center*

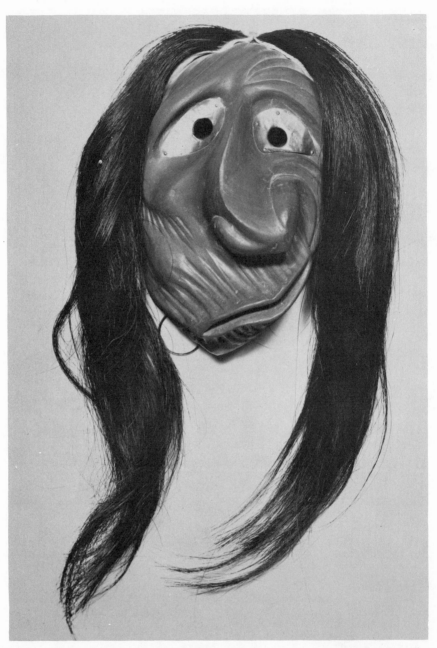

False Face Mask: "Crooked-mouth" type. *Rochester Museum and Science Center*

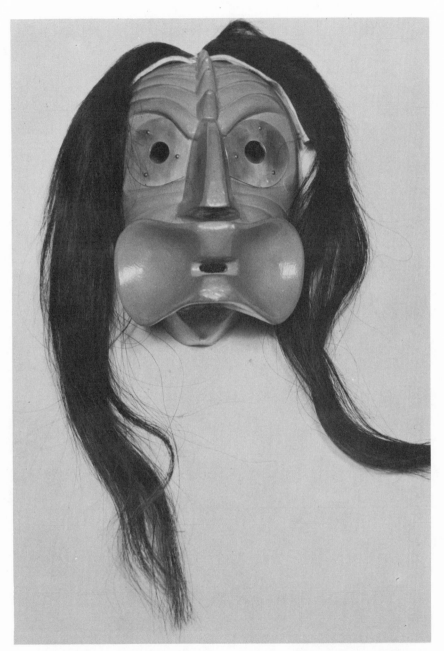

False Face Mask: "Spoon-lipped" type.　　*Rochester Museum and Science Center*

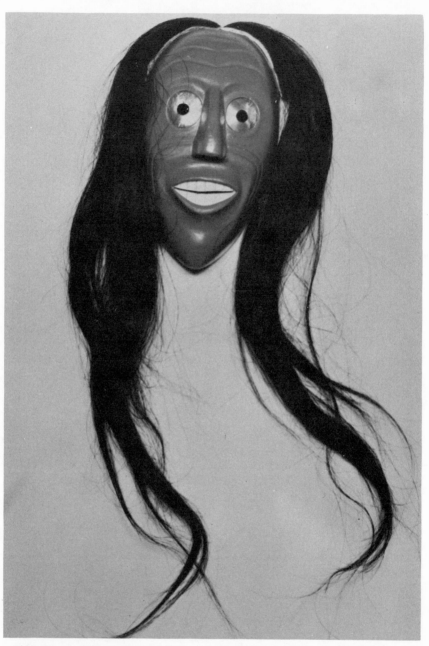

False Face Mask: "Straight-lipped" type.   *Rochester Museum and Science Center*

Husk Face Mask. *Rochester Museum and Science Center*

Diorama in the Rochester Museum and Science Center depicting the Iroquois Midwinter Ceremonial: False Face Society Dance (left) and White Dog Sacrifice (right). *Rochester Museum and Science Center*

They then institute a dance round or near a wooden image, which stands a little distance from the Chief's door, being formed of a huge block of wood into the similitude of a man, and artfully painted; embellished with skins, handkerchiefs, fine ribands, and feathers of a variety of colours. Both sexes join promiscuously in the dance—two men being seated near the feet of the image make music by pounding on a skin drawn over the mouth of a kettle, or some other vessel, the sound of which has some resemblance to that of a drum. As they move round in a circle, each one has a spoon, ladle, or some other instrument in the left hand, and frequently gives a frightful halloo or scream. All men are naked from the waist up, and their bodies painted a variety of hues. They have also various kinds of trinkets suspended from their ears and noses, and abundance of ornaments, such as belts and deer's hoofs strung like beads, fastened about their legs, which make a great rattle during the process of the dance.

For the next several days, companies of dancers went around the houses in the settlement. Halliday Jackson, in describing these companies, particularly stresses the False Faces, who wear masks and carry turtle shell rattles that they rub against wood. (Even today the False Faces rub their rattles against the door frames as they enter a house.) It seems likely that at this time also other dancers went around the houses, although Jackson does not mention them, perhaps through oversight.

After a day spent at this general rendezvous, they divide into smaller companies, men and women apart, and keep up the dance in each house in the town. These dancing companies are preceded by two men appointed for the purpose, who are dressed in the most frightful manner imaginable, being covered with bear skins, and a bag of ashes tied round their middle, behind them, with a hole to suffer the ashes to fly about as they move. Their faces are covered with a large painted mask, having a high mane on the crown, made of long coarse hair standing almost erect, and with large eyes encircled with a flame-coloured ring. The mouth is open, and shows their own teeth with which they grin in a terrific manner, and their hands are blackened so as to leave marks on every person they lay them on. They carry the shell of a mud tortoise, which has been dried for the purpose, with a stick thrust through it, which stretches the neck and a large head to their full extent, and inside of the shell are a quantity of pebbles, with which they make a wonderful rattle.

These men go from house to house and rub this shell on the side up and down the door posts. They frequently enter into the house, but say nothing, nor do any injury. As they travel about, if they meet with any person, male or female, in their way, they pursue them—those who turn and receive them in a friendly way, they shake hands with, but say nothing—but it is rather as expected that many should run as if terrified; these are pursued, and if overtaken before they get into a house, are laid hold of, and blackened with their hands, but no other injury is offered, and, except a frightful yelling noise, nothing is spoken.

The design of these frightful representations is to personify and imitate the bad spirit, and to remind the Indians of the necessity to amend their ways, and avoid all wrong things.

Then the white dog was sacrificed and a tobacco invocation offered.

After the concert of heathenish superstition has continued for several days, they assemble again around wooden image near the council house, and sacrifice a dog, first decorating him with strings of wampum, fine ribands, and some paintings; after hanging him on the image, burn him to ashes, on a fire kindled near him for the purpose. On some extraordinary occasions, they eat the flesh of the dog, and a white dog is always preferred, as being deemed a more acceptable offering.

While the dog is consuming, they dance round the fire, making a dreadful yelling and whooping, and during the process of the dance, about one pound of tobacco, of a particular kind, rubbed fine, which they consider as peculiarly agreeable to the Great Spirit, is thrown on the fire in the smoke whereof, their aspirations, as they suppose, ascending, they believe are heard by the Great Spirit, and are offered, together with their dancing, under a profession of pleasing him.

During this ascension of the smoke, a chief whom they call their minister, and who appears to have command and superintendence of this ceremony, addresses the Great Spirit in a speech, the purport of which is an acknowledgment for favours received, thanks for preservation in times past, and imploring his continued care and protection.

He then addresses the people, advising them how they ought to conduct, and pointing out some of the prominent evils which they ought to avoid; one of the greatest of these is stealing and another is for the husband to desert and separate himself from his wife during pregnancy; but the taking of the life of another is not considered a crime so capital, as they are left at liberty to revenge it by taking the life of the murderer. This may be done with impunity by the nearest relative of the deceased, and they then consider the cries of blood to be done away.

Preparatory to these sacrifices they are careful to procure a sufficiency of provisions.

This is done by deputing a certain number of their warriors to hunt, who encircle a large space of hunting ground, and all the game taken thereon is devoted to this feast. Previously to that which was held in the summer of 1799, thirty men were sent out, who returned the day following with seventeen deer. Great attention is paid to the cooking, and certain places are appointed where the entertainment shall be given. Spirituous liquors are not allowed on these occasions, although near the conclusion there are instances, at times, of some of them getting intoxicated.

Their stated time, according to ancient custom, for holding these sacrifices, is four days at a time, twice in the year; but they frequently continue their feasting and dancing at intervals and by companies, for eight or ten days; and, after the last day being spent in playing at games of chance, they generally conclude by the firing of guns.

Their reason for performing these ceremonious rites at these two seasons of the year, they say, is to return thanks to the Great Spirit for sending them plenty of bread and meat—that it was the way their forefathers had taught them, and they knew of no better; and although the feast is conducted with considerable noise, and apparent confusion, it is also attended at intervals with much solemnity, and on the part of many of them, purely on a religious ground, and from sincere and good motives. But, at the same time, they are willing to acknowledge that their worship was not performed with so much solemnity as their forefathers practiced.[13]

It should be noted that in this description of Midwinter Jackson states that anciently the ceremony lasted four days, but that at least by the end of the nineteenth century it lasted four or six days longer and ended with the playing of games of chance.

MARY JEMISON'S DESCRIPTION OF THE SENECA MIDWINTER CEREMONIAL

In 1823, James Seaver recorded the life of Mary Jemison; his account was published the following year. Mary Jemison was a white woman who had been captured by the Iroquois in 1758 (she thought the year was 1755) when she was fifteen years old and spent the remaining years of her long life (she died at the age of ninety) among

the Senecas. She had married two Indian men and had children by
both of them, but only those by her second husband survived her.
Her descendants still live on Indian reservations today. Seaver's account of Mary Jemison's life—recorded when she was eighty years
old—became one of the most popular captivity narratives of the time,
and the many editions of it that have been published (one appeared
in 1961) attest to its continuing interest to many.

Some account of Seneca customs—also by Mary Jemison—are
given in the appendix of Seaver's book. These include a description
of the Seneca Midwinter ceremony. Although no date is given, it
seems likely that the description is of the Genesee Seneca practice before the time of Handsome Lake—that is, of practice Mary Jemison
remembered from her young adulthood (she was probably in her fif-
ties when Handsome Lake first began to preach on the Allegheny).

Mary Jemison states, as does present Seneca tradition and Halliday Jackson, that the Midwinter ceremonial was held after the Indians had returned from the fall hunt.

The Indians having returned from hunting, and having brought in
all the venison and skins that they have taken, a committee is appointed,
says Mrs. Jemison, consisting of from ten to twenty active men, to
superintend the festivities of the great sacrifice and thanksgiving that
is to be immediately celebrated. This being done, preparations are made
at the council-house, or place of meeting, for the reception and accommodation of the whole tribe; and then the ceremonies are commenced,
and the whole is conducted with a great degree of order and harmony,
under the direction of the committee.

On the first day of the ceremonial, two white dogs were
strangled, painted red, decorated with ribbons and feathers, and hung
on a pole near the council house. Then a group of men, each carrying
a paddle went around the houses stirring the ashes in each. Mary Jemison said that during the course of the ceremony, all the fires were
extinguished and new fires lit, that is, that this ashes-stirring rite
was also a New Fire one.

Two white dogs, without spot or blemish, are selected (if such can
be found, and if not, two that have the fewest spots) from those belonging to the tribe, and killed near the door of the council-house by
being strangled. A wound on the animal or an effusion of blood, would
spoil the victim and render the sacrifice useless. The dogs are then

painted red on their faces, edges of their ears, and on various parts of their bodies, and are curiously decorated with ribbons of different colors, and fine feathers, which are tied and fastened on in such a manner as to make the most elegant appearance. They are then hung on a post near the door of the council-house, at a height of twenty feet from the ground.

This being done, the frolic is commenced by those who are present, while the committee run through the tribe or town, and hurry the people to assemble by knocking on their houses. At this time the committee are naked (wearing only a breech-clout), and each carries a paddle, with which he takes up ashes and scatters them about the house in every direction. In the course of the ceremonies, all the fire is extinguished in every hut throughout the tribe, and new fire, struck from the flint on each hearth, is kindled, after having removed the whole of the ashes, old coals, &c. Having done this, and discharged one or two guns, they go on, and in this manner they proceed till they have visited every house in the tribe. This finishes the business of the first day.

On the second day of the ceremonial, a group of men went around the houses. From Mary Jemison's description, these men were False Faces, who also collected tobacco.

On the second day the committee dance, go through the town with bear-skin on their legs, and at every time they start they fire a gun. They also beg through the tribe, each carrying a basket in which to receive whatever may be bestowed. The alms consist of Indian tobacco and other articles that are used for incense at the sacrifice. Each manager at this time carries a dried tortoise or turtle shell, containing a few beans, which he frequently rubs on the walls of the houses, both inside and out. This kind of maneuvering by the committee continues two or three days, during which time the people at the council-house recreate themselves by dancing.

On the fourth or fifth day, the Husk Faces went around the houses. (It should be noted that this was at the midpoint of the ceremonial and as has been seen, some kind of Husk Face rite now is often performed midway through the Midwinter ceremonial.)

On the fourth or fifth day the committee make false faces of husks, in which they run about, making a frightful but ludicrous appearance. In this dress (still wearing the bear-skin), they run to the council-house, smearing themselves with dirt and bedaubing every one who refuses to contribute something toward filling the baskets of incense, which they

continue to carry, soliciting alms. During all this time they collect the
evil spirit, or drive it off entirely, for the present, and also concentrate
within themselves all the sins of their tribe, however numerous or
heinous.

At the end of the ceremonial, the dogs were taken down and put
on the fire and a tobacco invocation offered. There followed a feast,
then a War Dance and a Peace Dance.

On the eighth or ninth day, the committee having received all the
sin, as before observed, into their own bodies, they take down the dogs,
and after having transfused the whole of it into one of their own number,
he, by a peculiar slight of hand, or kind of magic, works it all out of himself into the dogs. The dogs, thus loaded with all the sins of the people,
are placed upon a pile of wood that is directly set on fire. Here they
are burnt, together with the sins with which they were loaded, surrounded
by the multitude, who throw incense of tobacco or the like into the fire,
the scent of which they say, goes up to Nauwaneu [Great Good Spirit
or Creator], to whom it is pleasant and acceptable.

This feast continues nine days, and during that time the Chiefs review the national affairs of the year past; agree upon the best plan to
be pursued through the next year, and attend to all internal regulations.

On the last day, the whole company partake of an elegant dinner,
consisting of meat, corn, and beans, boiled together in large kettles,
and stirred till the whole is completely mixed and soft. This mess is
devoured without much ceremony—some eat with a spoon, by dipping
out of the kettles; others serve themselves in small dippers; some in
one way, and some in another, till the whole is consumed. After this
they perform the war dance, the peace dance, and smoke the pipe of
peace; and then, free from iniquity, each repairs to his place of abode,
prepared to commence the business of a new year. In this feast, tem-
perance is observed, and commonly, order prevails in a greater degree
than would naturally be expected.

Seaver adds two notes. First, that at the time of his writing only
one dog was sacrificed and, second, that although previously the ceremonial lasted nine days, it was then not commonly held for more
than five to seven days.

THADDEUS OSGOOD'S DESCRIPTION OF THE SENECA
MIDWINTER CEREMONIAL IN THE EARLY PART
OF THE NINETEENTH CENTURY

As has been noted above, in 1812 the Reverend Thaddeus Osgood, a missionary among the Iroquois, sent Timothy Dwight a description of the Seneca Midwinter ceremony that Dwight published in his "Travels." This description differs in no important respect from Halliday Jackson's or Mary Jemison's. The few differences in the description (as that pertaining to the disposal of the dogs) probably reflect regional or temporal differences and should not be construed as inaccuracies in the description.

The following is the pertinent information contained in Dwight's "Travels" (1822[4]:213–14):

The following account of this subject, as it exists among the Senecas, was give me, in August, 1812, by the Reverend Thaddeus Osgood, who has spent several years as a missionary, partly in the United States and partly in Canada. Mr. Osgood was present at one of these solemn festivals, and acquired additional information, such as he wished, from the national interpreter.

At the time when the Senecas return from hunting in January or February they annually keep a feast seven days; the professed object of which is to render thanks to the Great Spirit for the benefits which they have received from him during the preceding year, and to solicit the continuance of them through the year to come. On the evening before the feast commences, they kill two dogs, and after painting them with various colours and dressing them with ornaments, suspend them in the center of the camp, or in some conspicious place in the village.

The whole of this solemn season is spent in feasting and dancing. Two select bands, one of men and another of women, ornamented with a variety of trinkets, and furnished each with an ear of corn, which is held in the right hand, begin the dance at the Council-house. Both choirs, the men leading the way, dance in a circle around the council-fire, which is kindled for the occasion, and regulate their steps by music. Hence they proceed to every house in the village, and in the same manner dance in a circle around each fire.

On one of the festival days they perform a peculiar religious ceremony, for the purpose of driving away evil spirits from their habitations.

Three men clothe themselves in the skins of wild beasts, and cover their faces with masks of a hideous appearance, and their hands with the shell of the tortoise. In this garb they go from house to house, making a horrid noise, and in every house take the fuel from the fire, and scatter the embers and ashes about the floor with their hands.

Toward the close of the festival they erect a funeral pile, place upon it the two dogs, and set it on fire. When they are partly consumed, one of them is taken off and put into a large kettle, with vegetables of every kind which they have cultivated during the preceding year. The other dog is consumed in the fire. The ashes of the pile are then gathered up, carried through the village, and sprinkled at the door of every house. When this ceremony is ended, which is always near the close of the seventh day, all the inhabitants feast together upon the contents of the kettle; and thus the festival is terminated.

DESCRIPTION OF THE MIDWINTER CEREMONIAL
AT SQUAKIE HILL IN 1816 AND 1819

In 1876 Lockwood Doty published a description of the Midwinter ceremonial held at Squakie Hill. He states that he obtained this description from Jerediah Horsford who was present at the ceremony in 1816 and recorded the events in his diary. Doty also states that he obtained some information from Governor George W. Patterson who had attended the ceremonial three years later. Although Squakie Hill was supposedly a settlement of Fox Indians (from which the settlement got its name—the Fox were also called Squakies) in the Genesee Valley, the ceremonial described is much like that earlier described for the Senecas. Doty's (1876:53–56) description follows:

The New Year's festival at Squakie Hill, in 1816, opened on the morning of the 7th of February. A white dog was brought to the council-house and strangled, care being taken not to break its bones or shed its blood, and hanged to a post. Its body was then striped with red paint, and five strings of purple beads were fastened about the neck. A stem of hedge-hog quills was attached to the body, from which hung a clump of feathers, a rag filled with something like fine tobacco being placed under them. To each leg was tied a bunch of feathers with red and yellow ribbons. The day was spent in short speeches and dream-telling. Near night, two Indians, with blackened faces, appeared in bear skins with long braids of corn husks about their ankles and heads. Keeping time to a dolorous song, they begun a tour of the village. Entering a house, they would pound the benches and sides and then proceed to the next, and so on throughout the village.

The discharge of three guns opened the second day's proceedings, when five Indians appeared with long wooden shovels, and began to scatter fire and ashes until the council-house became filled with dust and smoke. This ceremony was repeated at each house several times during the day, but to a different tune at each round.

Speeches, exciting levity, and dreams occupied the third morning. About noon the fire-shovelling was repeated with increased vigor. This over, the clothing of the actors and others was changed, their heads were adorned with feathers and their faces with paint. A number of squaws in calico short gowns and blue broadcloth petticoats, ornamented with bead-work and a profusion of silver brooches, joined in the dance, which, beginning at the council-house, was repeated at every hut several times during the day. A species of gambling with a wooden dish and six wooden balls and a like number of white beans was practiced from house to house. In the evening a party of dancers would enter a dwelling, and soon a person dressed in bear-skin and false face would come in, when the dancers, as if afraid, beat a retreat to the next house.

The fourth day was devoted to ceremonies in which false faces and dancing held the principal place.

The members reappeared on the fifth day. They approached every person for a trifling gift. An apple, a plug of tobacco, or a few pennies was enough, in default of which the party refusing was often roughly handled. Two Indians, disguised as bears, came next. On their entering a house the inmates would at once quit it, when the mock bears pretended a disposition to tear everything in pieces or to overturn whatever fell in their way. A number of Indians followed them, flashing guns, as though forcibly to drive out the simulated bears. Next in order was a game of ball upon the ice, played with great life by a party of seven on each side. Many a hard fall occurred, which always drew forth shouts of laughter. Three Indians then appeared in deer-skins and rags, one of whom, personating the evil one, had his clothing literally torn from his body by his companions, who quickly covered him with skins, and then led him from hut to hut. In each hut he would lie down and roll along the ground, tumble into the fire, paw out the ashes and scatter it about the room, all the while groaning and making great ado. A dancing group next entered the council-house with painted faces, attired in skins, with feathers around their heads and with deer's hoofs or pieces of tin fastened about their legs. A large Indian, with bow and arrows, soon came in, bringing three lads. The four enacted a rude drama of hunter and dogs. The boys got down on hands and knees, barking, growling and snapping at whatever came in their way, as they passed from door to door, demanding bread for the final feast, which two girls gathered into baskets.

On the morning of the sixth day, seven lads, one of whom was covered with wolf-skins and used two short sticks for forelegs, went from house to house. The dwellers brought out corn and placed it in a basket carried by an aged female. Next followed a dance at the council-house. "The female dancers," says an eye witness, "were the most graceful, and, I may add, the most modest I ever saw tripping the fantastic toe upon the bare ground." An old squaw stepped into the ring with a live pig under her arms. She would strike it upon the head, when the dancers would spat their hands and sing. [*Quis-quis,* meaning pigs, swine, was a word constantly repeated.] About noon preparations were made for burning the white dog, which was taken down and laid upon a small pile of dry wood, ornaments and all. An Indian gave three yells. The wood was then placed around and over the dog. When old and young had gathered quite near Jim Washington, a favorite speaker, he applied the fire, and, as it begun to burn, he walked around inside the circle, occasionally throwing pulverized mint into the flames, all the while talking as if to some invisible being. The spectators appeared quite solemn, and at length joined in singing. When the pile was partly consumed Jim stopped. After a moment's pause, he put a question which met with loud response from the circle, and then all dispersed.

A general feast was now prepared at the council-house. Two brass kettles, filled with squash, corn, beans, pumpkins and venison, which had been boiling for hours over fires in the center of the room, were placed on the ground, and the contents dipped away in calabashes and eaten with spoons, or from wooden sticks, with the bread gathered the day before. The evening was devoted to dancing, in which all joined. At length, one after another withdrew, and by ten o'clock the council-house was empty and silent. The ceremonial part of the festival was over, and though the seventh and last day was to follow, it was mainly spent in petty gambling and feats of strength.

LEWIS HENRY MORGAN'S DESCRIPTION OF THE
SENECA MIDWINTER CEREMONIAL

The most detailed nineteenth-century description of a Midwinter ceremonial is contained in Lewis Henry Morgan's *League of the Ho-de-no-sau-nee or Iroquois*. This description is probably of practice at the now defunct Sand Hill Longhouse on the Tonawanda Reservation about 1846. The family of Morgan's principal informant, Ely S. Parker, lived near this longhouse.[14] It was torn down about 1870 (Fenton 1941:144) with the intention of building a larger one. Although it was never built, for a time its congregation held its ceremonials at a private house.

Morgan's description of the Seneca Midwinter ceremonial is much like those describing earlier Seneca practice with one exception. Morgan notes that the last days of the ceremonial were devoted to the performance of the Four Sacred Rituals which tradition states were added by Handsome Lake.

Morgan (1901[1]:199–213) states that before Midwinter began a rite of confession was held. On the first day of Midwinter, the Bigheads went around the houses twice, once in the morning and again in the afternoon, and the white dog was strangled. (Morgan's statement that the Bigheads were Faithkeepers may be in error.)

Several days before the time appointed for the jubilee, the people assembled for the confession of their sins. On this occasion they were more thorough in the work than at any other season, that they might enter upon the new year with a firm purpose of amendment. This council not unfrequently lasted three days, before all the people had performed this act of religious duty.

The observances of the new year were commenced, on the day appointed, by two of the keepers of the faith, who visited every house in and about the Indian village, morning and evening. They were disguised in bear skins or buffalo robes, which were secured around their heads with wreaths of corn-husks, and then gathered in loose folds about the body. Wreaths of corn-husks were also adjusted around their arms and ankles. They were robed in this manner, and painted by the matrons, who, like themselves, were keepers of the faith, and by them were they commissioned to go forth in this formidable attire, to announce the commencement of the jubilee. Taking corn-pounders in their hands, they went out in company, on the morning of the day, to perform their duty. Upon entering a house, they saluted the inmates in a formal manner, after which, one of them, striking upon the floor, to restore silence and secure attention, thus addressed them:

"Listen, Listen, Listen: The ceremonies which the Great Spirit has commanded us to perform, are about to commence. Prepare your houses. Clear away the rubbish. Drive out all evil animals. We wish nothing to hinder or obstruct the coming observances. We enjoin upon every one to obey our requirements. Should any of your friends be taken sick and die, we command you not to mourn for them, nor allow any of your friends to mourn. But lay the body aside, and enjoy the coming ceremonies with us. When they are over, we will mourn with you."

After singing a short thanksgiving song, they passed out.

In the afternoon this visit was repeated in the same manner. After saluting the family as before, one of the keepers of the faith thus addressed them:

"My Nephews, my Nephews, my Nephews: We now announce to you that the New Year's ceremonies have commenced, according to our ancient custom. You are, each of you, now required to go forth, and participate in their observance. This is the will of the Great Spirit. Your first duty will be to prepare your wooden blades (*Gä-ger-we-sä*) with which to stir up the ashes upon your neighbors' hearths. Then return to the Great Spirit your individual thanks for the return of this season, and for the enjoyment of this privilege."

Having sung another song, appropriate to the occasion, they departed finally, and when they had in this way made the circuit of the village, the ceremonies of the first day were concluded.

On the first day, however, the white dog was strangled. They selected a dog, free from physical blemish, and of a pure white, if such an one could be found. The white deer, white squirrel, and other chance animals of the albino kind were regarded as consecrated to the Great Spirit. White was the Iroquois emblem of purity and of faith. In strangling the dog, they were careful neither to shed his blood nor break his bones. The dog was then spotted, in places, over his body and limbs, with red paint, and ornamented with feathers in various ways. Around his neck was hung a string of white wampum, the pledge of their sincerity. In modern times, the dog is ornamented with a profusion of many-colored ribbons, which are adjusted around his body and limbs. The ornaments placed upon the dog were the voluntary offerings of the pious; and for each gift thus bestowed, the giver was taught to expect a blessing. When the dog had been thus decorated, it was suspended by the neck about eight feet from the ground, on the branching prong of a pole erected for that purpose. Here it hung, night and day, until the morning of the fifth day, when it was taken down to be burned. Oftentimes two dogs were burned, one for each four of the tribes [clans]. In this case, the people separated into two divisions, and after going through separate preparatory ceremonies, they united around the same altar for the burning of the dogs, and the offering of the thanksgiving address to the Great Spirit.

The second day began in the morning with the circuit of the Bigheads uncostumed through the houses. They stirred the ashes in each. Then parties of people visited the houses stirring ashes. The Bigheads uncostumed went around stirring the ashes again at noon and in the evening, and following them were other parties of people who also stirred the ashes.

On the second day all the people went forth, and visited in turn the houses of their neighbors, either in the morning, at noon, or in the evening. They went in small parties apparelled in their best attire. It was customary, however, for the people to be preceded by the two keepers of the faith who made the recitations the day previous, as a matter of etiquette; the houses not being open to all, until these personages had made their call. At this time was performed the ceremony of stirring the ashes upon the hearth, which appears to have no particular idea attached to it, beyond that of a formal visitation. Putting aside the disguise of the day before, the keepers of the faith assumed the costume of warriors, plumed and painted, in which attire they visited every family three times, in the morning, at noon, and in the evening. Taking in their hands wooden blades or shovels, they entered the lodge and saluted the family. One of them then stirred the ashes, and having taken up a quantity upon the blade of the shovel, and sprinkled them upon the hearth, he thus addressed the inmates, as they were in the act of falling: "I thank the Great Spirit that he has spared your lives again to witness this New Year's celebration." Then repeating the process with another shovel full of ashes, he continued: "I thank the Great Spirit that he has spared my life, again to be an actor in this ceremony. And now I do this to please the Great Spirit." The two then united in a thanksgiving song prepared for the occasion, upon the conclusion of which they took their departure. Other parties of the people then came in successively, and each went through the same performances. In this manner every house was thrice visited on the second day, by the keepers of the faith in the first instance, and afterwards by the whole community.

On the third and fourth days, various groups of people went around the houses performing rituals, including the Feather Dance, Fish Dance, Trotting Dance, and War Dance. A man might go around the houses requesting that his dream be guessed. Also young boys, the Beggars, might go around the houses requesting gifts.

The proceedings upon the third and fourth days were alike. Small dancing parties were organized, which visited from house to house, and danced at the domestic fireside. Each set selected a different dance, appointed their own leader, and furnished their own music. One party, for instance, took the Feather Dance, another the Fish Dance, another the Trotting Dance, to give variety to the short entertainments which succeeded each other at every house. It was not uncommon, on such occasions, to see a party of juveniles, about a dozen in number, dressed in full costume, feathered and painted, dancing the War Dance, from house to house, with all the zeal and enthusiasm which this dance was so eminently calculated to excite. In this manner every house was made a scene of gaiety and amusement, for none was so humble or so retired as to remain unvisited.

Another pastime incident to these days was the formation of a "thieving party," as it was called, a band of mischievous boys, disguised with false faces, paint and rags, to collect materials for a feast. This vagrant company strolled from house to house, accompanied by an old woman carrying a huge basket. If the family received them kindly, and made them presents, they handed the latter to the female carrier, and having given the family a dance in acknowledgment of the present, they retired without committing any depredations. But if no presents were made, or such as were insufficient, they purloined whatever articles they could most adroitly and easily conceal. If detected, they at once made restitution, but if not, it was considered a fair win. On the return of this party from their rounds, all the articles collected were deposited in a place open to public examination; where any one who had lost an article which he particularly prized, was allowed to redeem it, on paying an equivalent. But no one was permitted to reclaim, as the owner, any article successfully taken by this thieving party on its professional round. Upon the proceeds of this forced collection, a feast was eventually given, together with a dance in some private family.

Guessing dreams was another of the novel practices of the Iroquois, which distinguished these festive days. It is difficult to understand pre-

cisely how far the self-delusion under which the dreamer appeared to
act was real. A person with a melancholy and dejected countenance,
entering a house, announced that he had a dream, and requested the inmates to guess it. He thus wandered from house to house, until he found
a solution which suited him. This was either received as an interpretation of an actual dream, or suggested such a dream as the person was
willing to adopt as his own. He at once avowed that his dream had been
correctly guessed; and if the dream, as interpreted, prescribed any future conduct, he fulfilled it to the letter at whatever sacrifice. The celebrated Cornplanter, *Gy-ant'-wä-ka,* resigned his chiefship in consequence
of a dream. In relation to dreams, the Iroquois had ever been prone to
extravagant and supernatural beliefs. They often regarded a dream as
a divine monition, and followed its injunctions to the utmost extremity.
Their notions upon this subject recall to remembrance the conceit of
Homer, that "dreams descend from Jove."

During the first four days the people were without a feast, from the
fact that the observances themselves did not require the assembling of
the people at the council-house. But entertainments were given in the
evenings at private houses, where the night was devoted to the dance.
Another amusement at this particular season was the Snow-snake game,
which, like all Indian games, was wont to arouse considerable interest.

On the morning of the fifth day, the white dog was burned and
the tobacco invocation with the Thanksgiving Address given. Then
the people returned to the council house and performed the Feather
Dance and other (social?) dances.

On the morning of the fifth day, soon after dawn, the white dog
was burned on an altar of wood erected by the keepers of the faith near
the council-house. It is difficult, from outward observation, to draw forth
the true intent with which the dog was burned. The obscurity with
which the object was veiled has led to various conjectures. Among other
things, it has been pronounced a sacrifice for sin. In the religious system
of the Iroquois, there is no recognition of the doctrine of atonement for
sin, or of the absolution or forgiveness of sins. Upon this whole subject
their system is silent. An act once done was registered beyond the power
of change. The greatest advance upon this point of faith was the belief
that good deeds cancelled the evil, thus placing heaven, through good
works, within the reach of all. The notion that this was a expiation for
sin is thus refuted by their system of theology itself. The other idea, that
the sins of the people, by some mystic process, were transferred to the
dog, and by him thus borne away, on the principle of the scapegoat of the

Hebrews, is also without any foundation in truth. The burning of the dog had not the slightest connection with the sins of the people. On the contrary, the simple idea of the sacrifice was to send up the spirit of the dog as a messenger to the Great Spirit, to announce their continued fidelity to his service, and also to convey to him their united thanks for the blessings of the year. The fidelity of the dog, the companion of the Indian, as a hunter, was emblematical of their fidelity. No messenger so trusty could be found to bear their petitions to the Master of life. The Iroquois believed that the Great Spirit made a covenant with their fathers to the effect that when they should send up to him the spirit of a dog, of a spotless white, he would receive it as the pledge of their adherence to his worship, and his ears would thus be opened in a special manner to their petitions. To approach *Hä-wen-né-yu* [Great Spirit] in the most acceptable manner, and to gain attention to their thanksgiving acknowledgments and supplications in the way of his own appointing, was the end and object of burning the dog. They hung around his neck a string of white wampum, the pledge of their faith. They believed that the spirit of the dog hovered around the body until it was committed to the flames, when it ascended into the presence of the Great Spirit, itself the acknowledged evidence of their fidelity, and bearing also to him the united thanks and supplications of the people. This sacrifice was the most solemn and impressive manner of drawing near to the Great Spirit known to the Iroquois. They used the spirit of the dog in precisely the same manner that they did the incense of tobacco, as an instrumentality through which to commune with their Maker. This sacrifice was their highest act of piety.

The burning of the dog was attended with many ceremonies. It was first taken down and laid out upon a bench in the council-house, while the fire of the altar was kindling. A speech was then made over it by one of the keepers of the faith, in which he spoke of the antiquity of this institution of their fathers, of its importance and solemnity, and finally enjoined upon them all to direct their thoughts to the Great Spirit, and unite with the keepers of the faith in these observances. He concluded with thanking the Great Spirit, that the lives of so many of them had been spared through another year. A chant or song, appropriate to the occasion, was then sung, the people joining in chorus. By the time this was over, the altar was blazing up on every side ready for the offering. A procession was then formed, the officiating keeper of the faith preceding, followed by four others bearing the dog upon a kind of bark litter, behind which came the people in Indian file. A loud exclamation, in the nature of a war-whoop, announced the starting of the procession. They moved on towards the altar, and having marched around it, the keepers of the faith halted, facing the rising sun. With some immaterial ceremonies, the dog was laid upon the burning altar, and as the flames surrounded the offering, the officiating keeper of the faith, by a species of ejaculation, upon a high key, thrice repeated, invoked the attention of the Great Spirit.

"*Quä, quä, quä* (Hail, hail, hail) : Thou who hast created all things, who rulest all things, and who givest laws and commands to thy creatures, listen to our words. We now obey thy commands. That which thou hast made is returning unto thee. It is rising to thee, by which it will appear that our words are true." [Some leaves of tobacco were attached to the wampum around the dog's neck, with the incense of which this invocation was made.]

Several thanksgiving songs or chants, in measured verse, were then sung by the keepers of the faith, the people joining in chorus. After this, was made the great thanksgiving address of the Iroquois. The keeper of the faith appointed to deliver it, invoked the attention of *Hä-wen-né-yu* by the same thrice-repeated exclamation. As the speech progressed, he threw leaves of tobacco into the fire from time to time, that its incense might constantly ascend during the whole address. The following is the address, as delivered among the Senecas :

"Hail, Hail, Hail: Listen now, with an open ear, to the words of thy people, as they ascend to thy dwelling, in the smoke of our offering. Behold thy people here assembled. Behold, they have come up to celebrate anew the sacred rites thou hast given them. Look down upon us beneficently. Give us wisdom faithfully to execute thy commands.

"Continue to listen: The united voice of thy people continues to ascend to thee. Forbid, by thy wisdom, all things which shall tempt thy people to relinquish their ancient faith. Give us power to celebrate at all times, with zeal and fidelity, the sacred ceremonies which thou hast given us.

"Continue to listen: Give to the keepers of the faith wisdom to execute properly thy commands. Give to our warriors, and our mothers, strength to perform the sacred ceremonies of thy institution. We thank thee that, in thy wisdom, thou hast given to us these commands. We thank thee that thou hast preserved them pure unto this day.

"Continue to listen: We thank thee that the lives of so many of thy children are spared, to participate in the exercises of this occasion. Our minds are gladdened to be made partakers in the execution of thy commands.

"We return thanks to our mother, the earth, which sustains us. We thank thee that thou hast caused her to yield so plentifully of her fruits. Cause that, in the season coming, she may not withhold of her fullness, and leave any to suffer for want.

"We return thanks to the rivers and streams, which run their courses upon the bosom of our mother the earth. We thank thee that thou hast supplied them with life, for our comfort and support. Grant that this blessing may continue.

"We return thanks to all the herbs and plants of the earth. We thank thee that in thy goodness thou hast blest them all, and given them strength to preserve our bodies healthy, and to cure us of the diseases inflicted upon us by evil spirits. We ask thee not to take from us these blessings.

"We return thanks to the Three Sisters. We thank thee that thou hast provided them as the main supporters of our lives. We thank thee for the abundant harvest gathered in during the past season. We ask that Our Supporters may never fail us, and cause our children to suffer from want.

"We return thanks to the bushes and trees which provide us with fruit. We thank thee that thou hast blessed them, and made them to produce for the good of thy creatures. We ask that they may not refuse to yield plentifully for our enjoyment.

"We return thanks to the winds, which, moving, have banished all diseases. We thank thee that thou hast thus ordered. We ask the continuation of this great blessing.

"We return thanks to our grandfather *Hé-no*. We thank thee that thou hast so wisely provided for our happiness and comfort, in ordering the rain to descend upon the earth, giving us water, and causing all plants to grow. We thank thee that thou hast given us *Hé-no,* our grandfather, to do thy will in the protection of thy people. We ask that this great blessing may be continued to us.

"We return thanks to the moon and stars, which give us light when the sun has gone to his rest. We thank thee that thy wisdom has so kindly provided, that light is never wanting to us. Continue unto us this goodness.

"We return thanks to the sun, that he has looked upon the earth with a beneficent eye. We thank thee that thou hast, in thy unbounded wisdom, commanded the sun to regulate the return of the seasons, to dispense heat and cold, and to watch over the comfort of thy people. Give unto us that wisdom which will guide us in the path of truth. Keep us from all evil ways, that the sun may never hide his face from us for shame and leave us in darkness.

"We return thanks to the *Ho-no-che-nó-keh* [other spirits]. We thank thee that thou hast provided so many agencies for our good and happiness.

"Lastly, we return thanks to thee, our Creator and Ruler. In thee are embodied all things. We believe thou canst do no evil; that thou doest all things for our good and happiness. Should thy people disobey thy commands, deal not harshly with them; but be kind to us, as thou hast been to our fathers in times long gone by. Harken unto our words as they have ascended, and may they be pleasing to thee our Creator, the Preserver and Ruler of all things, visible and invisible. *Na-hó.*"

After the delivery of this address, the people, leaving the partly consumed offering, returned to the council-house, where the Feather dance was performed. With this the religious exercises of the day were concluded. Other dances, however, followed, for the entertainment of the people, and the day and evening were given up to this amusement. Last of all came the feast, with which the proceedings of the day were terminated.

The important ritual of the sixth day was the dancing of the Thanksgiving Dance.

On the morning of the sixth day, the people again assembled at the place of council. This day was observed in about the same manner as one of their ordinary religious days, at which the Thanksgiving dance was introduced.

The rituals of the seventh day began with the rite of Personal Chant. There followed the playing of the Bowl Game.

The seventh and last day was commenced with the *Ah-dó-weh;* after which the Peach-stone game was introduced, with the determination of which ended the New Year's jubilee.

Here however Morgan seems to be describing newer practice. He states in his description of the Green Corn ceremony that although the Feather Dance, Thanksgiving Dance, Personal Chant, and Bowl Game were once given on separate days, the latter two are now given on the same day (Morgan 1901[1]:195–96).

The differences between Morgan's account of practice on the Tonawanda Reservation and present practice there probably do not reflect changes in the Midwinter ceremonial over the one-hundred-year period, but rather differences in the practice of two longhouses. As has been noted, Morgan's description is probably of practice at the Sand Hill Longhouse, now defunct, and it seems likely that even as early as the 1840's, there were differences in the ritual of Midwinter in these two longhouses on the Tonawanda Reservation. Some of these differences and the changes that they may indicate can be noted.

Morgan states that the Bigheads went around twice the first day in costume and three times (morning, noon, and afternoon) not in costume on the second day, stirring the ashes in the houses. This apparently indicates early change from older Seneca practice in the Sand Hill Longhouse. The Bigheads in costume stir the ashes three times (morning, noon, and afternoon) on the first day at the Tonawanda and Newtown Longhouses and twice (morning and noon) in costume and once (afternoon) not in costume on the first day at the Coldspring Longhouse. They do not now circuit the houses *three* times on the second day. That they do not suggests that perhaps they never did and that the variant form Morgan describes reflects early change in the Sand Hill Longhouse ceremonial, although there are other explanations for the difference.

The costume Morgan describes for the Bigheads is much as it is today, with the exception that bear or buffalo robes were used instead of blankets. However, it is still remembered at Tonawanda that buffalo robes were once used instead of blankets.

Morgan indicates that the Bigheads and the women dressers were Faithkeepers, which, if true, is unlike modern practice at Tonawanda. Morgan, however, probably underestimating the importance of the dream to the Seneca at that time, may have been in error with his statement that these individuals were Faithkeepers; it may be a kind of euphemism for what actually occurred. Even today at Tonawanda there is some reluctance to speak of the choice of the Bigheads as depending on dreams.

Morgan indicates that parties followed the Bigheads on each of these rounds on the second day, repeating their ritual. This is no longer the practice at Tonawanda, but since it does have parallels in the practice at other Iroquois longhouses, where parties representing the moieties stir ashes, it may have been older practice at Tonawanda.

Morgan's description of the "thieving parties" is probably a description of the Beggars. The Beggars still go around at Tonawanda, and it is still said that, if not given tobacco, they may take what they can steal. Morgan does not mention tobacco as being the gift to them, but this may be an oversight. An older woman no longer accompanies the Beggars; each Beggar collects for himself. They still dance, having been given gifts.

Although Morgan does not indicate that the dances and games given on the third and fourth days of Midwinter were in response to dreams, they probably were. Again, Morgan probably underestimated the importance of dreaming at this time. His mention of the Fish Dance being given is perhaps significant, for this is the dance my informants seem to miss most on these days. Morgan's inclusion of the dream-guessing rite in his description of these days, which was more important at Tonawanda previously than it is now, is undoubtedly correct.

The other events Morgan mentions as being held on the second day and on the third and fourth days differ in no important respect from those now held on these days. He does omit mention of the Dawn Song and of the circuits of the Feather Dance, Thanksgiving Dance, Bowl Game, and Women's Dance. This may have been due to oversight. On the other hand, it seems likely that these were introduced into the Midwinter ceremonial sometime in the nineteenth century, and it is quite possible that they had not been introduced into the ceremonial at the time of Morgan's writing.

The events Morgan describes for the fifth day are also essentially those of the sixth day at Tonawanda. The white dog is, of course, no longer sacrificed, but the Thanksgiving Speech once said over the white dog is still performed. A brief Rite of Personal Chant now follows this speech, those singing their personal chants being the various leaders in the events of the preceding days. Morgan is apparently describing a comparable practice when he mentions that several Faithkeepers sang thanksgiving songs or chants before the dog was burned. The mention of "people joining in chorus" is probably a reference to the usual accompaniment to personal chants, he: he:, by the men and hand clapping by the women. Then, as now, all went to the longhouse after the tobacco invocation for the Feather Dance. Now no other dances except the Thanksgiving Dance follow the performance of this Feather Dance, but it is not unlikely that they once did. It seems likely that the dances Morgan mentioned were social dances; in the old days when more people took part and it was not necessary to go to town and buy supplies (many people at Tonawanda now take advantage of this lull in ritual activity to shop), it is not unlikely that the people attending amused themselves by dancing social dances.

The rituals of the sixth and succeeding days also differ in no important respects from present practice. Morgan indicates that the Four Sacred Rituals were given in the order: Feather Dance—fifth day, Thanksgiving Dance—sixth day, Rite of Personal Chant and Bowl Game—seventh day.

Although this is somewhat unlike present Tonawanda practice (both the Feather and Thanksgiving Dances are given on the fifth day and both the Rite of Personal Chant and Bowl Game on the sixth), the order is the same. Morgan himself indicates that former practice was to devote a separate day to each of these rituals for the Green Corn ceremony (Morgan 1901[1]:191–96, 233) and this is also suggested by modern practice: the similar order in other longhouses suggests that at one time a day was devoted to each of the Four Sacred Rituals, and that in the process of shortening the ceremonial the various longhouses made different choices as to which of these ceremonies to include on the same day.

Other rituals now given on these last days of Midwinter are not included in Morgan's brief description: the announcement of new names after the Feather Dance, the social dances in the evening on those days when the Bowl Game is played, the Our Life Supporter Dances at the end of the ceremonial, or the Husk Face rite (Morgan virtually ignores the Husk Faces in his description).

CHANGES INTRODUCED INTO THE MIDWINTER CEREMONIAL
DURING THE NINETEENTH AND TWENTIETH CENTURIES

It seems likely that at one time both the Green Corn and Midwinter ceremonials were solstice ceremonies and that their specific associations with the solstices were forgotten as the two ceremonials came to be identified with two seasons of relative plenty: the time following the ripening of corn, the staple cultivated food, and the time following the fall hunt, the principle hunt of the year. In their turn, these associations with agriculture and hunting are being lost as the basic subsistence activities of the Iroquois are changing. Something of this process can be ascertained at Tonawanda: now in setting the date for the Green Corn ceremony the date of the State Fair is uppermost in the minds of the people, not when the corn is first ripe. Similarly, a story is told at Tonawanda that one year the Green Bean ceremony was put off so long that it was only with some difficulty that the beans for the feast were obtained.

The association of the Midwinter ceremonial with the fall hunt has also become obscured. At the time of Handsome Lake and for some years after, the Midwinter ceremonial was held after the fall hunt and a special final hunt to obtain meat for the feast preceded the ceremonial. Later, as hunting became less important and it was no longer possible to obtain supplies for the feast in this manner, other methods came to be used. The first modification seems to have been to collect the needed supplies by going around the houses collecting gifts from the households. Later, as this method became inadequate, money to buy supplies was collected by individuals who did jobs for pay and gave "socials." This was older practice at Tonawanda and is still that at the Sour Springs Longhouse. Now at Tonawanda a similar method, but one perhaps reflecting more recent conditions is used: the money necessary to buy the feast foods is raised at a summer Field Day open to both whites and Indians.

The old method of setting the date of Midwinter by observation of the Pleiades and the moon served to place the ceremonial after the fall hunt, although there may also be an ancient association of the ceremonial with the Pleiades: in what was probably the comparable Aztec ceremonial, the new fire was kindled as the Pleiades approached the zenith (Prescott 1843[1]:125–27).

Now, in part as a result of disagreements engendered by this method of setting the date and in part probably also because of the availability of printed calendars, the date is set by referring to these printed calendars.

Like other solstice ceremonies such as those of the Pueblos in the American Southwest, the Iroquois Midwinter and Green Corn ceremonies are similar in form—a not unexpected result of the similar concern of both ceremonials. Both are concerned with the apparent change in the movement of the sun north and south, that is, to and

away from the people and their land. The principal difference between the summer and winter ceremonials may also be grounded in
the nature of the solstices. The greater complexity of the winter solstice results from the addition of rites that mark the winter solstice
as the beginning of the New Year; the winter solstice marks the beginning of the warming of the earth and the beginning of the renewal
of life on the earth.

Since Handsome Lake undoubtedly added the Four Sacred Rituals to both the Green Corn and Midwinter ceremonials, it might be
concluded that the present similarities of these two ceremonials are
the result of an accident of relatively recent history. However, the
probable ancient association of these ceremonies with the solstices
and the similarity of the summer and winter solstice ceremonies in
other cultures suggests that the Green Corn and Midwinter ceremonials were also similar in some respects before the time of Handsome Lake and that Handsome Lake, in "adding" the Four Sacred
Rituals to both the Green Corn and Midwinter ceremonials, was
merely substituting these rites for others that were already present
in both. The historical documents neither confirm or deny such an
interpretation. With the exception of Halliday Jackson, who indicates that the Green Corn and Midwinter ceremonials of the Allegheny River Seneca were similar just before Handsome Lake's first
vision, and a mention of the Green Corn ceremony by Mary Jemison
that probably refers to the period before Handsome Lake, the historical documents are silent regarding even the presence of the Green
Corn ceremony in the Iroquois ritual calendar let alone the nature
of the ritual.

Although it is impossible to know what rites the Four Sacred
Rituals are substitutes for, it seems likely that, if in fact they are substitutes, they are substitutes for rites that had associations with the
sun. Such is indicated in the evidence that the Four Sacred Rituals
once had war associations, as well as the evidence that the Green
Corn and Midwinter ceremonials once had stronger associations with
the solstices. Among the Iroquoians, as among other North American Indians, the sun had war associations. Apparently, for example,
the Hurons killed previously tortured captives at daybreak (Tooker
1964:36–38) to honor the sun. In the course of the centuries following contact of the Iroquois with white Christians, the Iroquois sun

deity seems to have become partly identified with the Creator—a relatively new idea to the Iroquois. Handsome Lake's substitution of the Four Sacred Rituals, then, may have served to de-emphasize the sun and enhance the Creator as the important deity in the Iroquois pantheon.

The evidence also suggests that when the Four Sacred Rituals were added to the Green Corn and Midwinter ceremonials a separate day was devoted to each of the four. For example, Morgan (1901[1]:196), in his account of practice at the Sand Hill Longhouse in the 1840's, stated that though once each of the Four Sacred Rituals was given on a separate day, at that time the Rite of Personal Chant and Bowl Game were given on the same day. A similar process of combining two of the Four Sacred Rituals into a single day's ritual seems to have occurred in other longhouses with the result that the ceremonials have been shortened by one or two days. Table 1 summarizes the available data.

In fact, a comparison of present practice alone suggests both that the Four Sacred Rituals were added as a unit and that at one time each was performed on a separate day. If each of these rituals had been introduced separately, it seems unlikely that the order would be the same in all the longhouses. Yet, if the order in which the rites are given on a particular day is ignored, the order in which the Four Sacred Rituals are performed is the same: Feather Dance, Thanksgiving Dance, Rite of Personal Chant, and Bowl Game. And, if they had been combined very soon after the Four Sacred Rituals had been added by Handsome Lake, it seems likely that the combinations would have been the same in all or most of the longhouses.

The rituals distinctive to Midwinter are those that are or were renewal ones, rites that appropriately mark the beginning of a New Year. The first of these, the ashes-stirring rites, do not now have strong renewal connotations, but there is some evidence that they once did: they seem to be survivals of an old New Fire rite. The documentary evidence suggests that such a rite of extinguishing old fires and rekindling new ones was still practiced in at least some longhouses in the earlier part of the nineteenth century, although by the end of the nineteenth century, this rite seems to have generally become merely one of ashes-stirring. The practice of parties composed of members of the same moiety going through the houses to stir the

TABLE I. ORDER OF THE FOUR SACRED RITUALS IN VARIOUS WESTERN IROQUOIS LONGHOUSES

	Tonawanda Longhouse	*Newtown Longhouse*	*Coldspring and Sour Springs Longhouses*	*Canadian Onondaga and Tonawanda Sand Hill Longhouses*	*Reconstructed*
FIRST DAY	Feather Dance Thanksgiving Dance	Feather Dance Thanksgiving Dance	Feather Dance	Feather Dance	Feather Dance
SECOND DAY	Bowl Game begun Rite of Personal Chant	Bowl Game Begun	Rite of Personal Chant Thanksgiving Dance	Thanksgiving Dance	Thanksgiving Dance
THIRD DAY	Bowl Game finished	Bowl Game con't.	Bowl Game begun	Rite of Personal Chant Bowl Game begun	Rite of Personal Chant
FOURTH DAY			Bowl Game con't.	Bowl Game con't.	Bowl Game begun

ashes in each seems to be an old practice, being well-established in the nineteenth century and perhaps earlier.

The rites of dream fulfillment and renewal are still quite obviously rites of renewal. However, present practice in respect to these rituals may reflect two divergent, but related traditions: an eastern or Onondaga practice of renewing and fulfilling dreams through a long rite of dream-guessing, and a western or Seneca practice of renewal and fulfillment of dreams through individually sponsored rites, one of which is the dream-guessing ceremony. This difference may well be an old one for the Jesuits in the seventeenth century mention that the dream-guessing ceremony was held annually, and they are silent on this point in respect to other Iroquoians.

In the nineteenth and twentieth centuries there seems to have been a gradual decrease in the number of dreams renewed. In this period also and as a result of changing settlement patterns, the rituals of dream-renewal have come in most instances to be held in the longhouse only. At present, the older practice of fulfilling and renewing dreams through performances circuiting the houses of the community survives most strongly at Tonawanda, but even there the number of houses so visited has declined within memory of living Iroquois.

Other rites were undoubtedly added during the nineteenth century. These include the singing of the Dawn Song at the Newtown and Tonawanda Longhouses on those days devoted to individually sponsored dream fulfillment and renewal rites, and the performance of the Feather Dance, Thanksgiving Dance, Bowl Game, and Women's Dance as stated rites on these days. Since its introduction, the principal change in the Dawn Song seems to have been the time at which it is given; now it is given a few hours after dawn rather than at dawn. But, in general, the timing of Iroquois rituals seems to have gradually changed to approximate a more white-oriented notion of the day's activities. An instance of such change has taken place at Tonawanda within recent times: the present speaker begins the ceremony "on time," that is, when he said it would start and the ceremony is begun early enough so that it is usually concluded about 11 o'clock—an hour early enough to insure a good night's sleep, although the previous speaker often started a few hours late, with the result that the ceremony ended late.

The addition of the Feather Dance, Thanksgiving Dance, Bowl

Game, and Women's Dance to the first portion of Midwinter in the Seneca Longhouses seems to have been suggested by their inclusion in the second portion. The Feather Dance, Thanksgiving Dance, and Bowl Game are, of course, the Four Sacred Rituals with the exception of Personal Chants. The Women's Dance is one, and, if distributional evidence is to be trusted, the oldest dance of the Our Life Supporters ceremony. The particular times at which these rites are given—virtually always a duplication of when they are given on the last days of Midwinter—also suggest their inclusion after the addition of the Four Sacred Rituals to Midwinter.

A Husk Face rite often concludes the individually sponsored dream fulfillment and renewal section of Midwinter, and this suggests that the practice may well be a very old one. However, the inclusion of a Husk Face rite in the second portion of the Seneca ceremonial seems to be a relatively recent one, perhaps suggested by the duplication of the Feather Dance, Thanksgiving Dance, Bowl Game, and Women's Dance in the first section of these ceremonials.

The concluding and prominent part of the first part of the Midwinter ceremonial during much of the nineteenth century was the white dog sacrifice. At one time, this rite seems to have had war connotations and consequently sun associations. There is also a tradition that the sacrifice was in renewal of a dream by the Creator, and was thus a renewal rite. More poetically, renewal implies death and consequently a sacrifice symbolizing death is an appropriate part of a ceremonial stressing renewal.

The white dog sacrifice itself seems to have begun to lapse about 1880. It may have been that at one time each moiety among the western Iroquois and each clan among the Oneida sacrificed a dog, but that over the years each longhouse came to sacrifice only one dog. Finally, even this sacrifice was given up. The evidence indicates that the change was not sudden: for a period of time, the dog was sacrificed in some years, but not others.

Handsome Lake apparently preached against the inclusion of the white dog sacrifice in Midwinter, an admonition that was not followed at the time. It is difficult to know if this admonition had a delayed effect—finally coming to be accepted some eighty years after it was originally made. White observers of the white dog sacrifice during the period when it was being given up mention only that the white dog was or was not burned, and when the last burning occurred. They give no reason for this change other than the usual Indian explanation that the special breed of dogs used in the sacrifice had died out.

In some longhouses, after the white dog sacrifice had been given up, the tobacco invocation that once accompanied the burning of the dog was combined with the Rite of Personal Chant given as one of the Four Sacred Rituals. This change was apparently suggested by the old practice of holding a rite of Personal Chant following the white dog sacrifice.

In sum, although the greatest changes in the Iroquois Midwinter ceremonial during the last two centuries were introduced by the prophet Handsome Lake, other changes have taken place since then. But, despite the changes, the Midwinter ceremonial still continues to be performed—a testament to the vitality of Iroquois culture over many centuries.

Epilogue

The great mission of Handsome Lake was to infuse the traditional Iroquois religion with a new spirit and to adapt it to the changed situation the Iroquois found themselves in at the beginning of the last century. In this, he was successful; many Iroquois found his New Religion attractive and adopted it in place of the older form—an indication that it was suited to the kind of life the Iroquois had to live in the period after the American Revolution. But, although this and other evidence indicates that the religion of Handsome Lake was compatible with Iroquois life of the nineteenth century, is it also compatible with the life that Iroquois must now live of necessity—a life in a world that again has greatly changed? For a century, various observers of Iroquois life have predicted that in the next generation the religion of the Longhouse would die out. Thus far this dire prophecy has not come to pass—in each new generation, a portion of the Iroquois continue to practice the old ceremonies and to believe in the religion of their fathers. Will it continue?

When I first attended the Midwinter ceremonial in 1958, I thought this prediction of the imminent demise of the Iroquois religion to be false. I was most concerned then with gathering information about the ceremonial and learning what took place and the sequence of these events. Faced with the complexity of the ceremonial, I tried to find the patterns in the ritual, believing that there ought to be a simple pattern in the long sequence of these rituals that aided the Longhouse members in remembering what would happen next. True, there was some mention that the houses were no longer as full of people and the dancers going around were not as numerous as they had been in the youth of the older adults. I viewed these observations with skepticism—after all, contrasted with the stark lighting of the present, did not the olden days often appear to have a golden glow? In Elsina's house, where I was a guest, relatives still came to visit and watch the rituals of the troupes that "go around," albeit in smaller numbers than they had in the past. In fact, at the time, it seemed to me that there were many dances, that they came in a continual stream. And, most important, was I not seeing the rituals the Seneca still observed as their grandparents and great-grandparents and ancestors as far back as anyone could remember had done?

Nothing—until 1964—changed my mind. On my occasional visits to the longhouse in the interim, I only observed that the ceremonials were continuing in much the same manner I remembered from my first year's extended stay. As I saw more, I also saw more of the mechanisms used to select and train future leaders of the longhouse, mechanisms that help insure continuity. These confirmed my belief that the ceremonials would continue for at least another generation.

When I observed Midwinter in 1964, my impression was quite different. Outwardly, the forms were the same as those I had observed in previous years. But now, perhaps because I also had a standard against which to compare them, I also came to feel that the ceremonials may be dying. It so happened that the 1964 New Year's was a particularly sad one. The ceremonial, because it looks back over the previous year as well as forward to the coming one, reminds the participants of those who have died during the past twelve months; the deceased are not mentioned by name, but the phrasing of the speeches—the giving of thanks that those there are still alive—serves to recall the recent dead and their absence at this time. And not long before this New Year's, two deaths had occurred; one being that of a younger woman prominent in the longhouse who was related to others active in longhouse affairs. The death had its effect and on occasion during the first several days, those present could be seen weeping, the ritual itself reminding them of their recent loss.

Midwinter of 1964 was different from usual in another respect: it was quite warm for the entire week, a January thaw lasted until the last day of the ceremonial. There was virtually no snow on the ground—a circumstance that afforded a pleasant relief from the usual battles at that time of year with snowfall and snow accumulation whenever one undertook to travel. But a winter snow is also a happy occurrence: it makes one wish to draw up to a fire and, sheltered from the outside world, to enjoy the intimacy of family and close friends in a manner unthought-of in more clement weather. So it is usually during Midwinter. The difficulties of travel—the annoyances of getting stuck in the snow and slipping on the ice—are such that many do not wish to venture out often or far and are content to enjoy the pleasures of the fireside. During the first days of Midwinter when the troupes of dancers circuit the houses near the longhouse, this intimacy can be indulged in. It is quite enough to stay in the kitchen near the stove and wait for the dancers to come through, occasionally glancing out the window to see if anyone is coming down the path in the snow that earlier in the day has been swept for them. The world outside the reservation seems distant indeed, and even the nearby houses seem to be far away. An understanding of why winter is so often a time of ceremonial activity grows in the mind.

But it was not only these occurrences that gave me the overwhelming sense that perhaps the religion of the Longhouse might not survive. Objectively there really were fewer visitors in Elsina's house and fewer groups going around—to the extent that one afternoon we resorted to our individual games of solitaire to while away the time (solitaire because it is a more social activity than the alternative—reading). Thinking back, I realized that my impression of many dancers six years before was exaggerated, that my impression of activity resulted from incessant floor washing—for that year after almost every dance the floor was washed (each group of dancers tracked in snow and if there had been an ashing, ashes were also scattered on the floor). This domestic activity no longer filled in the time between the dances. Elsina, less able to do housework because of age, no longer washed the floor. Was it the same in other houses, and will diminishing numbers of participants finally end the observance of Midwinter?

Some other memories suggest it. While visiting that week in 1964, the telephone would ring occasionally and someone on the other end would inquire of Elsina as to the "doings" in the longhouse. Her position in the community and the location of her home made her a logical person to call for this information. In these conversations, she often remarked, "You should come and learn something," meaning,

"You should come and learn about your ways, the Indian ways."
During that week, also, there was usually no man visiting who could
serve as musician for those who came around to dance. For those
groups that circuit the houses with their own musicians, this is no
problem, and on one occasion, knowing there was no musician at the
house, one was sent over before the troupe itself arrived. The Beggars, however, were not so supplied and, on several occasions, Elsina
herself played for them—beating the stick on the bench with a vigor
that not only provided the accompaniment to their dancing, but also
was an attempt both to make them dance properly (children nowa-
days tend to take the dancing rather lightly) and to make them understand Indian ways, including the language that they did not
speak. This is not standard behavior for a Seneca woman. It was
that of a woman who, in spite of being very much imbued with the
Indian ideal of shyness, was attempting single-handedly to instill the
religion of her people into the children, an obligation that would not
have fallen to her if there were others about.

Such were my impressions, and I too came to feel that something
important was in the process of being lost.

I reflected on this driving into Buffalo. Surely, I decided, the ceremonials will end when too few speak the language. That one factor,
language, was *the* necessary condition for the maintenance of these
rituals—for, after all, are not the rituals conducted only in Seneca
and is not the use of the language dying out? Only a few of the children speak it.

In Buffalo, perspective returned. I discussed the problem with a
friend of mine. I maintained the ceremonials would die with the language. No, I was told, it is not necessary. Have not other religions
survived the demise of the language in which they were given? Has
not Roman Catholicism survived despite the fact that Latin is no
longer spoken by most of the believers? As had Latin, the Seneca
language could become the language of ritual, if not the language of
everyday conversation. This is quite correct, of course. Religion
changes; it does survive though in changed forms. Perhaps also the
religion of the Iroquois will continue to change as it has in the past.
It is change, not death, that is the essence of life.

In 1966, I returned to Tonawanda to see again the Midwinter
ceremonial. This time I stayed with friends in another part of the

reservation. But, Elsina and I had decided to go to Newtown to see the dances there on Sunday. It was the fifth day of Midwinter at Tonawanda and there were no "doings" in the afternoon and evening. Elsina had gotten up early in the morning and made a quantity of soup to take to Cattaraugus. But we did not go. By noontime, the snow was falling so heavily that I took my "pail" of soup down to Elsina's to eat it with her and to tell her I thought we should not go. I left without tarrying long and returned to the house where I was staying. I was lucky to get back. We were snowed in for two days, by what the radio and television were calling the Blizzard of 1966. All of upstate New York was shut down for these two days. It may have been that the doings at the longhouse were the only activities in western New York that took place as planned during those two days.

On October 9, I received a telephone call from Tonawanda saying that Elsina had died two days earlier and that her funeral was the following afternoon. The news itself was not unexpected. Elsina was seventy-six and had some kind of heart condition. But, as is often the case, the timing was such as to be unsettling. I had just returned from a professional meeting in Canada, and such a return always involves a readjustment to home. The process of readjustment was shattered by the call.

Early the next morning I took a plane to Buffalo. I was met at the airport and driven to Tonawanda. After a bite to eat, we went to Elsina's house. It seemed strange. A group of women had worked all day Saturday to clean it—Elsina had not been renowned for her housekeeping. One missed the piles of clothing and such on the tops of bureaus, the newspapers on the floor, the clutter on the kitchen table, the dusty jars in the small rear kitchen. It seemed too neat to be Elsina's house. The mirrors, the pictures in glass frames, and the television screen were covered with cloth, but two framed pictures had been forgotten by the women and one wondered if this would lead to some unknown harm.

Without her ever really saying it—one does not talk about important things—one knew that two things were important to Elsina: her deceased husband, Jesse, and her house. Her belief in Indian ways were important, too, but important only as the context in which the really important things happened. It was in the house, seemingly older than it actually was, in which activities took place and in which one dreamed of how it is to live on the reservation isolated from the nearby town of Akron. It was in this house that one dreamed of how things had been on the reservation for the last hundred years and how they now are—all comforted by the closeness of the longhouse. One looked out the windows from time to time to see what was going on at the longhouse—or rather delighted in guessing what might be going on, for the house is close enough to see certain activities, but not close enough to see everything.

We went through the formalities—the viewing of the body and the speech of the chief. Then Elsina left her beloved house for the last time, accompanied by her relatives. For the last time, she entered the longhouse—by the women's door. Every bench on one side of the longhouse was filled with mourners—most of whom I did not know; Elsina had many friends. There is little one can say about a speech in a language that one does not understand; this speech was the slowest, most hesitant I had ever heard in Seneca. Then we all paid our last respects and left for the cemetery. Although earlier the day had been clear and bright, it rained heavily as we left the longhouse.

Elsina was buried, as she had wished, next to Jesse. Several people reported that they had seen her smile while her body awaited the funeral. It was said that "she was happy to be going where she was going"—to see Jesse. I am inclined to think they were right.

Three months later, in January, it was time for Midwinter again, time to renew the rituals and a time to return thanks for all the beings and things on this earth and above for their existence, and the Midwinter ceremonial was held again in the Tonawanda Longhouse.

Appendix

J. V. H. Clark's Description of the New York
Onondaga Midwinter Ceremonial

(pp. 55–66 of Clark's *Onondaga; or Reminiscences of Earlier and Later Times*)

The fifth or last festival, the crowning one of the year, and the one
to which most importance is attached, is celebrated late in the month of
January, or early in the month of February, according to the phases
of the moon. The Indian year is reckoned by moons, and this great national festival is held in the old moon nearest to the first of our month
February.

The hunters having all returned from the chase, and having brought
in their venison and skins that have been taken, and a portion of these
trophies having been deposited in the council-house, two sets of managers are appointed, numbering from ten to twenty young men on a
side. These are chosen to superintend all the concerns relative to the
grand festival, thanksgiving and sacrifice, which are immediately to
take place. Arrangements are made at the council-house for the reception and accommodation of the whole nation. This being done, the managers are ready to commence their appropriate duties, during the whole
of which they act with great formality, order, and decorum.

On the first day a select number from each party of the managers,
some four or five, start from the council-house, and run with all possible
speed to every cabin in the nation, knocking on the doors and sides of
the houses, informing the people that all things are now ready, and that
they must immediately repair to the council-house and partake of the
festivities of the occasion. At this time, this portion of the committee
of arrangements are nearly naked, covered only by a waistcloth girded
about the loins reaching down nearly to the knee, with moccasins on
their feet, their faces and bodies painted, and plumes upon their heads.
The fire is now extinguished in every cabin, the committee enter the

dwellings (the inmates expecting them), and with a small wooden shovel scatter the ashes about in every direction. The hearths are made clean; new fire is struck from the flint and rekindled; thus they proceed from house to house till every one is visited and purified. During these proceedings, the remaining part of the managers are engaged at the council-house, in firing guns, hallooing, shouting &c., to inform the people that the ceremonies have commenced. They meet all those who come to the festival, greet them most cordially, and conduct them into the council-house.

This is the course pursued on the first day. The second day, the managers assemble early at the council-house, and receive from the master of ceremonies instructions for the day. When ready to depart, several guns are usually fired accompanied by shouting and hallooing. On this day the managers are fantastically dressed, and proceed from house to house with baskets, collecting the gifts of the people with which to grace the festival. These gifts consist of pork, beef, bread, beans, peas, ears of corn, tobacco, savory herbs, small handfuls of straw nicely bound, and every article is received that is useful for food, for incense or for sacrifice. Every one is bound to give something, or he is not to be included in the general absolution. Each manager in his round of alms-gathering, carries a large rattle made of dried tortoise-shell in which are small stones, peas or beans. These they rattle violently in the several cabins, earnestly inviting the people to bestow their gifts. These proceedings are continued for several days, according to the time allotted for the continuance of the festival. During all this time, the people who are assembled at the council-house are engaged in leaping, running, dancing, and their native sports.

On the first of the last three days, the committee cover their faces with masks, dress themselves in old blankets, fragments of old buffalo robes, &c., bedaubing themselves with soot and grease, in which frightful and ludicrous appearance they run from house to house with baskets, crying, "give, give." Every individual who refuses to comply with this reasonable request is saluted with a *rub* from these solicitors, which leaves a mark of disgrace not easily effaced.

While these things are going on, it is supposed they are collecting the sins of the people, and concentrating all the evils of the nation within themselves, which are to be expiated by the approaching sacrifice. On the evening of this day, they hold a most ludicrous dance, called by the white people "the devil's dance," in which they "dance off the witches." Nothing can appear more loathsome and abhorrent than do the participators in this dance. Covered with grease, coal-dust, and soot, dressed in old worn-out rags of blankets, tattered buffalo robes, hair side out, with masks of paper, bark, and husks of corn; add to this the yells and rude music of the savage, and indeed it may well be styled "a dance of devils."

On the day preceding the last, the managers having gathered all the ills of the nation to themselves, and made a full report of all their proceedings to the person who officiates as high priest or master of ceremonies, the day is spent in preparation for the great day of sacrifice which is to take place on the morrow. This day is concluded with demonstrations of joy, festivity and dancing.

The last day, and the one to which most consequence is attached, being the great day of sacrifice, the people assemble at the council-house in great numbers. The exercises commence by building large fires early in the morning, by firing guns and loud hallooing. The wood for the sacrificial offering is arranged near the council-house, by laying near half a cord, in alternate layers crosswise. This is done by a select committee of the managers, who proceed with considerable ceremony.

A house near the council-house is selected as a place in which to make preparation. To this the managers proceed, and prepare themselves for the occasion. One from each party is selected as a leader. They are dressed in long loose shirts of white, and others are appropriately dressed, as managers &c., according to the duties they are expected to perform. The grand master of ceremonies, or high priest, takes his station at the council-house, and to him reports are made of the progress of proceedings, and he in turn gives new directions. Messengers are continually passing and repassing from the council-house to the house of preparation. On the occasion at which notes for this article were taken, the venerable Captain Honnos (*Oh-he-nu*) presided with great dignity. Having arrived at an early hour, we found this gray-headed chief, gravely seated near the center of the council-house, discoursing to his people, receiving messages, and giving directions. One of these messengers, a female, particularly attracted attention. She was dressed throughout in a new suit of fine blue woolen cloth. Her leggings (pantalets) were most fancifully adorned with small white beads and brooches, and the lower part of the skirt, which came below the knee, was ornamented in the same manner. Over the whole was an ample covering of plain blue cloth, sweeping the ground at every step. Upon her seemed to devolve the duty of superintending the feast. She had as associates two young maidens dressed precisely like herself. To these every one gave way, and throughout the ceremonies they were treated with the greatest deference and respect.

About 9 o'clock, the managers rushed out of the house of preparation, and two white dogs fantastically painted with red figures and adorned with small belts of wampum, feathers, and ribbons tied around their necks, legs and tails, followed them. A long rope with a single knot in the center was instantly passed over the head of one of them, when some eight or ten of the managers seized the rope on either side, commenced pulling lustily, each party occasionally yielding to the other, as if to give greater force to their operations. After a few struggles, the dog was suffocated and hung up on a ladder which leaned against the house. The other dog was disposed of in precisely the same manner, and hung beside his fellow. Guns were now fired, and some thirty or forty persons rushed out of the council-house, gave three tremendous yells, and retired. After about half an hour, the dogs were taken down and carried into the house of preparation. To this house spectators were not admitted, and what particular ceremonies were there performed we have no means of knowing.

These dogs are always white, or as nearly so as they can procure them; spot or blemish renders them unsuitable for sacrifice. A wound producing an effusion of blood would be productive of the same consequences.

By some peculiar maneuvering, the sins of the people which had become concentrated in the managers are now transferred to the two individuals who are clad in the white garments. These, by some peculiar ceremony, again work them off into the dogs. These animals, thus laden with the sins of the nation, are raised upon the shoulders of two persons appointed for the purpose (their legs being tied so as to admit of their being slung like a pack). A procession is formed in ranks of double files, preceded by the two men dressed in white, and others of the managers, followed by as many others as may choose to join them. The procession moves slowly and silently with measured step around the house of preparation, through the council-house which has two doors, one opposite the other, and around it. After which, they are brought in, and the dogs laid upon a platform about a foot from the floor. As they enter the council-house for the last time, they break into single file. While these ceremonies were going on at the house of preparation and out of doors, others of importance were observed at the council-house.

The offerings which had been collected were disposed of upon pins around the council-room. The master of ceremonies, during the whole progress of proceedings, remained stationary, seated in the center of the council-room. To him were brought, at different times, at intervals of about two minutes, every article which had been deposited. Every person who brought a piece of pork, a paper of tobacco, a bunch of herbs, or handful of straw, stopped about three paces from him, holding it towards him, looking him full in the face with the greatest attention. After he had said a few words, the old chief took it in his hands, over which he uttered a short ejaculatory prayer or thanksgiving, after which a hearty response was made by all present. It was then returned to the place from which it had been taken. Every article of the offerings was presented and returned in like manner. The females present participated in these ceremonies. All the messengers who addressed the chief halted at a respectful distance, and stood a moment in silence before they made their communications. These events all transpired at the council-house before the dogs were brought in. After the dogs were brought in, the procession, in single file, moved three times around the platform, before they were laid down. At each round, the master of ceremonies rose in a sedate and dignified manner, clapped his hands on the shoulders of the bearer of the dog, who was foremost in the procession. He stopped in the precise position he was in, when the hand of the chief was laid upon his shoulder, and there remained as motionless as a statue, for the space of a minute, during which he was addressed in a whisper by the master of ceremonies. Several other chiefs addressed those who carried the dogs in the same manner, and again the procession moved on. After this the dogs were laid upon the platform, and all joined in loud singing and chanting, while the procession continued slowly moving around the dead carcasses of the dogs, with the most devout solemnity.

While these ceremonies were proceeding in the council-house, fire had been applied to the altar of wood outside. The pile had become nearly half consumed and yielded great heat; while around it, in a circle, had been drawn a line, within which it was not intended spectators should pass. This, however, availed nothing, for the moment the procession had drawn around the fire, the area was crowded to its utmost capacity.

Under the direction of Captain Honnos, the bearers of the dogs again resumed their burdens; a procession was formed in single file, the master of ceremonies taking the lead. Then followed the men in white robes, the persons who carried the dogs, the managers, and others, promiscuously. As the procession moved along, the principal actors in the scene commenced singing, which continued while the whole marched around the council-house to the place of sacrifice. Around the burning pile they moved three several times, the last of which, the master of ceremonies stopped on the west side, with his face to the east and towards the fire. The remainder of the procession formed around the circle; the persons in white being on the left hand of the high priest, and those bearing the dogs near to them.

The leader of ceremonies offered a short prayer to the Great Spirit, a sacrificial chant was sung, the dogs were laid at the feet of the officiating priest, another prayer was offered, another chant was sung, when one of the dogs was cast into the fire by the high priest. A like ceremony was performed and the remaining dog was also thrown upon the burning pile, and again followed the chanting. Different individuals now brought forward baskets of herbs, tobacco, and such like, which were at intervals thrown upon the fire, and with the consuming dogs produced a variety of scents, not easily comprehended. After the dogs were nearly consumed, the procession was again formed and returned to the council-house, and the committee were directed to go to the preparation house. The solemnities of this day being concluded, they formally adjourned. The accustomed ceremonies of this interesting season are usually concluded by a War Dance and feast, on the same day, after the sacrifice. But on this occasion it was adjourned till the following day, when the season of oblations, invocation, sacrifice, and thanksgiving were concluded with the War Dance.

This most singular and interesting of all the Indian ceremonies is worthy of particular remark.

For this important ceremony about thirty young braves were selected, each of whom provided himself with a horse, and left the Indian village alone, and by different ways approached a place previously appointed. When all were gathered at the place agreed upon, painted in the most frightful manner, they mounted on horseback, without saddles, with no clothing except a short and scanty garment extending from the waist nearly to the knee. Each man was armed with a rifle, tomahawk, and scalping knife, and adorned with a bundle of scalps, or something resembling them, hanging from his girdle, and a few rude ornaments besides. They proceeded leisurely along, till within sight of the council-house, when the deafening war-whoop was raised and thrice repeated, and their horses were at once put to their utmost speed. On arriving at the council-house, the horses were speedily tied, the warriors during the time maintaining an air of immovable gravity. They proceeded in a body to the council-room, where the chiefs and aged men, who had all the while been anxiously waiting their return, most cordially received them; asked them what success upon the war-path; how many trophies of victims slain they had secured; of the fortitude of the tortured captives; the snares and ambuscades they had escaped; the feats of daring they had themselves performed; and if they were still willing and resolved again to try their skill and courage, and to strive to add new trophies of valor to enrich their former fame.

All was gone through with in the most solemn and affecting manner. Their stories were told with much gesticulation and earnestness. After the preceding ceremony commenced the War Dance, which, for singularity and effect, and the thrilling animation it imparts to the actors, cannot be surpassed by any rite of modern times. The fantastic figures and devices painted on their almost naked bodies, the rude headdresses and ornaments, consisting of bells, brooches, rings, a profusion of ear and nose jewels, with deers' hoofs dangling about their ankles, gave the performers a most singular and grotesque appearance. Each warrior held in his hand a hatchet, a war-club, or a bow and quiver full of arrows. One of the party was firmly bound to the stove pipe as if to a tree, and personified a prisoner. A young brave, with long false beard and hair of perfect whiteness, represented by his appearance and movements an old and wrinkled man. He approached the supposed prisoner, and with great vehemence and earnestness of manner, addressed him, saying, "his glorious deeds were now at an end—that he must prepare himself for torture by fire—that no mercy could be shown him—that his character for heroism should be established by the fortitude with which he withstood his sufferings." After the old man had finished his speech, the whole party gave the tremendous war-whoop. It seemed as if the lower regions had been suddenly broken up, and that the inhabitants thereof had made a hasty and unceremonious ascent to the earth. The substitute beheld all their mock preparation for his manifest destruction with as much apparent seriousness as if the whole had been real, and appeared as perfectly unconcerned and indifferent to all their movements, as the coldest stoicism could make him. Their rude music now struck up, consisting of blows with a stick upon a barrelhead and a kind of half-drum, accompanied by the voice. It would be utterly impossible to describe the various attitudes in which they presented themselves, and the rapidity of the transition of one posture to another was so sudden, that the eye could not follow them. Look at a man in one position, and instantly his form would be imperceptibly changed to another. During the dance the prisoner was frequently menaced as if to be instantly dispatched with a war-club or hatchet. At another time a bow would be drawn with its arrow to the head, as if death was to be the immediate consequence.

Through the whole he stood as composed as if no threats had been made, and occasionally sung of his own achievements in the wars and of the ignorance of his enemies in the arts of torture. During the dance there was a continual flourishing of war-clubs and hatchets, and an unearthly exhibition of the most horrid grimaces, and protraction of the war-whoop. The warriors exerted themselves to the utmost of their capacity; the sweat rolled from their naked limbs and bodies in profusion; their breasts heaved from excessive fatigue; their nostrils were dilated to an unaccountable extent; their eyes flashed with delight; and their countenances showed the workings of passion intermingled with pleasure, and the whole scene was one of the most perfect enthusiasm and frenzy. Just at the close of the grand drama, which had lasted with short intervals for more than two hours, the prisoner was liberated, his bands having been cut by a stroke from a hatchet. He gazed wildly all around to see if the coast was clear; an opening was made for him to escape, he bounded like a panther to clear the ring, but the war-clubs and hatchets were flourished over his head; the most terrific yells were uttered, and he finally sunk, as if beneath their blows, and personified a dying man in the most perfect manner. An agonizing cry proclaimed his death; the slow, melancholy death song was chanted while the whole party moved solemnly in single file around the apparent dead body of their prostrate prisoner. After this, all passed out into the open air reeking with perspiration as they were, and after a short conversation they severally retired to their homes. After the warriors had left the council-room, the young man who had so really acted the part of a suffering captive gradually raised his head and groaned, as if in excruciating agony; and finally collected himself, passed out, and rejoiced with his companions. After a recess of about an hour large numbers of both sexes, young and old, assembled to participate in the Peace Dance. This interesting ceremony is performed to music without words, and females as well as males engage in it. In the performance, the males form as large a circle as the room will allow, facing inwards, the females then glide shyly into the circle and range themselves forward of the males. After these arrangements are made, the rude music strikes up, and the females proceed by placing their feet close together, then raising their toes, pass them about four inches to the right, and then their heels in the same manner, thus keeping time they pass noiselessly around the circle until the music ceases. During this movement of the females, the males retain their position, beating time with their heels and toes without moving at all, to the right or left.

This course is gone through with several times, which finally closes the dancing for the season.

Early in the morning, previous to the commencement of the War Dance, several large kettles had been placed over the fires in which were cooking the ingredients upon which the whole nation were at liberty to feast. The contents were composed of meat, corn, beans, peas, potatoes, turnips, some garden herbs which served for seasoning and other things which had been previously gathered in the baskets. After the close of the War Dance and the Peace Dance, the feast was made ready by removing the kettles to a convenient distance from the fires.

The mass was frequently stirred till the whole became completely mixed. The contents of the kettles were devoured without regard to politeness or ceremony; some dipped from the kettles with spoons, others skimmed out the more substantial parts, with chips, some were provided with bowls and spoons, while others as soon as the scalding aliment was sufficiently cooled, thrust in their fingers and thus obtained their share. After a reasonable time, the whole had vanished, and all appeared to be refreshed and satisfied. The pipe of peace was now lighted, and the presiding officer of the past ceremonies drew the first draught, puffed the first whiff, and was very careful that a large quantity of smoke should issue from his mouth at a time, which he took great pains to make ascend in graceful curls and watched them with peculiar enjoyment. The pipe was passed from him to the other chiefs present, and from them to the old men, who all partook of it with a commendable relish.

Having concluded the ceremonies of the great festival, and all its requirements being fulfilled, everyone feels himself absolved from the sins of the past year, and forms new resolutions for the time to come. Congratulations are exchanged, and new hopes excited—free from iniquity and resolved to follow the path of evil no more; each one repairs to his home, happy in the propitious commencement of a new year, in perfect readiness to embark in all the operations of war, the chase, the council, or the cabin.

Notes

Part I. Principles of Iroquois Ritualism

1. In fact, so many children on the Tonawanda Reservation do not know Seneca that for a time classes were held to teach them the language. A somewhat similar movement also took place on the Tuscarora Reservation (Graymont 1967), though there are now no longhouses on that reservation.

2. It is perhaps unfortunate that there are so many erudite discussions by college-educated middle-class whites regarding such questions as whether or not Indians should be assimilated. Implicit in many of these discussions is the hope that all Indians will become good upper-middle-class individuals, an expectation that is not possible for the whites themselves. The fact of the matter is that Indians are forced to make adjustments to the changed economic structure of the United States. Many of these adjustments are identical to those of the whites, though others, of course, are not. But, we should not hold unrealistic expectations for the Indians and then damn them if they achieve these goals and damn them if they do not.

It is sometimes said that conservatism "holds the Indians back," that, for example, belief in the religion of the Longhouse impedes the Iroquois's adjustment to the modern world. Such an argument often presumes that the world of the middle-class white person is the best of all possible worlds. It is not, of course. And, the extent of its preposterousness or pretentiousness, as well as its real value, is made clearer by the comments of those who are not full participants in it as many Indians are not. One characteristic of Senecas and of Indians generally is their sense of humor, and it is in their jokes about the white man that the foibles of our culture are most apparent. This may be reason enough to let the Indians alone to pursue their own destiny.

Only the most naive hope for no change in a culture over the course of time. The essential question is merely how much change, what kind, and when. It is perhaps fortunate that we know so little about how to introduce or impede such change, for since many of the wished-for changes do not take place for lack of knowledge of how to do it, Indians are often allowed to take the course they want to.

Not only are many of the suggested changes unworkable, but some also may have really dangerous consequences to ourselves. Abolishing the reservation system—the most frequent suggestion for helping the Indian assimilate —apart from scarcely enhancing our sense of legal morality, would not abolish the fact of cultural difference, the fact that some Indians are and always will be poor, or the fact that, in the course of our history, the Indians have at times been rather shabbily treated. To think otherwise would only harm ourselves.

3. However, New York Onondaga practice is somewhat different in this respect from that reported for the western Iroquois longhouses; Blau (1969) reports that both the dead and the False Faces are mentioned in the Thanksgiving Speech.

4. This is probably a description of the first longhouse at Tonawanda, now said to have been built in 1776, that was located on the flats of the feeder canal to the Barge Canal near the present "Iron Bridge" where the first settlement and the old village was located. This longhouse was moved and rebuilt at its present location in 1876 (Fenton 1941:144).

5. The Tonawanda "kitchen" was built in 1958 primarily as a place where people could be fed at the Six Nations meeting in September when numbers of people visit from other reservations.

6. This is practice as customarily described in the literature. I was told at Tonawanda that the clan mother in consultation with other women of the clan suggest two candidates for chief and the names of these two are presented to the chiefs for approval. If the chiefs do not approve the women's first choice, the second is considered. Usually the chiefs approve one of the two.

7. Parker's description is confusing as it might be read as indicating that the tobacco invocation follows the performance of the War Dance. My informant indicated that first the tobacco invocation is held outside the longhouse, and then all go to the longhouse to dance the War Dance.

Part II. The Structure of the Midwinter Ceremonial

1. During the Green Corn ceremony, Eastern Standard time is followed, not Eastern Daylight time—the two methods of counting time leading to some confusion and to some questions as to whether "old time" or "new time," "slow time" or "fast time" is to be followed in determining when to end the ritual.

2. This whole performance bears some resemblance to Halloween—the dressing up in odd disguise, the request for gifts, the banter between adults and children (who must remain mute) all remind one forcefully of Halloween. In fact, the resemblance is so strong that I consciously have to restrain myself from giving cigarettes to children who appear at my door on the evening of October 31; white mothers of three- and four-year-olds would

hardly appreciate such gifts of tobacco being given to their children in place of the usual candy. There is absolutely no evidence, however, for any historical connection between these two rituals.

3. The Seneca attitude towards gambling is not of the Protestant sort so prevalent in the United States. Gambling is not a sin to the Seneca, but rather on occasion a sacred obligation. Further, the Indians seem less concerned about losing games than do many whites. These attitudes may reflect an Iroquois disinterest in the accumulation of material things, an attitude given some sanction by Handsome Lake, who said that one should not be concerned with material possessions. At least, in my limited experience among the Seneca, it has been expressions of this casualness towards material possessions that gave me my most severe cases of "culture shock"—those occasions where the differences between my white Anglo-Saxon Protestant heritage and Seneca culture were most painfully apparent. It should be noted, however, that Handsome Lake condemned card playing.

4. I find that not all know that the customary seating by sex is disregarded on this morning in favor of seating by moiety, and so suspect that this blackening has not been done in recent years, though by all accounts it once was.

5. One feels, though such impressions as these are not of the sort that can be confirmed by informants, that the choice may fall on a man who is a poor speaker, but who is well-liked, for the humor that this choice may engender; or on a man who for one reason or another has potentialities for becoming a speaker in the longhouse as this gives him experience in "public speaking"; or on a man who for some other reason should be singled out for attention that year, such as recent renewed interest in Longhouse religion activities, or some combination of such factors. Who is chosen, then, becomes something of more than routine interest.

6. It may be of some minor interest that when I was "adopted" into the Beaver clan, the speaker deemed it appropriate that this adoption not take place at this point in the evening's activities, but at the very end. Such names given to whites now are not names belonging to the clan, but made-up names, although in the past they were apparently names belonging to the clan.

7. At several points, Shimony's (1961:173–91) description does not agree with Speck's outline of the ceremonial (Speck 1949:34–35), and in these instances Speck's outline does not agree with the description in the body of the text and in the appendix. In the following, Shimony's description and that in Speck's text and appendix have been used where these discrepancies exist.

8. In 1945, apparently various dances were also held on this day, and after they were concluded, the longhouse was scrubbed (Witthoft 1946:31–33). In 1933, the Feather Dance was given on this day (Speck 1949:35, 145 n; 180–81).

9. David Boyle attended parts of the Midwinter ceremonial at the Seneca Longhouse on the Six Nations Reserve in 1898 and published an incomplete

description of the ritual. In many ways, it is a tantalizing one—more complete in its account of certain details than many descriptions of Midwinter, but lacking mention of many crucial rituals of the ceremonial.

The best part of Boyle's (1898) description is that which recounts the burning of the white dog and the dances and other rituals of the dream-fulfillment segment of Midwinter the night before. Much else is either glossed over or omitted. According to Boyle, the Midwinter ceremonial began on the first day after the new moon occurring at the end of January and beginning of February (i.e., some preliminaries began; five days after the February new moon, the ceremonial proper began), runners were sent out to summon the people to the longhouse for what would appear to be a recitation of the "Code of Handsome Lake" and a rite of confession. At least, on these three or four days following the new moon "preachers" exhorted the people respecting their behavior and talked of the "goodness of the Master of Life or the Great Spirit" (a statement that easily serves as a brief characterization of the Code of Handsome Lake), and people made brief speeches in which they confessed their shortcomings. The following five days were devoted to songs, dances, dream interpretations (i.e., dream guessing), and ashing, and the last of these days the white dog was killed and burned.

All of this is familiar Iroquois practice; the ritual of the recitation of the "Code of Handsome Lake" and the confession of sins preceding Midwinter are well-known, if now often optional, preparations for the ceremonial, and the days of dream fulfillment before the burning of the white dog are also customary procedure.

What Boyle said happens next is not usual Iroquois practice. He states that on the day following the burning of the white dog, two runners (probably the Uncles) went through the houses scattering ashes and summoning people to the longhouse on the next day to stir the ashes. On that day, after the people had assembled in the longhouse, the runners stirred the ashes, and the speaker gave the Thanksgiving Speech. The people, divided into their respective moieties, then stirred the ashes. During this ashes-stirring rite, the exit from the longhouse and counterclockwise circuit entering by the opposite door described by Boyle is much as Shimony (1961:177) describes the same ritual for the Sour Springs Longhouse. After the ashes-stirring ritual, the next night's proceedings were announced: the Feather and Thanksgiving Dances.

This description—if true—would indicate that the Grand River Seneca Longhouse practice was unlike that of other longhouses. (Practice now at the Seneca Longhouse is much like that at the other longhouses [Michael K. Foster: personal communication].) It is possible, however, that Boyle misinterpreted his informants: he says that he was not present at this part of the ceremonial and his informants may have been telling him what happened the week before. It is possible, for example, that Boyle was told that the runners went around on Tuesday (the white dog was burned on Monday, January 31, 1898), and he took this to mean Tuesday, February 1, rather than Tuesday,

January 25 as intended. As the ceremonial probably lasted ten days this is a possible source of confusion. This would mean that the Uncles stirred ashes around the houses on Tuesday, January 25; in the longhouse on Wednesday, January 26; the following days being devoted to dream fulfillment, ending late Sunday night–early Monday morning, January 30–31.

It may be of some interest that Speck (1949:95 *n*) states that at the Seneca Longhouse (but not at the Sour Springs Longhouse) a Husk Face rite is held at the end of the medicine society rites on the fourth day. This performance has some resemblance to the New York Seneca ones, and gives some confirmation to the suggestion that this practice is an old one, at least among the Seneca.

PART III. The Midwinter Ceremonial in Historical Perspecitve

1. Hewitt (1910a:719; 1928:468) says that *Agatkonchoria* means "masked face."

2. The reference here is probably to Mardi Gras (Shrove Tuesday), indicating again that the *ononharia* was customarily given yearly in the month of February.

3. See especially Wallace (1952:47–51) for these dates. Although later accounts of the visions of Handsome Lake imply that the Prophet was given these messages in a single vision, the journals of Halliday Jackson and Henry Simmons (Wallace 1952) indicate that Handsome Lake had three in 1799–1800 that formed the basis of his Good Message. The journal of the third member of this group, Joel Swayne, has not been found. All three men were living in these years among the Senecas on the Allegheny River, Henry Simmons at the Cornplanter settlement where Handsome Lake also was living.

4. I am indebted to Marian E. White for bringing this reference to my attention.

5. Houghton (1920:130–31) noted: "Mr. Buckingham, in 1813, witnessed in Rochester a 'White Dog Dance,' the yearly sacrifice such as was noted by Mr. Hyde in 1820. It included dances and a feast identical in every particular with those now held every mid-winter on the Cattaraugus Reservation, and also the sacrifice of the white dog, the distinguishing rite of this ceremony." The Mr. Buckingham mentioned by Houghton is probably J. S. Buckingham, who toured the United States in 1837–38, arriving in Rochester August 25, 1838, and leaving September 5, 1838 (Buckingham 1841[3]:45, 98). After his return to England, he published an account of his travels in which he included much information he had gained through his extensive reading. In this account, Buckingham (1841[3]:51–52) included O'Reilly's material, citing him. Houghton, then, merely misconstrued this reference to mean that Buckingham actually saw the ceremonial.

Houghton's reference to Mr. Hyde is probably to Jabez Backus Hyde, a missionary who wrote an account of his experiences in 1820 which was published in 1903. Hyde (1903:242) states: "They have annually the feast of first fruits, the feast of ingathering, the feast of atonement or yearly sacrifice, a feast in the Spring in which they present the different seeds they purpose to plant." This mention of a "feast of atonement or yearly sacrifice" by Hyde is probably what Houghton refers to. There is no other mention of a Midwinter ceremonial in Hyde's narrative.

6. Asher Wright (Fenton 1957:307) also said that the white dog provided clothing for the Creator: "The devil being thus disposed of, God soon after thought it best to leave the world and take up his abode in heaven, but because he was born here on earth, the people call him, 'Our son.' And they say, 'Our son in heaven likes to smoke,' and so they offer him, at their yearly festival, the incense of burning tobacco; and in like manner they say, 'Our son needs a new coat,' and they burn the white dog in sacrifice, that he may clothe himself in the skies with the skin, and tie them upon the deer's hoof rattles worn around the ankle in the dance, and then they say, 'Our son is with us, for here is a piece of his garment.' "

7. See Fenton (1945:91–92) for identification of this village.

8. M. H. Deardorff (personal communication) suggests that "seven" is a misreading of "several" in the now lost original manuscript.

9. The following is quoted with permission of the University of Rochester. I am indebted to Henrietta Blueye for helping me read Morgan's handwriting.

10. Among the Seneca and Onondaga, each of the two dogs represented a moiety. As the Oneida have only three clans and moieties are not important, each of these three dogs seems to have represented a clan.

11. Two copies of Samuel Kirkland's journal for 1800 (designated as 1800B and 1800D) now in the Hamilton College Library, contain a description of the white dog sacrifice at the end of the journal. The 1800B journal is followed here rather than the 1800D journal which also contains the same material; it seems to be a copy, somewhat edited, of the 1800B journal. I have made certain changes in punctuation, capitalization, and spelling for purposes of readability. Kirkland liberally uses dashes instead of other forms of punctuation, omits periods, strews commas about, and capitalizes certain words no longer capitalized. It seems unwise to burden the reader with these difficulties in reading, especially as Hamilton College is planning to publish a definitive edition of the Kirkland papers. It is often difficult to read Kirkland's spelling of Oneida words in the manuscripts, and for many words the reading given here is only one of several possible interpretations.

12. The second and third editions of *Webster's New International Dictionary* define *nothingarian* as "one of no belief, creed, or particular sect." Apparently, it was a word more frequently used in the nineteenth than in the twentieth century. Kirkland seems to be saying in this passage that many of those who wished to have the dog sacrifice performed were neither those who were Christians nor those who took an active part in the Iroquois rituals.

13. It may be of some interest to note that comments similar to that con-

tained in this sentence by Jackson are made today on the Tonawanda Reservation about the ceremonial behavior now as contrasted to that in the previous generation.

14. Although Morgan visited Tonawanda at the time of the Midwinter ceremonial in 1846, it is not clear from his manuscript journals (n.d., Vol. 1, No. 1) how much of the ceremony he saw. His journals for this trip contain only the information that he saw the white dog hanging on a pole before the longhouse and an account of an interview with Jimmy Johnson on the ceremony. This latter contains no information not in Morgan's published account with the exception that Johnson said that the Religious Dance (i.e., the Feather Dance) was performed on the third day. It is also quite brief. Later in the journals there are similar brief descriptions of the ceremonial, and they also are of the sort that a field worker might obtain if he knew little about the ceremonial. This suggests that perhaps Morgan's description is not based on observation of the ceremonial in 1846, but on Ely Parker's description of it to Morgan sometime after October, 1846.

Bibliography

Abrams, George. "Moving of the Fire: A Case of Iroquois Ritual Innova-
tion." In *Iroquois Culture, History, and Prehistory: Proceedings of
the 1965 Conference on Iroquois Research,* edited by Elisabeth Tooker,
pp. 23–24. Albany: New York State Museum and Science Service, 1967.
Alden, Timothy. *An Account of Sundry Missions Performed among the
Senecas and Munsees.* New York, 1827.
Bartram, John. *Observations on the Inhabitants, Climate, Soil, Rivers, Pro-
ductions, Animals, and Other Matters Worthy of Notice.* London, 1751.
Reprint. Rochester: George Perkins Humphrey, 1895.
Beauchamp, W. M. "The Iroquois White Dog Feast." *American Antiquarian*
7 (1885): 235–39.
———. "Onondaga Customs." *Journal of American Folklore* 1 (1888): 195–
203.
———. "Iroquois Notes." *Journal of American Folklore* 4 (1891): 39–46.
———. "The Early Religion of the Iroquois." *American Antiquarian* 14:
(1892): 344–49.
———. "Onondaga Notes." *Journal of American Folklore* 8 (1895): 209–16.
———. "The New Religion of the Iroquois." *Journal of American Folklore*
10 (1897): 169–80.
———. "Civil, Religious and Mourning Councils and Ceremonies of Adoption
of the New York Indians." *New York State Museum Bulletin* 113
(1907): 341–451.
———. *Moravian Journals relating to Central New York, 1745–66.* Syracuse,
1916.
Biggar, H. P., ed. *The Works of Samuel de Champlain.* 6 vols. Toronto,
1929.
Blau, Harold. "Dream Guessing: A Comparative Analysis." *Ethnohistory*
10 (1963): 233–49.
———. "The Iroquois White Dog Sacrifice: Its Evolution and Symbolism."
Ethnohistory 11 (1964): 97–119.
———. "Function and the False Faces: A Classification of Onondaga Masked
Rituals and Themes." *Journal of American Folklore* 79 (1966): 564–80.

179

——. "Notes on the Onondaga Bowl Game." In *Iroquois Culture, History, and Prehistory: Proceedings of the 1965 Conference on Iroquois Research*, edited by Elisabeth Tooker, pp. 35–49. Albany: New York Museum and Science Service, 1967.

——. "Calendric Ceremonies of the New York Onondaga." Ph.D. dissertation, New School for Social Research, 1969.

Boyle, David. "The Pagan Iroquois." *Annual Archaeological Report*, Minister of Education, Ontario, 1898: 54–196.

Brush, Edward Hale. *Iroquois, Past and Present*. Buffalo, 1901.

Buckingham, J. S. *America, Historical, Statistic, and Descriptive*. 3 vols. London, 1841.

Campbell, William W. *Annals of Tryon County; or, the Border Warfare of New-York, During the Revolution*. New York, 1841.

Caswell, Harriet S. *Our Life among the Iroquois Indians*. Boston, 1892.

Chafe, Wallace L. "Seneca Thanksgiving Rituals." *Bureau of American Ethnology Bulletin 183*, 1961.

——. "Handbook of the Seneca Language." *New York State Museum and Science Service Bulletin 388*, 1963.

——. "Linguistic Evidence for the Relative Age of Iroquois Religious Practices." *Southwestern Journal of Anthropology* 20 (1964): 278–85.

Charlevoix, P. F. X. de. *History and General Description of New France*. John Gilmary Shea, trans., 1870. Reprint. Chicago: Loyola University, 1962.

Clark, Joshua V. H. *Onondaga; or Reminiscences of Earlier and Later Times*. 2 vols. Syracuse, 1849.

Conklin, Harold C., and William C. Sturtevant. "Seneca Singing Tools at the Coldspring Longhouse." *Proceedings of the American Philosophical Society* 97 (1953): 262–90.

Converse, Harriet Maxwell. "The Seneca New-Year Ceremony and Other Customs." *Indian Notes, Heye Foundation* 7 (1930): 69–89.

Cook, Frederick. *Journals of the Military Expedition of Major Gen. John Sullivan Against the Six Nations Indians in 1779*. Auburn, N.Y., 1887.

Crowell, Samuel P. "The Dog Sacrifice of the Seneca." In *Indian Miscellany*, edited by W. W. Beach, pp. 323–32. Albany, 1877. Reprint. *Primitive Heritage*, edited by Margaret Mead and Nicolas Calas, New York, 1953.

Deardorff, Merle H. "The Religion of Handsome Lake: Its Origin and Development." *Bureau of American Ethnology Bulletin* 149 (1951): 77–107.

Deardorff, Merle H. and George S. Snyderman, eds. "A Nineteenth Century Journal of a Visit to the Indians of New York." *Proceedings of the American Philosophical Society* 100 (1956): 582–612.

Doty, Lockwood L. *A History of Livingston County, New York*. Geneseo, N.Y., 1876.

Driver, Harold E., and William C. Massey. "Comparative Studies of North American Indians." *Transactions of the American Philosophical Society*, n.s. 47 (1957) (2).

Dwight, Timothy. *Travels; in New-England and New-York*. 4 vols. New Haven, 1821–22.

Fenton, William N. "An Outline of Seneca Ceremonies at Coldspring Longhouse." *Yale University Publications in Anthropology* 9 (1936).

——. "The Seneca Society of Faces." *Scientific Monthly* 44 (1937) : 215–38.

——. "Masked Medicine Societies of the Iroquois." *Annual Report of the Board of Regents of the Smithsonian Institution for 1940:* 397–430.

——. "Tonawanda Longhouse Ceremonies: Ninety Years after Lewis Henry Morgan." *Bureau of American Ethnology Bulletin* 128 (1941) : 139–66.

——. "Songs from the Iroquois Longhouse." *Smithsonian Publication* 3691 (1942).

——. "Place Names and Related Activities of the Cornplanter Senecas." *Pennsylvania Archaeologist* 15 (1945) : 25–29, 42–50, 88–96, 108–18; 16 (1946) : 42–57.

——. "The Iroquois Eagle Dance: An Offshoot of the Calumet Dance." *Bureau of American Ethnology Bulletin* 156 (1953).

——. "Seneca Indians by Asher Wright." *Ethnohistory* 4 (1957) : 302–21.

——. "The Seneca Green Corn Ceremony." *The Conservationist* 18 (1963) (2) : 20–22.

——. ed. *Parker on the Iroquois. Iroquois Use of Maize and Other Food Plants; The Code of Handsome Lake, The Seneca Prophet; The Constitution of the Five Nations.* Syracuse: Syracuse University Press, 1968.

Graymont, Barbara. "Problems of Tuscarora Language Survival." In *Iroquois Culture, History, and Prehistory: Proceedings of the 1965 Conference on Iroquois Research,* edited by Elisabeth Tooker, pp. 27–29. Albany: New York State Museum and Science Service, 1967.

——. "The Tuscarora New York Festival." *New York History* 50 (1969) : 143–64.

Hale, Horatio. "The Iroquois Sacrifice of the White Dog." *American Antiquarian* 7 (1885) : 7–14.

Hewitt, J. N. B. "New Fire among the Iroquois." *American Anthropologist* 2 (1889) : 319.

——. "Teharonhiawagon." *Bureau of American Ethnology Bulletin* 30 (1910[a]) (2) : 718–23.

——. "White Dog Sacrifice." *Bureau of American Ethnology Bulletin* 30 (1910[b]) (2) : 939–44.

——. Abstract of "The White-dog Feast of the Iroquois" published as part of the Proceedings of the Anthropological Society of Washington Meeting, March 29, 1910. *American Anthropologist* 12 (1910[c]) : 86–87.

——. "Iroquoian Cosmology; Second Part." *Bureau of American Ethnology Annual Report* 43 (1928) : 449–819.

Houghton, Frederick. "History of the Buffalo Creek Reservation." *Buffalo Historical Society Publications* 24 (1920) : 1–181.

Hyde, Jabez Backus. "A Teacher among the Senecas: Historical and Personal Narrative of Jabez Backus Hyde, Who Came to the Buffalo Creek

Mission in 1811, Written in 1820." *Buffalo Historical Society Publications* 6 (1903) : 239–74.

Jackson, Halliday. *Civilization of the Indian Natives.* Philadelphia, 1830(a).

——. *Sketch of the Manners, Customs, Religion and Government of the Seneca Indians, in 1800.* Philadelphia, 1830(b).

Jesuit Relations and Allied Documents (JR). See Thwaites, Reuben Gold.

Kirkland, Samuel. "Journals." Manuscripts in the Hamilton College Library, n.d.

Kluckhohn, Clyde, and Leland C. Wyman. "An Introduction to Navaho Chant Practice." *American Anthropological Association Memoir* 53 (1940).

Kurath, Gertrude P. "Onondaga Ritual Paradies." *Journal of American Folklore* 67 (1954) : 404–406.

——. "Iroquois Music and Dance: Ceremonial Arts of Two Seneca Longhouses." *Bureau of American Ethnology Bulletin* 187 (1964).

Mandelbaum, David G., ed. *Selected Writings of Edward Sapir in Language, Culture, and Personality.* Berkeley and Los Angeles: University of California Press, 1949.

Megapolensis, Johannes, Jr. "A Short Account of the Mohawk Indians . . . 1644." In *Narratives of New Netherland, 1609–1664,* edited by J. Franklin Jameson, pp. 163–80. New York, 1909.

Morgan, Lewis H. *League of the Ho-de-no-sau-nee or Iroquois.* 2 vols. New York, 1901. Reprint. New Haven: Human Relations Area Files, 1954.

——. "Journals." Manuscript in the University of Rochester Library, n.d.

O'Reilly [O'Rielly], Henry. *Settlement in the West: Sketches of Rochester.* Rochester, N.Y., 1838.

Parker, Arthur C. "The Code of Handsome Lake, the Seneca Prophet." *New York State Museum Bulletin* 163 (1913). Available in Fenton's *Parker on the Iroquois.*

Parkman, Francis. *The Jesuits in North America.* 1867. Reprint. Boston: Little, Brown, 1963

Prescott, William H. *History of the Conquest of Mexico.* 3 vols. New York, 1843.

Seaver, James E. *A Narrative of the Life of Mrs. Mary Jemison.* 1824. Reprint. Corinth Books, 1961.

Shimony, Annemarie Anrod. "Conservatism among the Iroquois at the Six Nations Reserve." *Yale University Publications in Anthropology* 65 (1961).

Skinner, Alanson. "Some Seneca Masks and their Uses." *Indian Notes, Heye Foundation* 2 (1925) : 191–207.

Smith, De Cost. "Witchcraft and Demonism of the Modern Iroquois." *Journal of American Folklore* 1 (1888) : 184–94.

Smith, Erminnie A. "Myths of the Iroquois." *Bureau of American Ethnology Annual Report* 2 (1883) : 47–116.

Speck, Frank G. *Midwinter Rites of the Cayuga Long House.* Philadelphia, 1949.

Swanton, John R. "Sacrifice." *Bureau of American Ethnology Bulletin* 30 (1910) (2) : 402–407.

Thwaites, Reuben Gold, ed. *The Jesuit Relations and Allied Documents*. 73 vols. Cleveland, 1896–1901.

Tooker, Elisabeth. "The Iroquois Defeat of the Huron: A Review of Causes." *Pennsylvania Archaeologist* 33 (1963) : 115–23.

———. "An Ethnography of the Huron Indians, 1615–1649." *Bureau of American Ethnology Bulletin* 190 (1964).

———. "The Iroquois White Dog Sacrifice in the Latter Part of the Eighteenth Century." *Ethnohistory* 2 (1965) : 129–40.

———. "On the New Religion of Handsome Lake." *Anthropological Quarterly* 41 (1968) : 187–200.

Wallace, Anthony F. C., ed. "Halliday Jackson's Journal to the Seneca Indians, 1798–1800." *Pennsylvania History* 19 (1952) : 117–47, 325–49. Reprint. Pennsylvania Historical and Museum Commission.

Waugh, F. W. "Iroquois Foods and Food Preparation." *Canada Department of Mines, Geological Survey Memoir* 86 (1916).

Whittaker, Jane. "Narrative of the Captivity of Mrs. Jane Whittaker, Daughter of Sevastian Strope, a Revolutionary Soldier." *Quarterly Journal of New York State Historical Association* 11 (1930) : 237–51.

Witthoft, John. "Cayuga Midwinter Festival." *New York Folklore Quarterly* 2 (1946) : 24–39.

Index

Agriculture, 3, 8, 147
Alden, Timothy, 19
Allegeny Reservation. *See* Coldspring Longhouse
Alligator Dance, 26
Animals, 8, 11
Ashes-stirring rites, 43–46, 49–52, 67, 71, 75–78, 101–102, 128–29, 132–33, 136–37, 149
Aztec Indians, 83

Bartram, John, 18
Bean Dance, 26, 75, 79, 82
Beans. *See* Life Supporters
Bear disguise, 133
Bear Society, 16, 54, 57–58
Beauchamp, W. M., x, 102, 109, 114, 118
Beggar Faces, 28, 42–43, 45, 53–54, 58, 62, 71–72, 114–45
Bigheads, 24, 30, 41–45, 50–53, 59, 67, 70–71, 76, 78, 80, 108, 135–37, 144
Birds, 8, 11–12
Blacksmith (Oneida Indian), 116
Blacksmith (Seneca Indian), 113
Blau, Harold, 91, 102
Bone game, 26
Bowl game, 24, 26, 31–35, 39–40, 44–49, 51, 55–56, 58–63, 66–75, 77–80, 82, 105–106, 115, 117, 143, 148–53
Brant, Joseph, 111, 116
Brodhead, Daniel, 112
Buffalo Society, 16, 54, 58
Bush ceremony, 75, 77, 78

Campbell, Jane, 109
Campbell, William, 114
Canadeseago, 109
Canandiagua, 110–11
Carheil, Father, 86
Caswell, Harriet, 107–108
Cat Nation, 89–90
Cattaraugus Reservation. *See* Newtown Longhouse
Caughnawauga Reserve, 1, 104
Chafe, Wallace L., 7, 9, 25, 83
Champlain, Samuel de, 84
Changing Ribs dance, 16
Chanters-for-the-dead, 4, 16, 28, 35
Charm Holders, Society of, 16
Chenesee, 111
Cherokee Dance, 26
Cherry Valley massacre, 109
Chicken dance, 26
Chiefs: duties of, 21–22; selection of, 22, 24–25
Choose-a-partner dance, 26
Christianity, 3, 4, 21, 27, 116
Clairvoyant, 17, 33, 34
Clan, 22–24, 77, 80–81, 137
Clark, Joshua V. H., 107–108
Coldspring Longhouse, 1, 5, 22, 24, 28, 34–35, 39, 44–45, 47, 57, 69–74, 104, 112–13, 144
Condolence ceremony, 16, 22
Confession of sins, 31, 34, 40, 42, 79–80, 124, 135
Conklin, Harold C., 27–28
Converse, Harriet, 107–108
Corn. *See* Life Supporters

185

Plank Road Longhouse, 24
Planting ceremony, 16, 48, 69, 79
Pleiades, 39–40, 147
Pole dance, 124
Pygmy society, 16

Quavering dance, 16
Quiver dance. *See* Stomp dance

Rabbit dance, 26
Raccoon dance, 26
Raspberry ceremony, 75
Rattles, 27–28, 54, 57, 125, 129, 132
Riddles. *See* Dream-guessing rite
Robin dance, 26
Rochester, N. Y., 107

Sagard, Gabriel, 84
St. Regis Longhouse, 1, 104
Sand Hill Longhouse, 106, 135, 144, 149
Sandusky "Senecas," 107, 118
Sap dance. *See* Maple ceremony
Sapir, Edward, 5, 83
Scrantom, Edwin, 107
Seaver, James, 127, 130
Seer, 17, 33, 34
Seneca Indians, 1, 76, 87, 106–14, 116, 123, 131–32, 135, 151. *See also* Cold-spring Longhouse; Newtown Long-house; Tonawanda Longhouse
Seneca (Six Nations Reserve) Long-house, 35, 46, 74, 104, 173–74. *See also* Six Nations Reserve Longhouses
Shake-the-pumpkin dance, 26, 66–67, 69
Shaking-the-jug dance, 26
Sharpening-a-stick dance, 26
Sharpless, Joshua, 123
Shimony, Annemarie, x, 24, 35, 77
Silverheels, Old, 107–108
Simmons, Henry, 105, 123
Sioux dance. *See* War dance
Six Nations Reserve Longhouses, 1, 22, 34–35, 44–45, 92, 115, 118. *See also* Lower Cayuga Longhouse; Onondaga (Six Nations Reserve) Longhouse; Seneca (Six Nations Reserve) Long-house; Sour Springs Longhouse
Skin dance. *See* Thanksgiving dance
Skin-beating dance, 26

Sky, 13–15
Smith, De Cost, x, 109
Smith, Erminnie, x, 109
Snow snake game, 26, 139
Solstice ceremonies, 40, 83, 146–48
Sour Springs Longhouse, x, 5, 24, 34–35, 39, 44, 74–76, 104, 147. *See also* Six Nations Reserve Longhouses
Speck, Frank G., x, 5, 35
Squakie Hill, 106, 132
Squash. *See* Life Supporters
Squash dance, 75
Standing Quiver dance. *See* Stomp dance
Stars, 8, 14, 142. *See also* Pleiades
Stomp dance, 26, 48–49, 64, 66–67, 69, 73, 75, 77
Strawberries, 8–10
Strawberry ceremony, 4, 16, 25, 32, 35, 69, 118
Striking-the-pole (stick) dance, 26, 34, 124
Sturtevant, William C., 27–28
Sullivan-Clinton expedition 2, 110
Sun, 4, 8, 13, 14, 84, 102, 143, 152
Sun ceremony, 16, 25, 32, 34–35, 124
Susquehanna, 87
Swayne, Joel, 123

Taronhiaouagon. *See* Holder-of-the-Heavens
Ten-day feast, 16
Thanksgiving dance, 26, 29, 34, 39, 42, 44–45, 47–49, 53, 59, 66–71, 75, 77–79, 81, 84, 105–106, 125, 143, 145–46, 148–53
Thanksgiving speech (address), 7–17, 25, 48–50, 52, 58–59, 61, 64, 106, 108, 137, 139–43
Three Sisters. *See* Life Supporters
Thunder ceremony, 16, 25, 34
Thunderers, 4, 8, 12–14, 142
Tiyendinaga Reserve, 1
Tobacco, 19, 20, 43, 52–53, 55, 61–63, 81, 133, 145
Tobacco invocation, 4, 17, 20, 25, 34–35, 43, 46–47, 49, 51, 55–56, 58–59, 62, 65, 67–68, 70, 73, 76, 79–82, 115–17, 126, 129–30, 139–41, 153